Caravan & Camping Holidays in Britain

- Campsites and Caravan Parks
- Facilities fully listed

Honeybridge Park, Dial Post, West Sussex. page 82

© FHG Guides Ltd, 2010
ISBN 978-1-85055-426-4

Maps: ©MAPS IN MINUTES™ / Collins Bartholomew (2009)

Typeset by FHG Guides Ltd, Paisley.
Printed and bound in China by Imago.

Distribution. Book Trade: ORCA Book Services, Stanley House,
3 Fleets Lane, Poole, Dorset BH15 3AJ
(Tel: 01202 665432; Fax: 01202 666219)
e-mail: mail@orcabookservices.co.uk
Published by FHG Guides Ltd., Abbey Mill Business Centre,
Seedhill, Paisley PA1 ITJ (Tel: 0141-887 0428 Fax: 0141-889 7204).
e-mail: admin@fhguides.co.uk

Guide to Caravan & Camping Holidays is published by FHG Guides Ltd,
part of Kuperard Group.

Cover design: FHG Guides
Cover Pictures: With thanks to
Trevean Caravan and Camping Park, Padstow, Cornwall (see p 26)

symbols

	Caravans for Hire
	Holiday Parks & Centres
$	Caravan Sites and Touring Parks
	Camping Sites

	Electric hook-ups available		Facilities for disabled visitors
	Children's play area		Pets welcome
	Laundry facilities		Shop on site
	Licensed bar on site	W	Wifi access available

Contents

Editorial Section	2-10
Foreword	4
Tourist Board Ratings	10, 172
Directory of Website Addresses	195
Readers' Offer Vouchers	211

SOUTH WEST ENGLAND
11

Cornwall and Isles of Scilly, Devon, Dorset, Gloucestershire, Somerset, Wiltshire

LONDON & SOUTH EAST ENGLAND
67

London, Berkshire, Buckinghamshire, Hampshire, Kent, East Sussex, West Sussex

EAST OF ENGLAND
83

Cambridgeshire, Essex, Hertfordshire, Norfolk, Suffolk

MIDLANDS
94

Derbyshire, Herefordshire, Leicestershire & Rutland, Lincolnshire, Nottinghamshire, Shropshire, Staffordshire, Warwickshire, West Midlands

YORKSHIRE
108

East Yorkshire, North Yorkshire

NORTH EAST ENGLAND
119

Durham, Northumberland, Tyne & Wear

NORTH WEST ENGLAND
125

Cheshire, Cumbria, Lancashire,

SCOTLAND

Aberdeen, Banff & Moray	145
Angus & Dundee	146
Argyll & Bute	147
Ayrshire & Arran	151
Borders	152
Dumfries & Galloway	153
Edinburgh & Lothians	155
Fife	156
Highlands	157
Lanarkshire	164
Perth & Kinross	165
Stirling & The Trossachs	169
Scottish Islands	170

WALES

Anglesey & Gwynedd	176
North Wales	184
Ceredigion	185
Pembrokeshire	186
Powys	187
South Wales	189

NORTHERN IRELAND
191

Antrim, Down, Fermanagh, Londonderry

REPUBLIC OF IRELAND
194

Kerry

Foreword

Having tried a caravan holiday for the first time, we find that most people are keen to repeat the adventure. Children, especially, really enjoy caravanning, and many of the sites provide play areas and other facilities especially for them. Adults are not neglected either and larger sites usually have a club or licensed bar with entertainment. Many of the larger holiday parks will also have swimming pools, access to beaches, entertainment, shops and eating facilities.

As a long term holiday investment, some people are opting for touring caravans, and find that the smaller sites and touring parks offer peace and tranquillity, variety and the opportunity to travel the length and breadth of the country.

Of course there is also the option to enjoy a holiday "under canvas" and you will find that many camping sites nowadays also provide facilities such as electric hook-ups, water on tap, and shower and toilet blocks. A recent concept is the timber tent, or wigwam, a great adventure for the youngsters and with the advantage of being ready and waiting for your arrival on site.

Whatever your preference, you will find a full selection of caravan holiday opportunities in the pages of **The FHG Guide to Caravan and Camping Holidays 2010.**

ENQUIRIES AND BOOKINGS Give full details of dates (with an alternative), numbers and any special requirements. Ask about any points in the holiday description which are not clear and make sure that prices and conditions are clearly explained. You should receive confirmation in writing and a receipt for any deposit or advance payment.

CANCELLATIONS A holiday booking is a form of contract with obligations on both sides. If you have to cancel, give as much notice as possible.

COMPLAINTS It's best if any problems can be sorted out at the start of your holiday. You should therefore try to raise any complaints on the spot. If you do not, or if the problem is not solved, you can contact the organisations mentioned above. You can also write to us. We will follow up the complaint with the advertiser – but we cannot act as intermediaries or accept responsibility for holiday arrangements.

FHG Guides Ltd. do not inspect accommodation and an entry in our guides does not imply a recommendation. However, our advertisers have signed their agreement to work for the holidaymaker's best interests and as their customer, you have the right to expect appropriate attention and service.

For popular locations, especially during the main holiday season, you should always book in advance. Please mention **The FHG Guide to Caravan and Camping Holidays** when you are making enquiries and bookings and don't forget to use our Readers' Offer Vouchers (pages 211-234) if you're near any of the attractions which are kindly participating.

Anne Cuthbertson, **Editor**

Haven caravan +camping

Hook-up to Haven for great value Caravan & Camping breaks with a difference...

22 Holiday Parks offering superb Touring pitches and amenities at great coastal locations throughout the UK. Each one offering an exciting range of holiday facilities & activities, it's no wonder more and more people are making Haven their holiday choice!

Save up to 50%† off

Call or go online for a brochure & our latest offers!

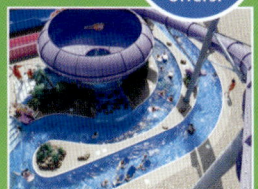

CAREFREE TOURING...
- Superb Touring areas with well maintained pitches
- 5 pitch types from Basic pitches to Premier pitches with electric hook up, water and drainage facility
- Convenient hot shower, toilet and dishwashing facilities
- 24-hour security
- Touring wardens*
- Pets welcome*

HOLIDAY FUN INCLUDED...
- Indoor & outdoor heated pool complexes
- Kids' clubs for all ages
- Sports facilities & activities
- Fantastic music, dance & stage entertainment - perfect for all the family!

Plus, there's a great range of 'pay as you go' activities including fencing*, archery*, golf* and more!

Haven caravan +camping

We Welcome | Tourers | Motorhomes | Tents | Trailer Tents

Call our UK Caravan & Camping Team on
0871 230 1933 Quote: TO_FHG

For 24/7 booking & information visit
caravancamping.co.uk/fhg

Open 7 days a week, 9am-9pm Calls to the number above will cost no more than 10p per minute from a BT landline - calls from other networks may vary.

Terms and conditions: †Save up to 50% off is available on selected Parks during Spring & Autumn excluding School & Bank Holiday periods. Offers are subject to availability, apply to new bookings only and are subject to the terms and conditions as shown in the current Haven Caravan & Camping brochure & website. We reserve the right to withdraw these offers from any Parks, dates and pitches without prior notice. *Vary by Park and may be subject to a moderate extra charge. Calls to the number shown will cost no more than 10p per minute from a BT landline - calls from other networks may vary. Bourne Leisure Limited is registered in England, no 04011660. 1 Park Lane, Hemel Hempstead, HP2 4YL.

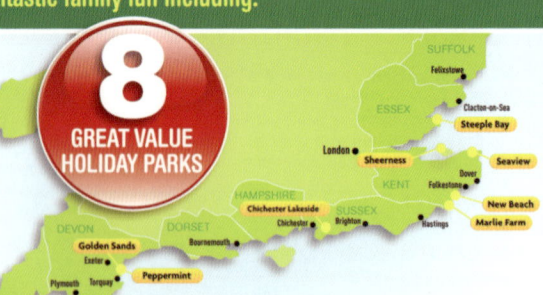

A sign of excellence.

Just one of 200 superb Caravan Club Sites to choose from

Broomfield Farm Caravan Club Site

Bunree Caravan Club Site

Burrs Country Park Caravan Club Site

Troutbeck Head Caravan Club Site

Caravan Club Sites are renowned for their excellence. With most of those graded achieving 4 or 5 stars from VisitBritain, you can be sure of consistently high standards. From lakes or mountains to city or sea, there are some 200 quality Club Sites throughout Britain & Ireland to choose from.

With over 40 fabulous Club Sites open all year, why stay at home?

Whichever site you choose, you can be assured of excellent facilities and a friendly welcome from our Resident Wardens. Just look for the signs.

You don't have to be a member to stay on most Caravan Club Sites, but members save up to £7 per night on pitch fees!

Call today for your FREE Touring Britain & Ireland brochure on 0800 521 161 quoting FHG10 or visit www.caravanclub.co.uk

THE CARAVAN CLUB

The Caravan Club, East Grinstead House, East Grinstead, West Sussex RH19 1UA

GREEN WOOD PARKS

CONTACT US FOR FREE BROCHURE

HOLIDAY HOMES
Buy a home away from home, with space to grow your own garden, from a selection of new and used luxury holiday caravans.

IN THE COUNTRY
• Itchenor, Oxford, Thirsk, York •
Four superb parks dedicated to peace and quiet. Riverside, lakeside or just beautiful countryside. The choice is yours.
Hire Vans at all Parks.
Tourers and Tents also in North Yorkshire.
Head Office: Tel: 01243 514433 • Fax: 01243 513053
E-mail: greenwood.parks@virgin.net • www.greenwoodparks.com

Visit the FHG website
www.holidayguides.com
for details of the wide choice of accommodation featured in the full range of FHG titles

---

Win

Getting out with your family is important and even if you have a little one to carry around why don't you try the holiday product of choice – **theBabaSling**™. It makes life much more spontaneous enabling mum, dad, grandparents or even friends to keep the baby happy and safe whilst joining in the fun of the holiday.

Walking and taking in the beautiful countryside or seaside is hassle free with **theBabaSling**™.
Simply use the sling on your front, back or side leaving your hands free to take the holiday snaps or keep the dog on a lead and away from those unsuspecting sheep!

It's a great solution for limited caravan or car boot storage space, leaving you more room for toys, games and clothes. **theBabaSling**™ can be used from birth until toddler, is very comfortable to wear, and has seven natural carrying positions.

Available in seven cheery colours and costing only £49.90 makes it the perfect holiday essential whatever the destination.

theBabaSling
www.theBabaSling.co.uk

You can win one of these by answering this simple question:
How many different carrying positions does **theBabaSling**™ have?

Name ....
Address ....
....
Postcode .... Date ....

To enter, cut out this slip and return to FHG GUIDES LTD, ABBEY MILL BUSINESS CENTRE, SEEDHILL, PAISLEY PA1 1TJ
Closing date JULY 30th 2010

England and Wales • Counties

Plymouth	12. Windsor & Maidenhead	23. Milton Keynes	34. Blackpool	
Torbay	13. Bracknell Forest	24. Peterborough	35. N.E. Lincolnshire	
Poole	14. Wokingham	25. Leicester	36. North Lincolnshire	
Bournemouth	15. Reading	26. Nottingham	37. Kingston-upon-Hull	
Southampton	16. West Berkshire	27. Derby	38. York	
Portsmouth	17. Swindon	28. Telford & Wrekin	39. Redcar & Cleveland	
Brighton & Hove	18. Bath & Northeast Somerset	29. Stoke-on-Trent	40. Middlesborough	
Medway	19. North Somerset	30. Warrington	41. Stockton-on-Tees	
Thurrock	20. Bristol	31. Halton	42. Darlington	
Southend	21. South Gloucestershire	32. Merseyside	43. Hartlepool	
Slough	22. Luton	33. Blackburn with Darwen		

NORTH WALES
a. Denbighshire
b. Flintshire
c. Wrexham

SOUTH WALES
d. Swansea
e. Neath & Port Talbot
f. Bridgend
g. Rhondda Cynon Taff
h. Merthyr Tydfil
i. Vale of Glamorgan
j. Cardiff
k. Caerphilly
l. Blaenau Gwent
m. Torfaen
n. Newport
o. Monmouthshire

Ratings & Awards

For the first time ever the AA, VisitBritain, VisitScotland, and the Wales Tourist Board will use a single method of assessing and rating serviced accommodation. Irrespective of which organisation inspects an establishment the rating awarded will be the same, using a common set of standards, giving a clear guide of what to expect. The RAC is no longer operating an Hotel inspection and accreditation business.

Accommodation Standards: Star Grading Scheme

Using a scale of 1-5 stars the objective quality ratings give a clear indication of accommodation standard, cleanliness, ambience, hospitality, service and food, This shows the full range of standards suitable for every budget and preference, and allows visitors to distinguish between the quality of accommodation and facilities on offer in different establishments. All types of board and self-catering accommodation are covered, including hotels, B&Bs, holiday parks, campus accommodation, hostels, caravans and camping, and boats.

VisitBritain and the regional tourist boards, enjoyEngland.com, VisitScotland and VisitWales, and the AA have full details of the grading system on their websites

The more stars, the higher level of quality

★★★★★
exceptional quality, with a degree of luxury

★★★★
excellent standard throughout

★★★
very good level of quality and comfort

★★
good quality, well presented and well run

★
acceptable quality; simple, practical, no frills

National Accessible Scheme

If you have particular mobility, visual or hearing needs, look out for the National Accessible Scheme. You can be confident of finding accommodation or attractions that meet your needs by looking for the following symbols.

Typically suitable for a person with sufficient mobility to climb a flight of steps but would benefit from fixtures and fittings to aid balance

Typically suitable for a person with restricted walking ability and for those that may need to use a wheelchair some of the time and can negotiate a maximum of three steps

Typically suitable for a person who depends on the use of a wheelchair and transfers unaided to and from the wheelchair in a seated position. This person may be an independent traveller

Typically suitable for a person who depends on the use of a wheelchair in a seated position. This person also requires personal or mechanical assistance (eg carer, hoist).

South West England

Porthminster Beach, Cornwall
Photo courtesy VisitCornwall

At the southernmost point of the British Isles, stretching from Gloucestershire and the Cotswolds in the north down to Dorset on the Channel coast, and west to Land's End, the South West offers a holiday to suit everyone. The mild climate, beaches, surf and moorland countryside are just some of the attractions of this region, along with stunning gardens, art galleries, four UNESCO World Heritage Sites, and miles of walking and cycling trails and bridle paths. There is history to explore in Iron Age villages and stone circles, and in the long marine heritage of the area, while the city of Bath shows what life was like in Roman times. For a more leisurely break there are medieval villages full of character, historic country pubs, and major centres for shopping. For families there are theme parks, farm parks, castles and zoos, as well as over 600 miles of coastline with golden beaches and rocky pools.

Cornwall, with the longest stretch of coastline in the UK, has become a major centre for watersports, whether sailing, surfing, windsurfing, water-skiing, diving in the clear waters to explore historic wrecks or enjoying a family beach holiday. There are busy fishing towns like Looe, Padstow, and traditional villages such as Polperro, with plenty of inns and restaurants where you can sample the fresh catch. There are gardens at Mount Edgcumbe and the Lost Garden of Heligan, as well as a wide choice of National Trust properties including Lanhydrock. The magnificent coast is ideal for birdwatchers, artists and photographers, while Bodmin Moor, one of Cornwall's 12 Areas of Outstanding Natural Beauty, is well worth a visit..

Think of moorland, and **Devon** immediately comes to mind. A county of contrasts, to the north are the wild moors of the Exmoor National Park, fringed by dramatic cliffs and combes, golden beaches and picturesque harbours, with busy market towns and sleepy villages near the coast. For family holidays, one of the best known of the many Blue Flag beaches on the north coast is at Woolacombe, with three miles of sand and a choice of holiday parks. Ilfracombe, originally a Victorian resort, with an annual Victorian festival, provides all kinds of family entertainment. In the centre of the county lies Dartmoor, with its wild open spaces, granite tors and spectacular moorland, rich in wildlife and ideal for walking, pony trekking and cycling. The Channel coast to

SOUTH WEST ENGLAND

the south, with its gentle climate and scenery, is an attractive destination at any time of year. The long stretches of beautiful sandy beaches, pebble and shingle are intersected by river estuaries which provide shelter for migrating birds and other wildlife, with fascinating towns full of history.

Somerset shares in the wild, heather-covered moorland of Exmoor, along with the Quantock Hills to the east, for walking, mountain biking, horse riding, fishing and wildlife holidays. Stretching inland from the Bristol Channel, historic villages and towns all provide ideal bases for exploring the area. The forty miles of coastline includes family resorts like Weston-super-Mare, with its famous donkey rides and all the other traditional seaside attractions. The city of Bath has all the features of a major 21st century centre: festivals, theatres, museums, galleries, gardens, sporting events and of course, shopping. Attracting visitors from all over the world, this designated World Heritage Site boasts wonderful examples of Georgian architecture and of course, the Roman Baths.

Italian Gardens, Budleigh Salterton, Devon

Photo courtesy English Riviera Tourist Board

Just to the north of Bath, **Gloucestershire** forms the major part of the Cotswolds Area of Outstanding Natural Beauty, with gently rolling hills, sleepy villages and market towns full of character, ideal for a relaxing break whatever the season. There are gardens to visit, country pubs, antique shops, cathedrals and castles, as well as all kinds of outdoor activities. The Forest of Dean is another area well worth visiting for the wide variety of spring flowers and amazing autumn colours in the ancient woodlands. Gloucester, the county town, offers plenty to see, including Roman remains, a Norman cathedral, and Victorian docklands, while the Regency spa town of Cheltenham is best known for its festivals of horse racing, music and literature.

For the greatest concentration of prehistoric sites in Europe, visit **Wiltshire.** Most famous is the World Heritage Site, Stonehenge, on Salisbury Plain, dating back at least five thousand years, and with evidence of even earlier work. Salisbury is the most well known centre in south Wiltshire, with its famous medieval cathedral, as well as individual shops in a historic setting. There is also the safari park at Longleat, farm parks, and stately homes and beautiful gardens to visit in the countryside, where there are also plenty of opportunities for walking and cycling.

Back on the south coast, **Dorset** has plenty to offer for an outdoor break. The spectacular cliffs of the Jurassic Coast, a World Heritage Site, form a major attraction for fossil hunters, particularly in the area around Charmouth and Lyme Regis. There are resorts to suit everyone, from traditional, busy Bournemouth with 10 kilometres of sandy beach and a wide choice of entertainment, shopping and dining, to the quieter seaside towns of Seatown, Mudeford and Barton-on-Sea, and Charmouth with its shingle beach. With almost half the county included in Areas of Outstanding Natural Beauty, walking enthusiasts have a choice of both coast and country, from cliff paths above the sea to rolling countryside, the Avon and Stour Valleys and fringes of the New Forest inland.

DEVON & CORNWALL
CHOICE OF 14 SUPERB HOLIDAY PARKS!
ALL CLOSE TO FANTASTIC BEACHES

BIG RANGE OF QUALITY HOLIDAY CARAVANS AND CHALETS
SLEEPS 2-12 PEOPLE
MANY HALF PRICE DEALS!

- **FREE!** Nightly Entertainment
- **FREE!** Linen
- **FREE!** Heated Pool
- **FREE!** Cancellation Plan
- **FREE!** Kids Club... and much more

JOHN FOWLER HOLIDAY PARKS

ALSO OUTSTANDING TENT & TOURING PITCHES

- **FREE!** Hot Showers
- **FREE!** Club Membership
- **FREE!** Awning Space

0844 576 4729
www.johnfowlerholidays.com
John Fowler Holiday Parks, Head Office, Ilfracombe EX34 8PF

14 SOUTH WEST ENGLAND

enjoy a family break at one of Darwin's award winning holiday parks across the beautiful South West

The range of facilities include*
- Lodges & Holiday Homes
- Grass Camping Pitches
- Fully Serviced Caravan Pitches
- Motor Home Facilities
- Pools, Activities & Playgrounds
- Seasonal Pitches
- Shops, Bars & Restaurants
- Family Entertainment
- Transport Links

special offers & discounts online — Pet Friendly

www.darwinholidays.co.uk
enquiries@darwinholidays.co.uk

darwin holiday parks

Other specialised holiday guides from FHG

PUBS & INNS OF BRITAIN

COUNTRY HOTELS OF BRITAIN

PETS WELCOME!

THE GOLF GUIDE WHERE TO PLAY, WHERE TO STAY

500 GREAT PLACES TO STAY

SELF-CATERING HOLIDAYS IN BRITAIN

BED & BREAKFAST STOPS IN BRITAIN

WEEKEND & SHORT BREAKS IN BRITAIN

FAMILY BREAKS IN BRITAIN

Published annually: available in all good bookshops or direct from the publisher:
FHG Guides, Abbey Mill Business Centre, Seedhill, Paisley PA1 1TJ
Tel: 0141 887 0428 • Fax: 0141 889 7204
e-mail: admin@fhguides.co.uk • www.holidayguides.com

Cornwall   **SOUTH WEST ENGLAND** 15

Cornwall

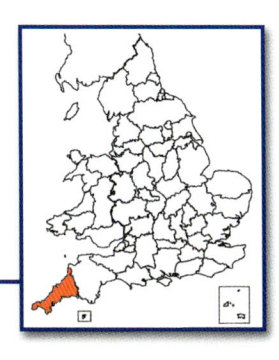

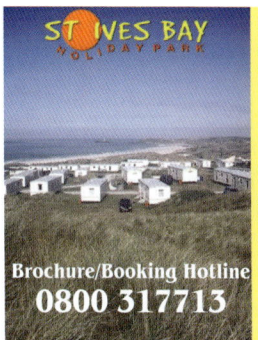

Located on one of Cornwall's finest beaches, **St Ives Bay Holiday Park** offers a fabulous holiday experience for all the family. The holiday park setting is simply stunning with rolling dunes leading down to 3 miles of beautiful sandy beach.

A wide choice of quality accommodation is available including modern caravans, recently refurbished chalets, and superb 4 bedroom houses. We also have camping and touring pitches.

St Ives Bay Holiday Park is exclusively for families and couples. Our facilities and entertainment are designed to ensure your family holiday in Cornwall is relaxed, enjoyable and most of all fun. We have a superb indoor swimming pool, bars, and a reasonably priced shop and takeaway on site.

Tel: 01736 752274 • Fax: 01736 754523
e-mail: stivesbay@btconnect.com • www.stivesbay.co.uk
St Ives Bay Holiday Park, Upton Towans, Hayle TR27 5BH

Brochure/Booking Hotline
0800 317713

Bodmin

Nestled in a beautiful wooded valley near Bodmin Moor, this holiday site offers a selection of accommodation styles, plus a fully equipped, designated camping and caravan area. There are timber cabins, cedar wood bungalows and static holiday caravans, all fully equipped. The touring and camping area has 29 pitches, 6 of which have electric hook-up; there is a shower and toilet block with solar hot water and laundry facilities. A recent addition is the Camping POD, a timber built, insulated wooden hut specially designed to be used like a tent but with the advantage of it being already set-up on the site, ready for your arrival and use. There is an on-site shop for basic groceries, confectionery, a selection of soft and alcoholic drinks plus camping gas and equipment. Ideal for families and centrally based so you can enjoy all that Cornwall has to offer. On Line Booking Available.

Ruthern Valley Holidays
Ruthernbridge, Near Bodmin PL30 5LU
Tel: 01208 831 395
E-mail: camping@ruthernvalley.com
E-mail: holidays@ruthernvalley.com
www.ruthernvalley.com

16 SOUTH WEST ENGLAND **Cornwall**
Bodmin, Botallack, Bude

Lanarth

Touring Caravan Park (nine-and-a-half acres), country setting, in landscaped fields and gardens. Easy access on A39, at St Kew Highway, between Wadebridge four miles and Camelford six miles. On site, toilet block, swimming pool and hotel with licensed bar. Wi-fi.. Dogs are welcome but must be on lead at all times (dog walking area). Caravan storage available. Some pitches have electricity, water and water disposal. Terms £10 to £14, pitch with two adults.

**St Kew Highway
Bodmin, Cornwall PL30 3EE
Tel: 01208 841315
www.lanarthhotel.co.uk**

Trevaylor Caravan & Camping Park
Botallack, Cornwall TR19 7PU

A sheltered grassy site located off the beaten track in a peaceful location at the western tip of Cornwall. The dramatic coastline and the pretty villages nearby are truly unspoilt. Clean, well maintained facilities and a good shop are offered, along with a bar serving bar meals. 6-acre site with 50 touring pitches.

**01736 787016 • www.cornishcamping.co.uk
trevaylor@cornishcamping.co.uk**

Upper Lynstone
Caravan and Camping Park

**Bude, Cornwall EX23 0LP
Tel: 01288 352017 • Fax: 01288 359034
e-mail: reception@upperlynstone.co.uk • www.upperlynstone.co.uk**

Upper Lynstone is a quiet family-run park situated just three-quarters of a mile from Bude's town centre on the coastal road to Widemouth Bay. Bude's shops, beaches with outdoor pool, bars and restaurants are all within walking distance.

Enjoy the breathtaking beauty of the Cornish Coast from the footpath that leads from our park. The park has modern caravans for hire and spacious camping and touring fields with electric hook-ups. Facilities include a small but well equipped shop, free showers, laundry room, and children's play area. Calor and Camping Gas stockists. Well-behaved dogs welcome.

We have four and six berth caravans at Upper Lynstone. All have mains services, colour TV, fridge etc. The caravans are well spaced with plenty of room for you to park. They have splendid views to distant villages and moors. Enjoy our NEW 35ft, 3-bedroom static caravans with panoramic views, designed to sleep six in comfort.

Cornwall

Bude

Budemeadows Touring Park

Widemouth Bay,
Bude, Cornwall. EX23 0NA
☎ 01288 361646 📠 08707 064825

A friendly family-run site in landscaped surroundings just 3 miles from Bude and a mile from Widemouth Bay.

- ✓ Heated Pool
- ✓ Children's Playgrounds
- ✓ Grumpy Pete's Bar
- ✓ Licensed Shop
- ✓ Laundrette
- ✓ Free Hot Water and Showers

Please ring or e-mail for a brochure.
Pool, bar and shop open mid and high season

Open all year

✉ holiday@budemeadows.com
🌐 www.budemeadows.com

Hedley Wood
Caravan & Camping Park

16 acre woodland family-run site with outstanding views, where you can enjoy a totally relaxing holiday with a laid-back atmosphere, sheltered and open camping areas.

Just 10 minutes' drive from the beaches, golf courses, riding stables and shops.

On site facilities include: Children's Adventure Areas, Bar, Clubroom, Shop, Laundry, Meals and all amenities. Free Hot Showers/Water. Nice dogs/pets are very welcome. Daily kennelling facility. Dog walks/nature trail.

Static caravans for hire. Caravan storage available. Open all year.

Visit our website: www.hedleywood.co.uk
or write or phone for comprehensive brochure
**Hedley wood Caravan & Camping Park
Bridgerule (Near Bude), Holsworthy, Devon EX22 7ED
Tel: 01288 381404 • Fax: 01288 382011**

The Camping and Caravanning Club
The Friendly Club

18 SOUTH WEST ENGLAND

Cornwall

Coverack, Crackington Haven

Little Trevothan
Caravan and Camping Park
Coverack • Cornwall TR12 6SD

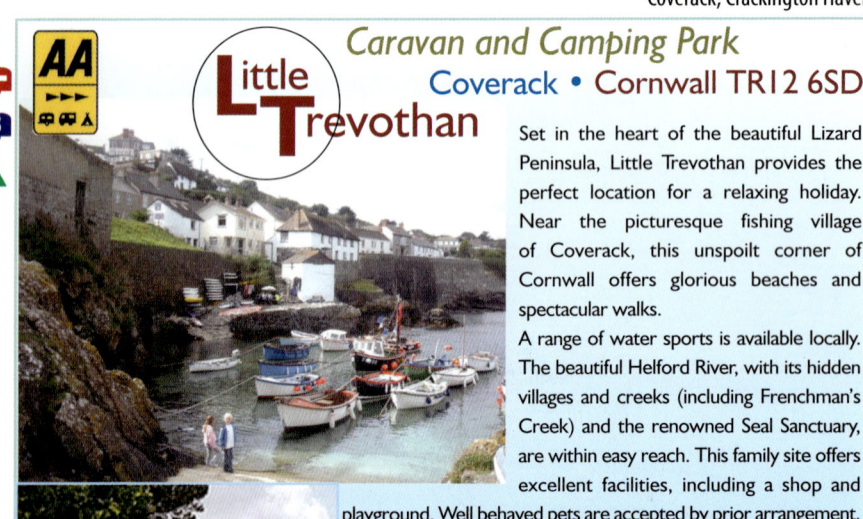

Set in the heart of the beautiful Lizard Peninsula, Little Trevothan provides the perfect location for a relaxing holiday. Near the picturesque fishing village of Coverack, this unspoilt corner of Cornwall offers glorious beaches and spectacular walks.

A range of water sports is available locally. The beautiful Helford River, with its hidden villages and creeks (including Frenchman's Creek) and the renowned Seal Sanctuary, are within easy reach. This family site offers excellent facilities, including a shop and playground. Well behaved pets are accepted by prior arrangement. Fully equipped four/six berth caravans for hire. Tents and tourers welcome. Please contact Rachel & Sean Flynn.

Tel: 01326 280260
e-mail: sales@littletrevothan.co.uk
www.littletrevothan.co.uk

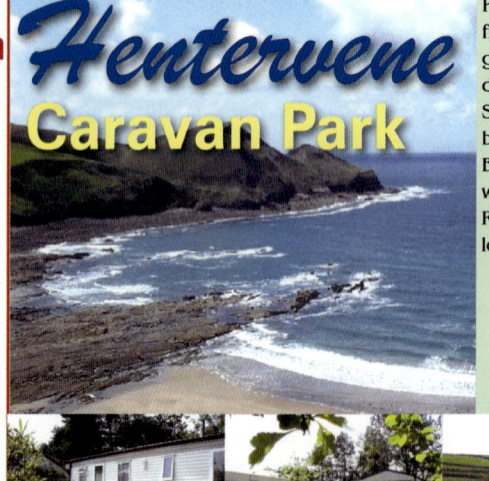

Hentervene
Caravan Park

Peaceful family-run caravan park two miles from Crackington Haven beach and glorious coastal footpath. Positively no bar, disco or bingo; just beautiful countryside. Short drive from Bodmin Moor, fine surfing beaches like Widemouth Bay, the Camel Estuary for sailing, windsurfing, cycling and within easy reach of Padstow, Polzeath, Rock, etc. Many attractive country pubs locally, plenty of attractions for children.

Luxury caravans and pine lodge to let. Caravan sales. Pets welcome – dog walk on site and dog-friendly woods, beaches etc. within a 5 to 10 minute drive.

Hentervene Caravan Park, Crackington Haven
Near Bude EX23 0LF • 01840 230365
e-mail: contact@hentervene.co.uk • www.hentervene.co.uk

Cornwall
Hayle, Helston

SOUTH WEST ENGLAND 19

Atlantic Coast *Holiday Park*

Tariff (touring and tents) from £17 per night. Hiring from £270 per week.

A small, friendly holiday park situated just minutes away from the glorious sands of Gwithian beach on St Ives Bay in West Cornwall. The park is perfectly located for exploring the natural coastal beauty of St Ives Bay and is within driving distance of many fine beaches, restaurants and tourist attractions including the Eden Project, Land's End and the Tate Gallery.

Atlantic Coast Holiday Park offers static caravans for sale, holiday caravans for hire (many with double glazing and central heating), short breaks and late availability deals.

There are fully serviced pitches for tourers, motorhomes and campers, and we offer refurbished toilets and showers, a launderette, and a well stocked shop.

• Wi-fi is also available on the park • Dogs and their owners are welcome • Open 1st March to first Sunday in January.

Atlantic Coast Holiday Park, Upton Towans Hayle, Cornwall TR27 5BL • 01736 752071
enquiries@atlanticcoastpark.co.uk
www.atlanticcoastpark.co.uk

Franchis Holiday Park • Helston • Cornwall

A warm welcome awaits you at Franchis, centrally positioned on the Lizard Peninsula, where beaches, coves and cliff walks abound.
Touring and camping or self-catering in our caravans or bungalows all surrounded by woodland and farmland.
Four acres of closely mown grass.
Electric hook-ups, hot showers, small shop.
No entertainment or bar.
Dogs welcome. Wreck and reef diving nearby.

Cury Cross Lanes, Mullion,
Helston TR12 7AZ
Tel: 01326 240301
e-mail: enquiries@franchis.co.uk
www.franchis.co.uk

Silver Sands
HOLIDAY PARK

Quiet, family-run park. Pets welcome with well-trained owners.
Short walk through woodland path to award-winning dog beach.
Ideal for families - no clubhouse or bar to disturb the peace.
Choice of holiday homes, touring and camping
in mature parkland setting.

SILVER SANDS HOLIDAY PARK
Gwendreath, near Kennack Sands, Ruan Minor, Helston TR12 7LZ
Tel/Fax: 01326 290631 • www.silversandsholidaypark.co.uk

20 SOUTH WEST ENGLAND **Cornwall**
Helston, Launceston

BOSCREGE
Caravan & Camping Park
Ashton, Nr Helston, Cornwall

from **£59** pppw

- Static caravans available for holidays
- Touring caravans, tents & motor homes
- Child's play area • Pets welcome
- Games room • Free showers

01736 762231
caravanparkcornwall.com

Lower Polladras
Touring Park

Carleen, near Helston, Cornwall TR13 9NX
An attractive, peaceful and friendly, family run park.
Just 10 minutes from the nearest beach, Spotless facilities,
free showers. Dog exercising and wildlife walks.
All year caravan storage. Low season special deals.

Tel: 01736 762220
e-mail: lowerpolladras@btinternet.com
www.lower-polladras.co.uk

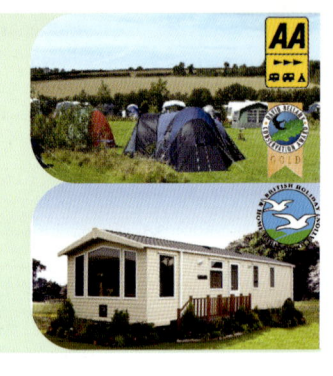

❖ Hollyvagg Farmhouse ❖

Part of cosy 17th century Listed Farmhouse in 80 acres of fields and woods. Working farm with sheep, geese, dogs and cats. Central to North and South coasts, Bodmin Moor, and the fabulous Eden Project. Golf and riding nearby. All modern conveniences.
Sleeps 4

Also available, LAKEVIEW, luxury mobile home with large verandah set in a secluded position overlooking a wooded valley and ponds with views of Dartmoor in the distance. There is a large parking area and enclosed garden suitable for large dogs only.
Sleeps 4.

Hollyvagg Farm
Lewannick, Launceston, Cornwall PL15 7QH
Mrs Anne Moore • 01566 782309
www.hollyvaggfarm.co.uk

Cornwall
Looe

SOUTH WEST ENGLAND 21

Tregoad Park

A unique Cornish 4 star holiday experience

Set in 55 acres of rolling countryside well away from the road and with stunning views of Looe Island and the sea beyond Tregoad Park offers the ideal location for both fun filled family holidays and quiet relaxing out of season breaks. Close to the pretty fishing town of Looe and beaches we can guarantee you a beautiful location, all the facilities and a very warm and friendly welcome.

We have 190 large flat & terraced pitches of which 60 are hardstanding ideal for touring caravans, motorhomes and tents. Most are southerly facing and all pitches have electric hook-up.

There are ample water and waste points around the park and access roads are tarmac so getting on and off your pitch is easy.

The toilet and shower facilities are modern, clean and free of charge and there is a launderette at the lower block. The reception building contains a well stocked shop and visitor information centre together with internet access point and post box.

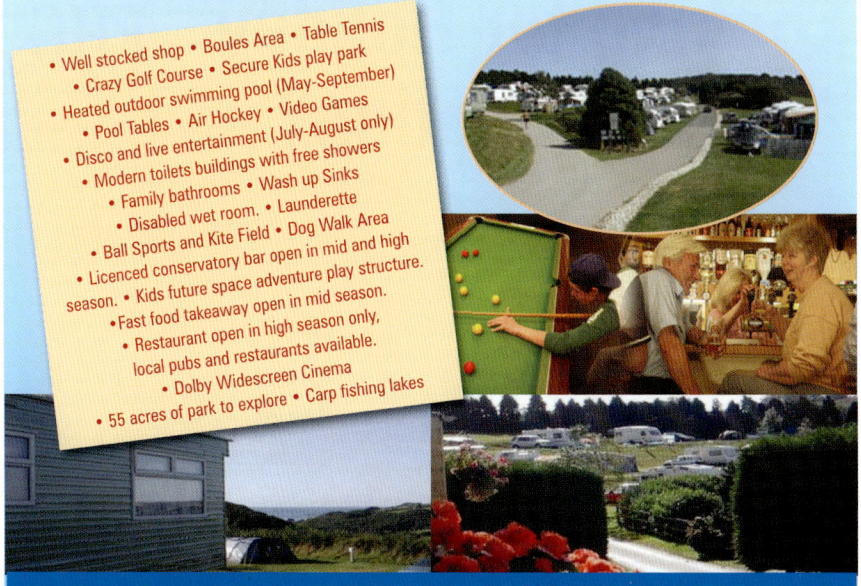

- Well stocked shop
- Boules Area
- Table Tennis
- Crazy Golf Course
- Secure Kids play park
- Heated outdoor swimming pool (May-September)
- Pool Tables
- Air Hockey
- Video Games
- Disco and live entertainment (July-August only)
- Modern toilets buildings with free showers
- Family bathrooms
- Wash up Sinks
- Disabled wet room
- Launderette
- Ball Sports and Kite Field
- Dog Walk Area
- Licenced conservatory bar open in mid and high season.
- Kids future space adventure play structure.
- Fast food takeaway open in mid season.
- Restaurant open in high season only, local pubs and restaurants available.
- Dolby Widescreen Cinema
- 55 acres of park to explore
- Carp fishing lakes

Tregoad Park, St Martin, Near Looe, Cornwall PL13 1PB
Tel: 01503 262718 • Fax: 01503 264777 • e-mail: info@tregoadpark.co.uk
www.tregoadpark.co.uk

22 SOUTH WEST ENGLAND Cornwall
Looe

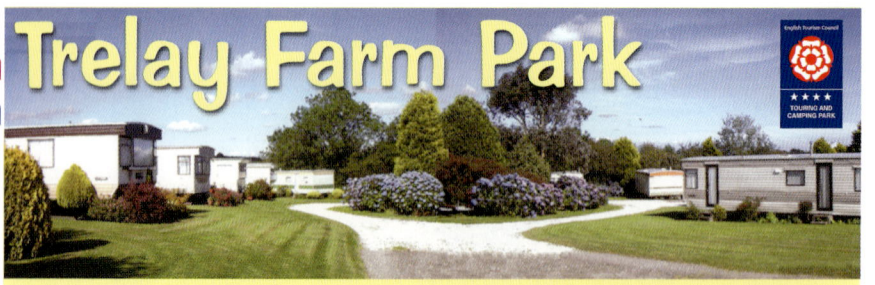

Trelay Farm Park

A small, peaceful, friendly, family-run site. It is quiet, uncommercialised and surrounded by farmland. The park lies on a gentle south-facing slope offering wide views of open countryside. Excellent new facilities include hot showers/launderette and disabled suite with wheelchair access. The three-acre camping field is licensed for 55 tourers/tents etc. Good access, generous pitches, hook ups. In adjoining area (1.5 acres) are 20 holiday caravans in a garden-like setting. The nearby village of Pelynt has shops, Post Office, restaurants, pub. Looe and Polperro are both just three miles away. The renowned Eden Project is 12 miles west. Luxury caravans for sale and rental. Pets welcome. New for 2008 – Child's Play Area.

Pelynt, Looe PL13 2JX
Tel: 01503 220 900
e-mail: stay@trelay.co.uk
www.trelay.co.uk

Looking for Holiday Accommodation?

FHG · K·U·P·E·R·A·R·D

for details of hundreds of properties throughout the UK, visit our website

www.holidayguides.com

Cornwall
Mawgan Porth

SOUTH WEST ENGLAND   23

Marver Holiday Park
**Mawgan Porth,
Near Newquay TR8 4BB**

Small, quiet family-run site, offering beautiful views of the Lanherne Valley. Approximately 150 yards from the beach, which is excellent for children, surfers and fishing. Only five miles from Newquay and eight miles from the historic fishing port of Padstow.

The site offers chalets and static caravans for hire and a level campsite suitable for caravans, motor homes and tents.

On site there is a toilet and shower block, sauna and launderette, in which there is a payphone, washing up facilities and a freezer for the use of our guests.

Nearby fishing, surfing, horse riding, golf and shops, also good public houses, surf board and wet suit hire.

Tel: 01637 860493
e-mail: familyholidays@aol.com
www.marverholidaypark.co.uk

24 SOUTH WEST ENGLAND   Cornwall
                                                                  Newquay

Quarryfield HOLIDAY PARK

CAMPING AND TOURING • CARAVANS

Bar • Pool Children's Play Area

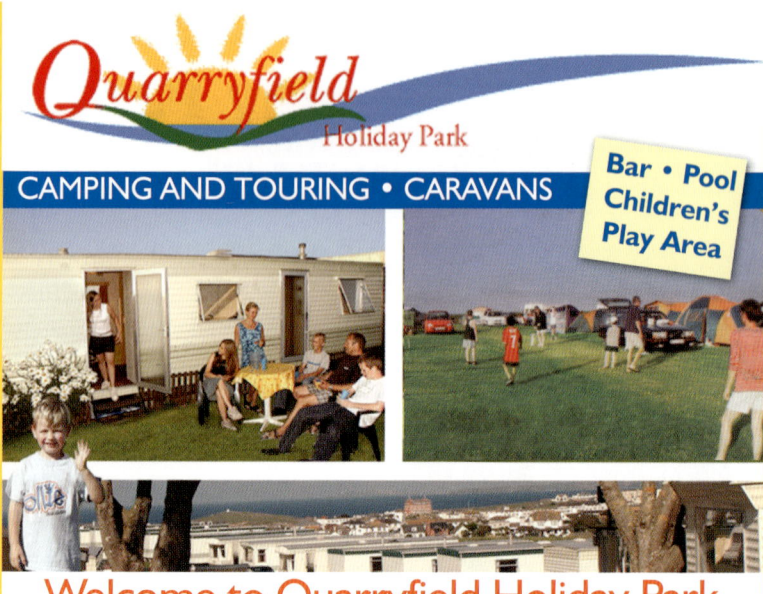

Welcome to Quarryfield Holiday Park

Quarryfield Holiday Park, situated in Crantock near Newquay, is the perfect location for your camping or touring holiday.

Situated overlooking the beautiful Crantock Beach, and next to the estuary of the River Gannel, you have plenty of choices on how to spend your time. You can relax on the beach, swim, surf or just play with the children, or you can walk up alongside the river, which is particularly beautiful. Newquay is just on the other side of the estuary and is within walking distance. If the tide is in then just take the row boat ferry to get across the river.

Quarryfield is a well established Holiday Park wtih 150 pitches, 50 hook up points, 42 Static Caravans and 2 chalets. With all this space and variety we are bound to have something to suit your needs!

The site itself is large enough to enjoy plenty of room for playing and for the family to spread out and enjoy their holiday. There are swings and a play area for the children and an outdoor swimming pool for them to let off steam on hot sunny days.

The on-site Inn allows the family to enjoy some drinks and food, as well as the shop which has plenty of supplies. And an amusement arcade with pool table and other facilities is also available to help keep the children busy and entertained.

Contact: MRS WINN, TRETHERRAS, NEWQUAY, CORNWALL TR7 2RE
Tel & Fax: 01637 872792
e-mail: quarryfield@crantockcaravans.orangehome.co.uk
www.quarryfield.co.uk

Cornwall
Newquay

SOUTH WEST ENGLAND 25

Trevarrian HOLIDAY PARK

Tel: 01637 860381
e-mail: holidays@trevarrian.co.uk
www.trevarrian.co.uk

Mawgan Porth, Newquay, Cornwall TR8 4AQ

Situated in quiet countryside close to fabulous beaches on the North coast of Cornwall between the bays of Mawgan Porth and Watergate Bay, Trevarrian Holiday Park has been owned and run by the Phillips family for over 35 years. Superb facilities include heated pool, self-service shop, launderette, TV/video and games room, children's play area, tennis court and pitch and putt. Free evening entertainment during peak season. "Stimbles" with club licence, bar snacks. Individual pitches, electric hook-ups available, modern toilets and hot showers.

No overcrowding, even at the busiest time of year, spacious pitches allow more privacy and comfort. Three fields are linked by well illuminated roads.

Cornwall's vast number of attractions are also within easy reach. Trevarrian Holiday Park caters exclusively for families and couples.

Write or phone for free colour brochure.

Treloy Touring Park

A friendly family site for touring caravans, tents and motor homes, just off the A3059 Newquay Road. A central location for touring the whole of Cornwall. Facilities include heated swimming pool, licensed bar/family room, entertainment, cafe/takeaway, shop, laundry, FREE showers, private washing cubicles, baby bathrooms, indoor dishwashing sinks, TV and games rooms, adventure playground. Facilities for the disabled. Electric hook-ups.

Coarse fishing nearby. Own superb 9-hole Par 32 golf course with concessionary green fees for our guests. Terms £8 to £15 per night for two adults, car and caravan. Please write or telephone for free colour brochure.

Treloy Touring Park • Newquay TR8 4JN
Tel: 01637 872063/876279
www.treloy.co.uk

Visit the FHG website
www.holidayguides.com
for details of the wide choice of accommodation featured in the full range of FHG titles

26 SOUTH WEST ENGLAND — Cornwall
Padstow, Penzance

Harlyn Sands HOLIDAY PARK

Family owned, family run for families

★ STRICTLY FAMILIES ONLY ★

Enjoy a good old family Bucket and Spade Holiday on this golden sandy beach. Miles of coastal walks and award-winning waters. Top class family entertainment*, immaculate luxurious accommodation.
Fish and Chippy, Arcade. Children's Play Park, Kids' Club mornings, afternoons and evenings.
On-site Shop, Launderette, Shower Block, Electric Hook-Ups.

SUPER SPLASH FUN POOL
with toddlers' pool, flume and rapids**

Situated right on Trevose Head, 3 miles from Padstow, 12 miles from Newquay, only 30 minutes from the Eden Project.

Lighthouse Road, Trevose Head, Padstow, Cornwall PL28 8SQ
e-mail: harlyn@freenet.co.uk
www.harlynsands.co.uk

RING OUR BROCHURE HOTLINE:
01841 520720

*main season; during quiet times limited services available. ** small charges apply; restrictions apply for non-swimmers.

Trevean Farm
St Merryn, Padstow PL28 8PR

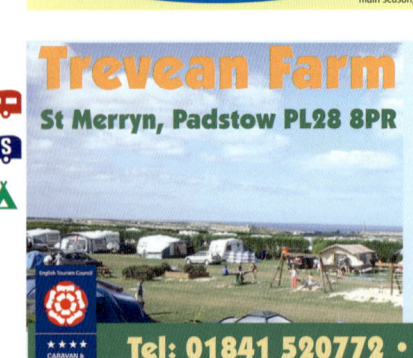

Small, pleasant site close to several sandy beaches with good surfing and lovely, golden sands. Splendid sea views. Riding school and golf club within 2 miles. Village shops one mile. Sea and river fishing nearby. Three static six-berth luxury caravans with cooker, fridge, mains water supply, flush toilet, shower and digital TV. Modern toilet/shower block with free showers. New family room with disabled facilities. Electric hook-ups. Pay phone, children's play area and small shop (Whitsun to September) on-site. Pets permitted in tents and tourers but not in static caravans. Weekly rates for static vans from £175 to £480 according to season. Touring caravans and tents welcome from £8 to £12 per night. Open Easter to October.

Tel: 01841 520772 • e-mail: trevean.info@virgin.net

Bone Valley Holiday Park

Situated in a pretty valley, ideal for exploring the countryside and coast of West Cornwall, this small, family-run park is surrounded by mature hedges and trees. There is also a pretty stream running along the park. We are located approx. ¾ mile from the centre of Penzance, in the village of Heamoor which has shops, a pub and a regular bus service.

17 pitches (some hardstanding) • Pitches for tents • Electric hook-ups available • Static Caravans, fully equipped • Budget Caravans
On-site facilities include: showers, kitchen/laundry room (microwave, electric kettle etc), shop, campers' lounge with digital TV, public telephone, free ice pack service, chemical disposal, gas and Camping Gaz, BBQ loan.

Bone Valley Holiday Park
Heamoor, Penzance TR20 8UJ
www.bonevalleyholidaypark.co.uk

Please contact Mr & Mrs Ward • Tel & Fax: 01736 360313

Cornwall — SOUTH WEST ENGLAND 27

Polzeath

www.polzeathcamping.co.uk

Cornish Camping... At its best

Tristram & Southwinds Camping and Caravan Parks @ Polzeath

For Southwinds email: Info@southwindscamping.co.uk or call: 01208 863267

For Tristram email: info@tristramcampsite.co.uk or call 01208 862215

One of the most spectacular, safest and best surfing beaches in Cornwall. Visitors return year after year to enjoy the beauty and safety of its golden sands, rolling surf and stunning views.

Tristram is one of the closest camp sites to the beach in the whole of Cornwall. Catering for both camping and caravans, It has stunning views of Polzeath with brilliant modern facilities. It is secure and safe for children with night security and ample car parking.

Families love Southwinds campsite because it is so quiet and peaceful. It has beautiful panoramic sea and rural views and is only a pleasant half mile stroll from the beach and town.

Visit Us Online Today

You can find rates, maps, information on local attractions and great photos. We also have two great live surf cams

MEMBER VisitCornwall southwesttourism

AA

28 SOUTH WEST ENGLAND

Cornwall

Penzance, Redruth

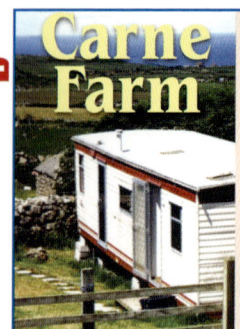

Carne Farm

is situated on the North Cornish Coast, one mile from the nearest beach at Portherras Cove. It is excellent for walking, close to coastal footpath and with climbing nearby. Visitors are only six miles from Penzance, eight miles from St Ives and two miles from the nearest village shop, pubs and restaurants at Pendeen. The spacious eight-berth caravan is located in the field above the farmhouse, with fenced lawn and garden furniture, and has lovely views of fields, moorland and sea. It has a double bedroom, twin bedroom/cot, shower and toilet. It is equipped with electricity, fridge, full sized cooker, fire and hot and cold water, duvets, pillows and kitchen equipment. Television. Linen provided. Visitors welcome on the farm • Babysitting available • Basic Camping available. *Ring for details* • *Rates: from £140 to £250 per week (gas & electricity included)*

C. Hichens, Carne Cottage, Morvah, Pendeen, Penzance TR19 7TT
Tel: 01736 788729 • Mobile: 07733 486347
• e-mail: andrewvlh@btopenworld.com

Globe Vale Holiday Park
Radnor, Redruth, Cornwall TR16 4BH

Globe Vale is a quiet countryside park situated close to the town of Redruth and the main A30. There are panoramic views across green fields to the coast; 10 minutes' drive to the nearest beach. Campers/tourers; static caravans for hire, and also plots available if you wish to buy your own new static holiday home. Facilities on site include fully serviced pitches, electric hook-ups, modern shower/toilet block, launderette and chemical disposal. Licensed bar with games room. Evening meals served. There is also a children's play area, and open spaces for ball games. We are happy to accept pets on site at extra charge. Caravan storage available.

Contact
Paul and Louise Owen on
01209 891183
www.globevale.co.uk
e-mail: info@globevale.co.uk

symbols

- ☼ Holiday Parks & Centres
- 🚐 Caravans for Hire
- $ Caravan Sites and Touring Parks
- ⛺ Camping Sites

Cornwall
Redruth

SOUTH WEST ENGLAND 29

Wheal Rose
Caravan & Camping Park

A secluded, 6-acre family-run touring park, central for all West Cornwall. Adjacent to the park is Mineral Tramway popular with walkers and cyclists. The park consists of 50 level, grassed pitches with electrical hook-ups. Spotlessly clean, purpose-built shower/toilet block, shop, children's play area, TV/games room, laundry and disabled facilities.

HEATED OPEN AIR SWIMMING POOL

Prices from £9.00 per night. Open March to December.

Scorrier, Redruth TR16 5DD
Tel/Fax: 01209 891496

e-mail: les@whealrosecaravanpark.co.uk
www.whealrosecaravanpark.co.uk

PLEASE CONTACT FOR SPECIAL OFFERS

AA

SOUTH WEST ENGLAND

Cornwall
Redruth

TEHIDY HOLIDAY PARK

Harris Mill, Illogan, Redruth, Cornwall TR16 4JQ

Welcome to one of Cornwall's finest small, family-owned 4 Star Parks

Clean, modern, well equipped facilities. Free showers, laundry, dish washing room, play area, games room and shop. Nestled in the heart of a wooded valley and a natural haven for wildlife. Near broad sandy beaches, hidden coves and the crystal clear ocean. An ideal base for exploring both the rugged North coast or the gentle South. Walks and buses from site. Something for everyone - beaches, surfing, cycling, walking, gardens, picturesque fishing villages, easy access to all the major attractions.

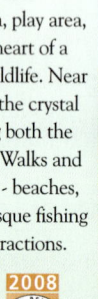

Telephone: 01209 216489
www.tehidy.co.uk

LANYON HOLIDAY PARK

explore south cornwall

For those wanting a memorable holiday look no further. We have lots to offer you. Superb central location surrounded by beautiful countryside. A range of caravans to suit all pockets. Indoor heated pool. All day games room. Bar/ Restaurant/Takeaway/Free entertainment in high season. Play area. Three upgraded toilet/bath/shower blocks. Launderette/dish washing facility/free hot water. Spacious level pitches and short grass. Best of all, you will be looked after by caring resident family. Pets welcome. A real gem of a park.

Loscombe Lane, Four Lanes, Redruth TR16 6LP
01209 313474
e-mail: info@lanyonholidaypark.co.uk
www.lanyonholidaypark.co.uk

Cornwall

St Agnes, St Austell

SOUTH WEST ENGLAND 31

Chiverton Park

- Caravan Holiday Homes
- Touring & Camping
- Families & Couples
- Pets Welcome
- Exclusive leisure facility:
- Gym, Sauna & Steamroom
- Shop • Laundry room
- Games room • Free WiFi
- Children's play area
- Multi-service hook-ups
- Satellite TV in all units
- No club, bar or disco

Set in the heart of Cornish countryside, yet only a short distance from superb beaches, this spacious, well-run park offers peace and relaxation in a delightful rural setting. Holiday homes are fully equipped (except linen, which may be hired)

Chiverton Park, Blackwater, Truro TR4 8HS • 01872 560667
info@chivertonpark.co.uk • www.chivertonpark.co.uk

Court Farm

Set in 30 acres of peaceful pasture land, with 4 acres designated for touring caravans and tents, to a limit of 20 pitches (between 50 and 100 pitches in August), with 20 EHUs.

The shower block has free hot showers, flush toilets, laundry facility, freezer, and dishwashing area. There is a chemical disposal point.

We have a small coarse fishing lake, and an astronomical telescope for star-gazing, lectures by arrangement.

Centrally based for beaches and all of Cornwall's attractions; the Eden Project and the Lost Gardens of Heligan are each 6 miles away.

Court Farm Caravan and Camping
St Stephen, St Austell PL26 7LE
e-mail: truscott@ctfarm.freeserve.co.uk • *www.courtfarmcornwall.co.uk* 
Tel & Fax: 01726 823684

Bill & Anne Truscott and Simon & Lisa Palmer

From £9.50 to £25.00 per night based on unit size.

Looking for holiday accommodation?
for details of hundreds of properties
throughout the UK including
comprehensive coverage of all areas of Scotland try:
www.holidayguides.com

32 SOUTH WEST ENGLAND   **Cornwall**
St Ives, Saltash

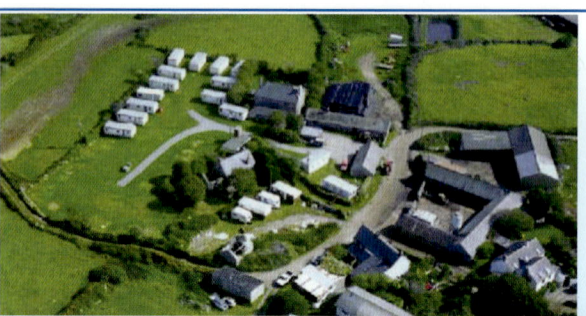

Small and welcoming, Hellesveor is an approved farm site situated just one mile from the sweeping beaches and town centre of St Ives. Located on the Land's End road and only five minutes from the bus route for touring the dramatic landscape of West Cornwall and taking spectacular countryside walks.

Hellesveor Caravan and Camping Site
Hellesveor Farm, St Ives TR26 3AD

Laundry facilities on site. Special terms for early and late season.
Campers and touring caravans welcome. Static Caravans for hire. Electrical hook-ups.
Dogs allowed under strict control.
Shop, pub, restaurant, indoor heated pool, tennis courts, fishing, horse riding, pony trekking, golf course, bowling greens and leisure centre all nearby.
SAE for further details.
• SHORT BREAKS - TELEPHONE FOR AVAILABILITY •
Contact G & H Rogers Tel: 01736 795738
www.caravancampingsites.co.uk/cornwall/hellesveor

Dolbeare Park
Caravan and Camping

An exceptional five star gold oasis in the Cornish countryside near to Plymouth the Eden Project and the unspoilt beaches of the Rame Peninsula

Open all year with refurbished amenity block
60 large gravel & grass pitches with electric
Children's Adventure Play Area • Wi-Fi
Shop & Off License • Takeaway • Calor Gas
Visit our website for reviews and Special Offers

Voted Regional Winner 2009 Practical Caravan Top 100
Awarded Silver – 2009 Best Holiday Park in Cornwall

01752 851332   **www.dolbeare.co.uk**   **PL12 5AF**

Cornwall

Truro

Summer Valley Touring Park
Shortlanesend, Truro TR4 9DW

Situated just two miles from Truro, Cornwall's cathedral city, and ideally placed as a centre for touring all parts of Cornwall. This quiet, small, secluded site is only one-and-a-half miles from the main A30 and its central situation is advantageous for North Cornwall's beautiful surfing beaches and rugged Atlantic coast or Falmouth's quieter and placid fishing coves. Horse riding, fishing and golf are all available within easy distance. This compact site is personally supervised by the owners. Facilities include a toilet block with free hot water, washing cubicles, showers, shaving points, launderette, iron, hairdryer, etc; caravan electric hook-ups; children's play area. Shop with dairy products, groceries, bread, confectionery, toys, Calor/Camping gas.

Mr and Mrs C.R. Simpkins • Tel: 01872 277878 • www.summervalley.co.uk

Two people, car, caravan/tent £12 to £15 per day

Treloan Coastal Holidays

Treloan is a friendly, relaxed family-run campsite and a perfect base for watersports, fishing and walking. Discover hidden, sandy, dog-friendly coves whichever way you turn along the picturesque South West Coastal Path. Open all year, offering static mobile homes as well as camping pitches. Close to shops, and dog-friendly pubs and beaches.
Half an hour to Truro and the Eden Project.
Our eight mobile homes are positioned on the highest point of the campsite with stunning views of the sea and countryside, sleep up to 9. Most pitches have 13 amp electrical hook-up if required. Water taps are regularly spaced, close to the pitches. Cars can be parked next to your tent / caravan or in the designated parking areas.
Facilities include: 2 toilet blocks with showers, toilets and basins, dishwashing facilities, ice pack service, laundry service.

Treloan Lane, Gerrans, Portscatho, Cornwall TR2 5EF
Tel: 01872 580989 • e-mail: info@treloancoastalholidays.co.uk
www.treloancoastalholidays.co.uk

34 SOUTH WEST ENGLAND   **Cornwall**

Truro, Wadebridge

TREVARTH HOLIDAY PARK

Trevarth is a small, well-kept family-run park excellently situated for north and south coast resorts. All our luxury caravan holiday homes are modern with all main services. Tourers and campers are well catered for with level pitches, some sheltered, with ample hook-ups.

Blackwater, Truro TR4 8FR
e-mail: trevarth@lineone.net
www.trevarth.co.uk
Tel: 01872 560266
Fax: 01872 560379

ROSE AWARD CARAVAN HOLIDAY PARK 2008

AA

English Tourism Council — HOLIDAY, TOURING AND CAMPING PARK

Gunvenna Holiday Park

Gunvenna Holiday Park is a well-drained site of level grassland on 10 acres commanding uninterrupted views of the countryside within five minutes' drive of safe golden sandy beaches. It makes the ideal holiday park for families and couples.

There are large spacious pitches some of which are fully serviced; mains water, gray waste, and electric. If you are looking to spend your holiday in a relaxing part of the south west of England this area will not disappoint.

Local activities include golf, fishing, tennis and cycle hire. Visit the Eden Centre or go karting at St Eval Kart Circuit.

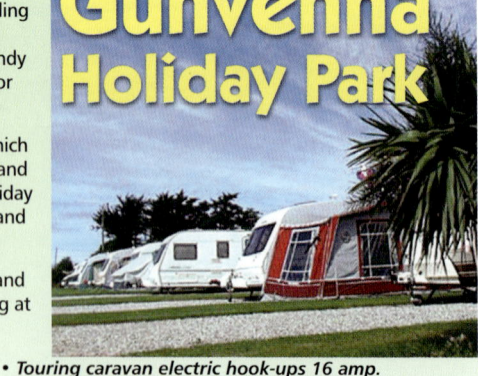

- Touring caravan electric hook-ups 16 amp.
- A modern toilet and shower block with FREE hot and cold water shaving points and hairdryers.
- Guests disabled toilet. • Launderette. • Post box.
- Ample mains water points. • Chemical disposal units.
- Waste water drains. • Children's play area on sand.
- Games room. • Telephone kiosk (outgoing only).
- Dog exercise area and shower. • On site shop.
- Indoor heated swimming pool.

St Minver, Wadebridge PL27 6QN
Tel: 01208 862405

Devon

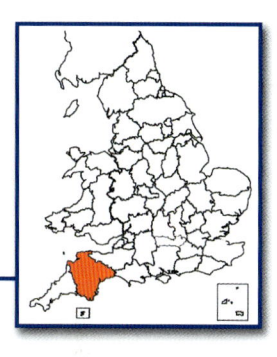

Branscombe, Chudleigh

Devon

SOUTH WEST ENGLAND 35

www.berrybarton.co.uk

Berry Barton Caravan Park
Branscombe, Near Seaton EX12 3BD
Tel: 01297 680208; Fax: 01297 680108

Modern six berth caravans to let from March to November on a 300 acre working farm, above the picturesque old village of Branscombe, with thatched cottages, bakery museum and smithy. A quiet, peaceful holiday for both retired people and families; there is a large area for children to play. Riding available nearby. There are two freehouses in the village, the nearest within easy walking distance. Many lovely walks, with golf and fishing within easy reach, as are Seaton and Sidmouth and the fishing village of Beer. All have mains electricity and water; flush toilets; colour TV; fridge, showers and hot water. 12ft wide and from 30-35ft long. Three touring caravan pitches available, campers and campervans welcome.

Holmans Wood Holiday Park

Delightful, personally managed Park set back in secluded wooded area. Easily accessed from the A38 and ideally situated for Dartmoor and Haldon Forest. Close to Exeter, Plymouth and Torquay, and sandy beaches at Dawlish and Teignmouth. Coarse fishing, golf, horse riding and bird watching are near by. **Quote FHG when booking.**

Our facilities: • *Deluxe all-weather pitches* • *Electric hook-ups* • *Excellent toilets/showers* • *Meadow for camping*
Seasonal pitches • *Storage available* • *Holiday homes for sale* • *Credit card facility for telephone bookings*

Chudleigh, Devon TQ13 0DZ • Tel: 01626 853785
e-mail: enquiries@holmanswood.co.uk • www.holmanswood.co.uk

Visit the FHG website
www.holidayguides.com
for details of the wide choice of accommodation featured in the full range of FHG titles

endless fun...

CAMPING FROM ONLY £5 per person a night

TOURING FROM ONLY £15 per van a night

Four award winning Holiday Parks set in Devon's breathtaking countryside next to Woolacombe's 3 miles of golden Blue flag sandy beach!

SEAVIEW Holiday Homes & Luxury Lodges plus great Camping & Touring

over 40 FREE activities...
- 10 Heated Indoor & Outdoor Pools
- Waterslides • Health Suite • Playzone
- Nightly Star Cabaret & Entertainment
- Snooker • Crazy Golf • Kid's Clubs
- Kid's Indoor & Outdoor Play Areas
- Tennis • Cinema • Coarse Fishing Ponds
...Plus so much more!

...and for just a little more
- 10 Pin Bowling • Affiliated Golf Club
- Waves Ceramic Studio • 17th Century Inn
- Indoor Bowls Rinks • Amusement Arcade
- Restaurants & Bars • WaterWalkerz
- Kiddy Karts • Sports Bar • Climbing Wall
- NEW All-Weather Pitches • Electric Hook-ups
- Laundry Facilities & Shop • Swim Lessons

REGISTER ONLINE FOR LATEST OFFERS!!
woolacombe.com/fcc
0844 770 0383
OR TEXT HOLIDAY TO 60800

WOOLACOMBE BAY
HOLIDAY PARKS • NORTH DEVON

Devon — Barnstaple

SOUTH WEST ENGLAND 37

Stay at Home
Affordable Holiday Homes
Have your own piece of Devon from ONLY £14500
50 Week Licence
Call 01271 343 691
www.tarkapark.com

Tarka Holiday Park
Barnstaple
North Devon
EX31 4AU

Overlooking the magnificent Taw Estuary with the famous Tarka Trail opposite, our Holiday Park is centrally situated and is only minutes away from some of the country's finest 'Blue Flag' beaches. Close to many of North Devon's superb attractions, Tarka Holiday Parkis on a direct route to Croyde, Ilfracombe and Woolacombe. Modern Holiday Caravans with full facilities for self-catering with separate fields for Tourers and Campers. Shower blocks and laundry area are centrally sited. We are proud to say that we hold 3 AA Pennants.

escape to the Stowford Life

Stowford Farm Meadows is a family owned, award winning touring **caravan and camping site** close to Combe Martin in the beautiful surroundings of the **North Devon** countryside.

Open all year round so come and enjoy the Stowford life.

SPECIAL OFFERS Available for low and mid season
check our website www.stowford.co.uk for vouchers

To book your holiday call us on
01271 882476
Combe Martin Devon EX34 0PW

Visit our website to request a free colour brochure
www.**stowford**.co.uk

Devon
Combe Martin, Crediton, Cullompton

SOUTH WEST ENGLAND 39

MANLEIGH HOLIDAY PARK

Graded ★★★★

COMBE MARTIN EX34 0NS
Tel: 01271 883353

Quiet, family-run site set in beautiful countryside near village, beaches, rocky coves and Exmoor. Chalets, caravans and log cabins tastefully sited on side of Combe Martin valley. Children's play area, laundry. Outdoor swimming pool. Dog walk.

Wine Bar serving delicious home-made food.

Colour Brochure:
Lynne & Craig Davey
www.manleighpark.co.uk

CREDITON. Beare Mill Caravan Site, Crediton EX17 3QP
Tel 01363 772973 • Fax 01363 772973
Secluded site, within easy reach of both north and south coasts of this popular holiday county. The level, lawned site has a river running through it and is just one mile from the historic market town of Crediton. Tourers welcome. Open May to October.

FOREST GLADE Caravan & Camping Park

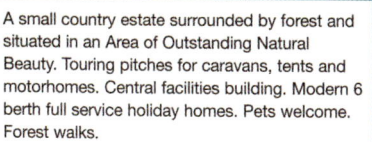

A small country estate surrounded by forest and situated in an Area of Outstanding Natural Beauty. Touring pitches for caravans, tents and motorhomes. Central facilities building. Modern 6 berth full service holiday homes. Pets welcome. Forest walks.

Motorhomes welcome. Facilities for the Disabled.

COLOUR BROCHURE AVAILABLE ON REQUEST

FOREST GLADE HOLIDAY PARK
CULLOMPTON DEVON EX15 2DT

FREE Indoor Heated Pool

Tel: (01404) 841381 (Evgs to 8pm) • Fax: (01404) 841593 • www.forest-glade.co.uk • email: enquiries@forest-glade.co.uk

---

Readers are requested to mention this FHG guidebook when seeking accommodation

40 SOUTH WEST ENGLAND — Devon

Dartmouth, Dawlish, Dawlish Warren

Woodlands Grove Caravan & Camping, Dartmouth

- Award Winning Facilities
- Spacious Pitches
- Licensed Shop
- Bath & Shower Rooms
- Superb setting and views
- Opposite 27 hole Golf Course
- Explore beaches, towns & moors

5 NIGHTS £40 ADULT BREAK
TERMS & CONDITIONS APPLY
in beautiful SOUTH DEVON

Blackawton, Totnes, South Devon TQ9 7DQ
www.woodlands-caravanpark.com • 01803 712598

Cofton Country Holidays

Superb family-run four star holiday park in a Glorious Corner of Devon

- swimming pools • Swan pub • play areas • fishing lakes
- blue flag beach five minutes • take-away • park shop • WiFi
- holiday homes • touring • camping • cottages • apartments

0800 085 8649   www.coftonholidays.co.uk

DAWLISH WARREN. Peppermint Holiday Park, Warren Road, Dawlish Warren EX7 0PQ
Tel 0845 815 9775 • www.ParkHolidaysUK.com
A well laid out site with some of the best facilities in the area and easy access from the M5. Regular family entertainment throughout the season. plus indoor and outdoor swimming pools. 250 tourer/motorhome pitches and 100 tent pitches. Tourers, motorhomes and tents welcome.

Electric hook-ups available		Facilities for disabled visitors
Children's play area		Pets welcome
Laundry facilities		Shop on site
Licensed bar on site		Wifi access available

Devon SOUTH WEST ENGLAND 41
Exmouth, Ilfracombe

St John's Farm
Caravan & Camping Park
St Johns Road
Withycombe,
Exmouth EX8 5EG

Our unique situation away from the hustle and bustle of the main town of Exmouth is ideal for those seeking a little peace and quiet, yet is ideally situated as a base to explore all the things that Devon is famous for, including Orcombe Point, the start of the East Devon Heritage Coast. The caravan park and camp site is situated in pleasant pasture land with rural views, yet only 10 minutes away from two miles of glorious sandy beaches or unspoilt heathland.

Stop overnight, spend a weekend with us, or stay for a month!
Whatever you choose you will be assured of a warm Devonshire welcome at this family-run site.

Facilities include: farm/site shop, electric hook-ups, toilets/disabled facilities, showers, hairdryers, water points, children's playground and pets corner. Dogs welcome - exercise area available.

Tel: 01395 263170
e-mail: stjohns.farm@virgin.net
www.stjohnscampsite.co.uk

Watermouth Cove Holiday Park
on the North Devon Coast

Nestling under Watermouth Castle and at the side of a wonderful secluded harbour, our campsite encourages you to relax and enjoy the dramatic North Devon scenery – reputed to be one of the most unspoilt areas in the UK.
• Modern showers and toilets • Deep washing-up sinks
• Electric hook-ups • Hard standings for motor homes • Launderette on site with washers, driers etc
• Harbour view (some pitches) • Extra camping field (open part July and August)
• Comfortable one and two bedroom chalets and apartments also available with shower, toilet, lounge/diner & kitchen area. All are fully equipped and bed linen is provided.
• Cots and high chairs are available.

Watermouth Cove Holiday Park, Watermouth, Berrynarbor, Near Ilfracombe, North Devon EX34 9SJ
Telephone 01271 862504 • e-mail: info@watermouthcoveholidays.co.uk
www.watermouthcoveholidays.co.uk

42 **SOUTH WEST ENGLAND** Devon
Kingsbridge

Alston Farm Camping & Caravan Site
Malborough, Kingsbridge TQ7 3BJ

The family-run site is set in a quiet secluded, sheltered valley adjoining the Salcombe Estuary in amongst Devon's loveliest countryside. Level pitches, ample space and conveniences.

Dish washing and clothes washing facilities. Electric hook-ups, Calor and Gaz stockists. Shop, (high season only), payphone on site. Children and pets welcome.

From £8 per night for two adults and caravan.

Please phone for brochure: Phil Shepherd.

Tel: 01548 561260

e-mail: info@alstoncampsite.co.uk

www.alstoncampsite.co.uk

Mounts Farm Touring Park
The Mounts, Near East Allington, Kingsbridge TQ9 7QJ
01548 521591 • www.mountsfarm.co.uk

MOUNTS FARM is a family-run site in the heart of South Devon. On-site facilities include **FREE** hot showers, flush toilets, **FREE** hot water in washing-up room, razor points, laundry and information room, electric hook-ups and site shop. We welcome tents, touring caravans and motor caravans.

- Large pitches in level, sheltered fields. • No charges for awnings.
- Children and pets welcome.

Situated three miles north of Kingsbridge, Mounts Farm is an ideal base for exploring Dartmouth, Salcombe, Totnes, Dartmoor and the many safe, sandy beaches nearby.

Self-catering cottage also available.

Devon — SOUTH WEST ENGLAND 43
Modbury, Newton Abbot

Pennymoor
Caravan & Camping Park
Modbury, Devon PL21 0SB

Welcome to the leisurely, relaxed atmosphere of Pennymoor, a delightful and spacious rural camping and caravanning site with panoramic views of Dartmoor and Devon countryside...

Immaculately maintained, well-drained, peaceful rural site with panoramic views, Midway between Plymouth and Kingsbridge (A379). An ideal centre for touring moors, towns and beaches, only five miles from Bigbury-on-Sea and nine miles from Salcombe. Golf courses at Bigbury and Thurlestone and boating at Salcombe, Newton Ferrers and Kingsbridge. Large, superb toilet/shower block with fully tiled walls and floors, and hairdryers. Facilities for the disabled holidaymaker. Dishwashing room - FREE hot water. Laundry room. Children's play area. Shop. Gas. Public telephone on site. Luxury caravans for hire, all services, fully equipped including colour TV. Ideal for touring caravans and tents.

Write, phone or e-mail quoting FHG for free colour brochure.

Tel & Fax: 01548 830542 • Tel: 01548 830020
e-mail: enquiries@pennymoor-camping.co.uk
www.pennymoor-camping.co.uk

Twelve Oaks Caravan Park
Twelve Oaks Farm, Teigngrace, Newton Abbot TQ12 6QT
Mrs M. A. Gale • Tel & Fax: 01626 352769 • www.twelveoaksfarm.co.uk

A unique experience
– set in quiet countryside –
a working farm and its animals!
- Serviced pitches with electric hook-up points
- TV hook-up
- On site shop • Luxury showers/toilets
- Free hot water
- Dish wash area • Laundry facilities
- Pets welcome at no extra charge
- Calor gas stockist • Heated swimming pool, ideal for all the family to relax and have fun
- Coarse fishing on site.

Open all year. Find us off the A38 Expressway.

ALSO: Two carefully converted cottages, each with one double and one twin room, bathroom and shower room. Heating, TV, fridge, microwave and laundry facilties. Parking.

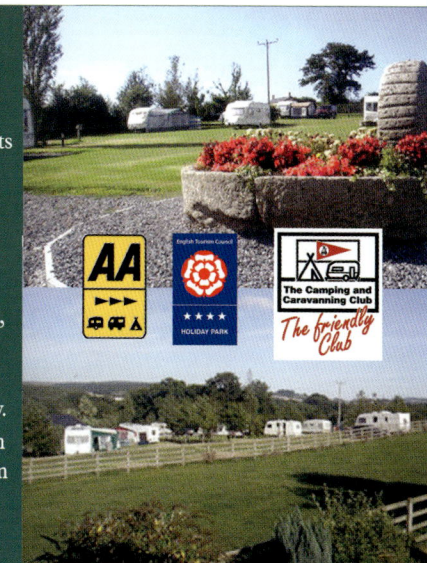

SOUTH WEST ENGLAND — Devon — Paignton

Beverley Holidays

holidays to remember

Escape to the perfect seaside resort and rediscover the things that really matter.

- Family run 5 star holidays
- Playground & children's room
- Indoor & outdoor pools
- Great nightly entertainment
- Crazy golf, tennis & snooker tables
- On site bars, restaurants & takeaway

HOLIDAY CARAVANS TOURING LODGES

Call for a brochure 01803 661955

Award winning holidays on The English Riviera

www.beverley-holidays.co.uk

• Hoburne Torbay •

Grange Court
Holiday Centre

Grange Road,
Goodrington
Paignton TQ4 7JP

Two and three-bedroom modern holiday caravans on this popular site. Some have sun decking with garden furniture. They are fully equipped with microwaves, electric cookers and heating. The site offers a licensed clubhouse with entertainments and children's play area, restaurant and indoor pool. Other facilities include an outdoor pool, launderette, shop for papers and groceries and a café. Goodrington Beach is 15 minutes' walk or there are two car parks. Sorry, no pets. Brochure available.

For further information & reservations contact:
M. Gould, 3 Pulteney Terrace, Bath BA2 4HJ
Tel: 01225 316578 • e-mail: murielg@live.co.uk

Devon — **SOUTH WEST ENGLAND** 45
Salcombe

Salcombe Regis

Camping & Caravan park
Sidmouth, Devon EX10 0JH
Tel: 01395 514303
Fax: 01395 514314
contact@salcombe-regis.co.uk
www.salcombe-regis.co.uk

Large Amenities Block
- FREE hot water to all Showers and Basins
- Shaver Points • Dishwashing Area
- Laundrette • Ironing facilities
- Hairdryers • Family Bathroom
- Baby Changing facilities

Shop and Reception
- Information Area • Payphone
- Calor Gas and Camping Gaz sales/refills
- Battery charging service • Basic camping supplies
- Basic General Stores • Freezer Pack Service
- Daily Newspapers (to order only) • Park Post Box

On Site
- Electric Hook-ups
- Chemical and Grey Water Disposal Points
- Children's Playground • Putting Green
- Badminton Net • Large Dog Exercise Field
- Barbeques permitted (NOT disposables)
- Parking on Departure Day (off pitch, small charge)
- Caravan storage subject to availability

The Hook Family Welcomes You

Adjoining our family home and covering 16 acres, Salcombe Regis Camping and Caravan Park offers unrivalled space and tranquillity.

Beautiful views of the combe, with the sea beyond, can be seen from our camping field where young and old may enjoy open expanses of grass ideal for picnics, ball games, flying a kite or just quiet reflection.

Paths lead to the world heritage coast, where Salcombe Mouth boasts a delightful pebble beach, forming part of the Jurassic Coastline, which at low tide gives access to Weston and Sidmouth beaches.

FREE COLOUR BROCHURE

46 SOUTH WEST ENGLAND   Devon
                                                                          Seaton

AXEVALE CARAVAN PARK

Beautiful views, first class facilities, and just a short walk from both the town and the beach, Axevale is the perfect choice for an easy going, relaxing holiday in Devon.

A quiet, family-run park with 68 modern and luxury caravans for hire.
The park overlooks the delightful River Axe Valley, and is just a 10 minute walk from the town with its wonderfully long, award-winning beach.

Ideal for children and families
The park is fenced and safe for children, who will love our extensive play area, with its sand pit, paddling pool, swings and slide. A reliable babysitting service is available so you can enjoy an evening out on your own

Quiet and peaceful
With no clubhouse, a relaxing atmosphere is ensured.
All of our caravans have a shower, toilet, fridge and TV.
Sited on hard standing which connect dry pathways and tarmac roads. Axevale is the perfect choice in spring and autumn too.

Shopping and Laundry
Laundry facilities are provided and there is a wide selection of goods on sale in the park shop which is open every day.

Prices from £80 per week; reductions for three or fewer persons early/late season.

Axevale Caravan Park, Colyford Road, Seaton, Devon EX12 2DF
Tel: 0800 0688816
e-mail: info@axevale.co.uk   www.axevale.co.uk

Devon — SOUTH WEST ENGLAND 47
South Molton

Riverside Caravan & Camping Park
Marsh Lane, North Molton Road, South Molton EX36 3HQ

A beautiful, family-owned caravan and camping park in 40 acres of flat meadow and woodland near the market town of South Molton, an ideal base for exploring Exmoor.

- Luxurious heated shower and toilet block with free hot showers.
- Laundry facilities and baby changing area.
- Children and pets welcome.
- Specimen carp fishing lakes.
- Coarse fishing lakes
- Barbecue and picnic tables.
- Hard standing, level Europitches.
- Electrical hook-up.
- Drinking water and grey waste outlet
- TV aerial sockets.
- Large open flat field available for rallies.
- Storage available

Tel: 01769 579269/574853
relax@exmoorriverside.co.uk
www.exmoorriverside.co.uk

48 SOUTH WEST ENGLAND — **Devon**

Tavistock, Thornbury

HARFORD BRIDGE
HOLIDAY PARK

1985 – 20 – 2005

Beautiful, award-winning family-run park set in Dartmoor National Park on the banks of the River Tavy, with delightful views of the moor. Riverside camping and other level pitches.

Luxury self-catering caravan holiday homes open all year.

(Off the A386 Okehampton Road, two miles from Tavistock. Take Peter Tavy turning).

A lovely, peaceful camping facility where you can be assured of warm personal care and attention. 120 pitches available for any mix of touring caravans, motor homes, trailer tents and tents.

Included in our charges is free hot water and showers, use of a hard tennis court, children's enclosed play area, table tennis and games room (no gaming machines), a quiet room with television and comprehensive library, a large recreation green for leisure facilities, a plentiful supply of picnic tables and 2 permanent barbecue facilities. All pitches are on a level plain with parking alongside for one car.

Harford Bridge Holiday Park
Peter Tavy, Tavistock, Devon PL19 9LS
Tel: 01822 810349 • Fax: 01822 810028
e-mail: enquiry@harfordbridge.co.uk
www.harfordbridge.co.uk

Woodacott Holiday Park
Woodacott, Thornbury, Devon EX22 7BT

Peaceful, rural Devon

A small site taking touring caravans and letting self-catering bungalows. Plenty of hard standing pitches, all with electric points. Toilets and shower rooms are available together with water taps and waste disposal.

We have two lakes for coarse fishing, and an indoor heated swimming pool together with jacuzzi and sauna.

Please telephone for further details:
01409 261 162

e-mail: stewartwoodacott@yahoo.co.uk

www.woodacottholidaypark.co.uk

Devon

SOUTH WEST ENGLAND 49

Totnes, Woolacombe

Delightful rural Devon farm just five minutes' drive to Paignton's beaches, shops and entertainments, thirty minutes to Dartmoor. The nearby village of Stoke Gabriel has pubs, shops, and a Post Office. Broadleigh Farm Park has a Caravan Club Certificate site, which is adjacent to its own main site, situated in the countryside in a beautiful setting close to Torbay and the River Dart.

The park occupies a field alongside the farmhouse where fresh farm produce is on sale, and also the farm's own traditional farmhouse cider. There are 68 pitches, all with mains hook-up. Newly built service block providing hot showers, hot and cold washing facilities, flush WC (including disabled & baby changing facilities), and a chemical disposal point. There are also cold water taps on site close to the pitches. A separate field is available for camping and for caravan rallies

Broadleigh Farm Park
Caravan & Camping

Coombe House Lane, Aish, Stoke Gabriel, Totnes TQ9 6PU
Tel: 01803 782309 • www.broadleighfarm.co.uk

endless fun...

Four award winning Holiday Parks set in Devon's breathtaking countryside next to Woolacombe's 3 miles of golden Blue Flag sandy beach!

over 40 FREE activities...
- 10 Heated Pools • Cinema • Waterslides
- Health Suite • Playzone • Crazy Golf
- Nightly Entertainment • Tennis • Snooker
- Kid's Clubs • Cinema ... Plus so much more!

...and for just a little more
- 10 Pin Bowling • Affiliated Golf Club
- Waves Ceramic Studio • 17th Century Inn
- Indoor Bowls Rinks • Amusement Arcade
- Kiddy Karts • Sports Bar • Climbing Wall
- NEW All-Weather Pitches • Electric Hook-ups
- Laundry Facilities & Shop • Swim Lessons

Seaview Camping and Touring plus Holiday Homes & Luxury Lodges

REGISTER ONLINE FOR LATEST OFFERS!!
woolacombe.com/fcc
0844 770 0383
OR TEXT **HOLIDAY** TO **60800**

WOOLACOMBE BAY
HOLIDAY PARKS · NORTH DEVON

symbols

- ☀ Holiday Parks & Centres
- 🚐 Caravans for Hire
- Ⓢ Caravan Sites and Touring Parks
- ⛺ Camping Sites

50 SOUTH WEST ENGLAND   Devon
                                                          Woolacombe

North Morte Farm Caravan & Camping
Dept. FHG, Mortehoe, Woolacombe EX34 7EG
(01271 870381)

The nearest camping and caravan park to the sea, in perfectly secluded beautiful coastal country.

Our family-run park, adjoining National Trust land, is only 500 yards from Rockham Beach, yet only five minutes' walk from the village of Mortehoe with a Post Office, shops, cafes and pubs – one of which has a children's room.

Four to six berth holiday caravans for hire and pitches for tents, dormobiles and touring caravans, electric hook-ups available.

We have hot showers and flush toilets, laundry room, shop and off-licence; Calor gas and Camping Gaz available; children's play area. Dogs accepted but must be kept on lead. Open April to end September. Brochure available.

e-mail: info@northmortefarm.co.uk
www.northmortefarm.co.uk

Dorset
Dorchester

Dorset

SOUTH WEST ENGLAND 51

Giant's Head

Caravan & Camping Park • Tel: 01300 341242
Old Sherborne Road, Cerne Abbas, Dorchester DT2 7TR

A quiet site with wonderful views of Dorset Downs and the Blackmoor Vale. Two miles north-east of Cerne Abbas. We are in an ideal position for a motoring, cycling or walking holiday. Discover hidden sites of Dorset through our Treasure Trails, available online at www.treasuretrails.co.uk or at Giants Head.

Fishing, boating and bathing at Weymouth and Portland.

Site facilities include toilets, water supply, showers. Electric hook-ups available. Laundry room. Hot water. Good approach road. Site holds 60 caravans and tents; campers and camper vans also welcome. Terms on request.

• Children welcome • Pets accepted on lead • Self Catering also available

e-mail: holidays@giantshead.co.uk • www.giantshead.co.uk

CAMPING SITES

DORCHESTER near. Home Farm, Rectory Lane, Puncknowle, Near Dorchester DT2 9BW (01308 897258). Small secluded site in beautiful area, one-and-a-half-miles from West Bexington, four miles from Abbotsbury and Burton Bradstock. We can accommodate tents, touring caravans, and motor caravans. Facilities include mains water, washbasins, toilets, washing-up sinks, showers, razor points, disposal point for chemical toilets, electric hook-ups; gas exchange. Sea fishing available locally. Good food served at the village inn. Must pre-book at all times. Further information on request.
• Dogs welcome, must be on a lead at all times.

www.holidayguides.com

THE INSIDE PARK

Touring Park, Blandford, Dorset

Dorset — Blandford

So Relaxing You Won't Want To Leave!

- ✪ Extra Large Pitches
- ✪ All modern Facilities
- ✪ Free Hot Water
- ✪ Shop
- ✪ Ideal Family Site
- ✪ Quiet & Secluded
- ✪ Children's Play Area
- ✪ Country Walks & Wildlife
- ✪ Cycle trails
- ✪ Caravan Storage

01258 453719
www.theinsidepark.co.uk

Dorset
Poole

Beacon Hill Touring Park

David Bellamy Gold Award Winners since 2001

Beacon Hill Touring Park enjoys the beauty of 30 acres of partly wooded heathland, together with a wide selection of wildlife. We are a Conservation Award winning park, three miles west of Poole town centre, and just five miles from some of the best beaches Britain has to offer.

- Well stocked shop
- Showers with free hot water
- Baby changing unit
- Laundry rooms with adjacent dishwashing facilities
- Electric hook-ups
- Ample water, waste and chemical disposal points
- Wireless internet
- Heated swimming pool
- Games rooms
- Children's adventure play areas
- All-weather tennis court
- Fishing, with horse riding nearby
- Take-Away/Coffee Shop
- Fully licensed bar

Our natural landscaping affords many unique pitch settings; a non-regimented feel is an aspect our customers return to enjoy.

Beacon Hill Touring Park, Blandford Road North, Poole, Dorset BH16 6AB
Tel: 01202 631631 • Fax: 01202 624388
www.beaconhilltouringpark.co.uk • bookings@beaconhilltouringpark.co.uk

picture perfect holidays...

...picture South Lytchett Manor

Set in over 20 acres of tranquil parkland, South Lytchett Manor is the ideal base for exploring outstanding local countryside, heritage coastline and nearby attractions. It is a friendly, family-run park just three miles from Poole, offering top quality amenities.

- **Practical Caravan's Best Park in Dorset, 2009**
- Close to Poole • Open until January 2nd - special winter rates • Fully stocked shop • Superb heated shower blocks • Large pitches available • Hard-standings, electric hook-ups, TV connections available • AA pet-friendly/dog walk • Bus service from main gates • Rallies welcome • Fantastic discounted Golf Weekend in October

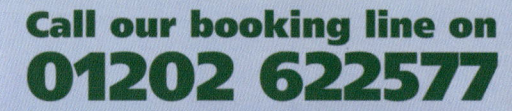

Call our booking line on
01202 622577

SOUTH LYTCHETT MANOR

South Lytchett Manor Caravan and Camping Park
Dorchester Road, Lytchett Minster, Poole, Dorset BH16 6JB.
Telephone: 01202 622577. Web: southlytchettmanor.co.uk
Email: info@southlytchettmanor.co.uk

Dorset — Wareham

SOUTH WEST ENGLAND 55

Wareham Forest Tourist Park

North Trigon, Wareham, Dorset, BH20 7NZ
Tel (01929) 551393 Fax (01929) 558321
email: holiday@warehamforest.co.uk
Owners: Tony & Sarah Birch
originally of Carnon Downs

www.warehamforest.co.uk

Enjoy the peace and tranquillity of Wareham Forest, together with the luxury of our tourist park. Located mid-way between Wareham and Bere Regis (off A35). We make an ideal base for exploring this unspoilt corner of Dorset.

- Heated Pool (High Season)
- Wi-fi Available
- Licensed Shop
- Disabled Facilities & Family Bathrooms
- Children's Adventure Playground
- Woodland Dog Walks
- Fully Serviced Luxury Pitches Available
- Heated Toilet Blocks
- Laundrette
- Long or Short Term Storage
- Table Tennis

OPEN ALL YEAR

AA Regional Campsite of the Year 2009
WiFi Available
Caravan Top 100 Parks 2009 Awards
The BEST OF BRITISH
SILVER
enjoyEngland.com TOURING & CAMPING PARK
AA

Manor Farm Caravan Park

We look forward to welcoming you at our quiet and clean Park in the Frome Valley. Situated just off the A352, in the village of East Stoke, mid-way between Wareham and Wool in an Area of Outstanding Natural Beauty. An ideal base from which to explore the beautiful Dorset countryside and the Jurassic coast.

60 units – seasonal pitches – storage.
Shower and toilet block, children's play area.
Ice blocks frozen. Calor Gas/Camping gaz exchange.
Site supervised 24 hours a day and the toilet block is lit all night.
Three quarters of pitches are electrical 240V – 16amp.
Although we allow dogs on site (1 per pitch), they have to be leashed at all times, exercised and toiletted off the site.

David and Gillian Topp
Manor Farm Caravan Park, Church Lane
East Stoke, Wareham, Dorset BH20 6AW
Tel : 01929 462870
e- mail info@manorfarmcp.co.uk
www.manorfarmcp.co.uk

OPEN ALL YEAR

SOUTH WEST ENGLAND — Dorset

West Bexington, Weymouth

Gorselands Caravan Park

Peace and Tranquillity

Small select park with stunning views over Jurassic Coastline

- Excellent beach fishing
- Pets Welcome • Caravans & Apartments
- Camping nearby mid July-August • Shop and Launderette
- Village Pub 100 yards • Beach and car park one mile

Tel: 01308 897232 • Fax: 01308 897239
www.gorselands.co.uk
e-mail: info@gorselands.co.uk
West Bexington-on-Sea, Near Bridport, Dorset DT2 9DJ

Pebble Bank Caravan Park
Camp Road, Wyke Regis, Weymouth DT4 9HF

Pebble Bank Caravan Park is situated 1½ miles from Weymouth town centre. The Park is broadly divided into two sections, one for touring vans/campers and recreational space, the other for privately owned static holiday vans, some of which are let for holiday bookings.

Facilities include numerous water points and electric hook-ups, first class toilet and shower facilities and chemical disposal points, laundry room, children's play area, etc. Dogs allowed provided they are well behaved and kept on leads.

Our aim is to give the discerning visitor the most relaxed, comfortable and enjoyable holiday possible. Brochure available.

e-mail: info@pebblebank.co.uk
www.pebblebank.co.uk
Tel & Fax: 01305 774844

FHG Guides

publish a large range of well-known accommodation guides.
We will be happy to send you details or you can use the order form at the back of this book.

Dorset
Wimborne, Wool

SOUTH WEST ENGLAND 57

Woolsbridge Manor Farm caravan park

Three Legged Cross,
Wimborne, Dorset BH21 6RA
Telephone: 01202 826369

Your base for exploring Dorset and the New Forest

Situated approximately three-and-a-half-miles from the New Forest market town of Ringwood – easy access to the south coast. Seven acres level, semi-sheltered, well-drained spacious pitches. Quiet country location on a working farm, ideal and safe for families. Showers, mother/baby area, laundry room, washing up area, chemical disposal, payphone, electric hook-ups, battery charging. Children's play area on site. Site shop. Dogs welcome on leads. Fishing adjacent. Moors Valley Country Park golf course one mile. Pub and restaurant 10 minutes' walk.

e-mail: woolsbridge@btconnect.com • www.woolsbridgemanorcaravanpark.co.uk

Whitemead Caravan Park

East Burton Road, Wool
Dorset BH20 6HG

Peaceful, family-run site set in mature woodland. New toilet block with excellent facilities for 2005/6 with free showers and hot water. We have two children's play areas, a games room. Our shop is open daily selling groceries, sweets, gas, newspapers and accessories. Takeaway food on site. Monkey World is within walking distance, as are the village pubs, restaurants and shops. The Tank Museum is also close by with Lulworth Cove only five miles away. Excellent walking and cycling all round. The perfect base to explore the beautiful county of Dorset. Dogs welcome.

Tel & Fax: 01929 462241
e-mail: whitemeadcp@aol.com • www.whitemeadcaravanpark.co.uk

symbols

- Holiday Parks & Centres
- Caravans for Hire
- Caravan Sites and Touring Parks
- Camping Sites

Gloucestershire

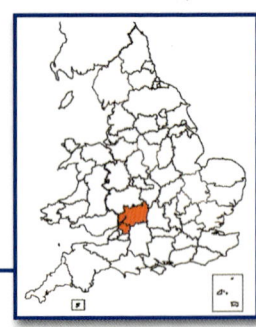

Cirencester, Coleford

CIRENCESTER. Hoburne Cotswold, Broadway Lane, South Cerney, Cirencester GL7 5UQ
Tel: 01285 860216 • www.hoburne.com/cotswold_main.asp
For those who love an aquatic adventure, Hoburne Cotswold is an ideal centre for water-based sports, with four lakes, indoor & outdoor pools, fishing, canoes and pedalos. No pets allowed. 302 touring pitches available. Caravans, motorhomes and tents welcome. Open all year round.

CIRENCESTER. Mayfield Park, Cheltenham Road, Cirencester GL7 7BH
Tel: 01285 831301 • www.mayfieldpark.co.uk
A warm welcome is given to everyone at this friendly site. Modern facilities including hot showers are provided, but no on-site entertainment. There are wildlife parks and stately homes to visit nearby, as well as bridlepaths and various eateries. Open all year round. 36 touring pitches available. Tents and caravans welcome.

COLEFORD. Christchurch Camping and Caravan Site, Bracelands Drive, Coleford GL16 7NN
Tel: 01594 833376
Come to Coleford for long woodland walks down to the river and visits to the Clearwell Caves and Ancient Iron Mines, just some of the attractions of the beautiful Wye Valley area. Open from March to January. 280 touring pitches available. Caravans, motorhomes and tents welcome.

COLEFORD. Braceland Camping & Caravan Park, Bracelands Drive, Coleford GL16 7NN
Tel: 01594 833376
This site provides spacious touring pitches with panoramic views of Highmeadow Woods and the Wye Valley. 530 touring pitches available. Caravans, motorhomes and tents welcome.

COLEFORD. Woodland Caravan and Camping Site, Coleford GL1 7NN
Tel: 01594 833376
Secluded pitches in a woodland setting, perfect for a peaceful holiday. No toilet/shower facilities. Open from March to November. Tents not permitted. 90 touring pitches available. Caravans and motorhomes welcome.

	Electric hook-ups available		Facilities for disabled visitors
	Children's play area		Pets welcome
	Laundry facilities		Shop on site
	Licensed bar on site	W	Wifi access available

Gloucestershire

Cotswolds, Lower Wick, Slimbridge, Tewkesbury

SOUTH WEST ENGLAND 59

The Red Lion Camping and Caravan Park
Wainlode Hill, Norton, Near Gloucester GL2 9LW
Tel & Fax: 01452 730251 • www.redlioninn-caravancampingpark.co.uk

Set in an idyllic riverside location in glorious countryside, the park provides an ideal base for exploring the surrounding countryside, and nearby historic towns of Gloucester, Tewkesbury and Cheltenham. Full facilities are available including electric hookups, toilets and showers, well-stocked shop on-site and launderette, with a wide range of food available at the neighbouring Red Lion Inn. Seasonal tourer pitches and static caravans available for sale.

'A warm and friendly welcome at all times of the season'

AA LISTED.

This site is set between the Cotswold Escarpment and Severn Vale, in open rural countryside. Many local amenities including swimming, golf, riding, fishing. Tourist attractions include Westonbirt Arboretum, Berkeley Castle, Slimbridge Wild Fowl Trust, Jenner Museum and Cotswold Way. Ideal for touring the many picturesque towns and villages on hills and vales and as a stopover for north/south journeys. Inn within walking distance and many inns and hotels within close proximity.

- Gas and electric hook-ups available • Elsan disposal
- Toilets and shower • washing-up facilities • Laundry
- Children's play area • Storage available all year.

Pets welcome under control. Terms from £8 to £10 tents, £9.50 caravans and motor homes.

Hogsdown Farm Camp Site, Dursley, Lower Wick GL11 6DB • 01453 810224

Welcome to Camping & Caravanning in Slimbridge
TUDOR CARAVAN PARK

- Quiet country site set in the beautiful Severn Vale, along the Cotswold Edge
- Beside the Gloucester-Sharpness canal with great fishing and cycling.
- A short walk to world famous SLIMBRIDGE WETLANDS CENTRE.
- Adjacent to the Tudor Arms pub & restaurant.
- Walking on the Severn Way alongside or the Cotswold Way, 4 miles away.
- Ideal base for touring the Cotswolds, visiting Bristol, Gloucester Docks, Westonbirt Arboretum, Berkeley Castle, & Forest of Dean.
- Electric hook-ups; Hard-standings; Toilets & Showers; Open All Year.

New Toilet & Shower Block for 2010

Shepherds Patch, Slimbridge, Gloucestershire, GL2 7BP   Tel: (01453) 890483
Email: fhg@tudorcaravanpark.co.uk   Web: www.tudorcaravanpark.co.uk

---

TEWKESBURY. Winchcombe Camping & Caravanning, Brooklands Farm, Near Tewkesbury GL20 8NX Tel: 01242 620259.
Winchombe is situated near Tewkesbury, a quaint little town with antique shops and tea rooms. The site is a perfect base for touring the surrounding area with its lakes and rolling countryside. 90 touring pitches available. Caravans and tents welcome. Open March to January.

TEWKESBURY. Croft Farm Leisure & Waterpark, Bredons Hardwick, Tewkesbury GL20 7EE Tel: 01684 772321 • Fax: 01684 773379 • www.croftfarmleisure.co.uk
Croft Farm is ideal for all the family, with facilities and activities to suit all ages. These include a fully equipped gym, sauna and sunbed, as well as a variety of watersports. The caravan pitches are situated on two sides of the waterpark's lake. Open from March to January. Caravans, motorhomes and trailer tents welcome.

60 SOUTH WEST ENGLAND   Somerset
                                                    Bridgwater

Somerset

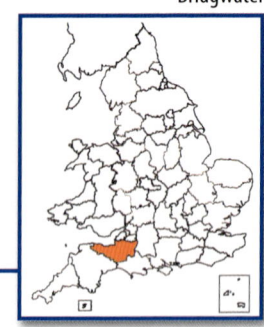

Mill Farm Caravan & Camping Park

FIDDINGTON, BRIDGWATER, SOMERSET TA5 1JQ

SWIMMING – TROPICAL INDOOR HEATED POOLS AND TWO OUTDOOR POOLS WITH GIANT WATER SLIDE ★ RIDING ★ WiFi ★ BOATING ★ HOLIDAY APARTMENTS TO LET

Attractive, sheltered farm site. Between beautiful Quantock Hills and the sea. Boating, swings, table tennis, TV, tourist information, large sand pit.

FOR HIRE: Canoes, trampolines and ponies.
★ Club Entertainment ★ Caravan storage available.

CLEAN TOILETS ETC, LAUNDRY ROOM, ELECTRIC HOOK-UPS, CAMP SHOP, GOOD LOCAL PUBS. OPEN ALL YEAR.

WRITE OR PHONE FOR BROCHURE

Tel: M. J. Evans:
01278 732286
www.millfarm.biz

symbols

- ☼ Holiday Parks & Centres
- 🚐 Caravans for Hire
- Ⓢ Caravan Sites and Touring Parks
- ⛺ Camping Sites

Somerset
Bridgwater

SOUTH WEST ENGLAND 61

the FAIRWAYS International Touring Camping & Caravan Park

A place to relax... for the holidaymaker who appreciates peace and serenity, this friendly, family-run park is an ideal centre to explore Somerset, and is close to Devon and Cornwall's stunning coastline.
Easy access off B3141 • Open all year.
• Shower block with washing up area and chemical disposal point
• Well equipped amenity blocks • Electric hook-ups • Secure caravan storage
• **Games room and children's play area**
• WiFi available • Kitchen area with stainless steel tables, ice cube dispenser, microwaves, upright freezers • Shop with caravan accessories, toys and foodstuffs.

Fairways International Touring, Camping and Caravan Park
Bath Road, Bawdrip, Bridgwater, Somerset TA7 8PP
Tel/Fax: 01278 685569
e-mail: holiday@fairwaysinternational.co.uk
www.fairwaysinternational.co.uk

ST AUDRIES BAY
Holiday Club

**West Quantoxhead,
Near Minehead,
Somerset TA4 4DY
Tel: 01984 632515**

- Family-owned and run award-winning Park near Exmoor and The Quantocks • 15 miles from the M5 • Fantastic views across the sea and beach access • Sport & leisure facilities • Entertainment • Licensed bars and restaurant • Coffee Shop • On-site shop • Children's play area

- Peaceful relaxing Park with family time in school holidays
- Self-Catering & Half-Board Holidays
- Touring Caravans & Camping
- Luxury Holiday Homes for sale

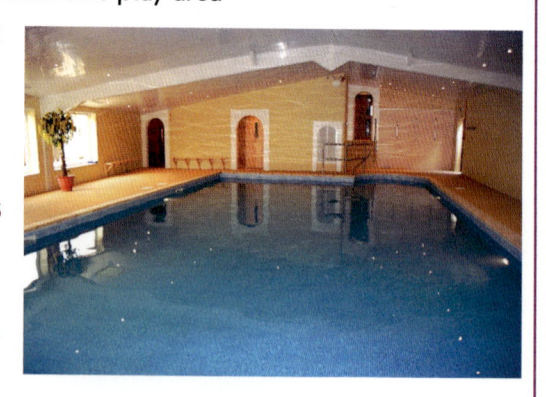

e-mail: info@staudriesbay.co.uk
www.staudriesbay.co.uk

Somerset
Porlock

SOUTH WEST ENGLAND 63

In the heart of Exmoor Country
BURROWHAYES FARM
Caravan & Camping Site and Riding Stables
West Luccombe, Porlock, Near Minehead, Somerset TA24 8HT
Tel: 01643 862463

A select family site in the heart of the Exmoor National Park, just 2 miles from the coast.

The surrounding moors and woods of the glorious Horner Valley provide a walker's paradise and children enjoy playing and exploring for hours.

Riding Stables offer pony trekking for all ages and abilities.

Heated shower block with disabled and baby changing facilities, launderette and pot wash. Shop on site.

Sites for Touring Caravans, tents and motorhomes with or without hook-ups. Caravan holiday homes for hire.

Proprietors Julian & Marion Dascombe
e-mail: info@burrowhayes.co.uk
www.burrowhayes.co.uk

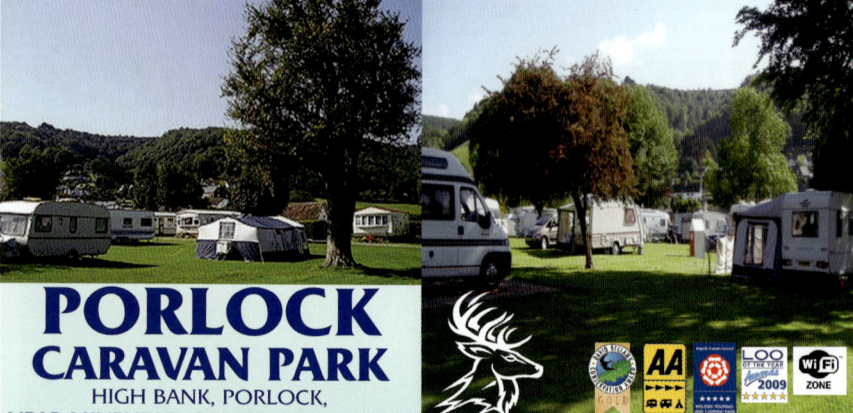

PORLOCK CARAVAN PARK
HIGH BANK, PORLOCK, NEAR MINEHEAD, SOMERSET TA24 8ND

- Small family-run park • A few minutes' walk from Porlock village, set in the heart of Exmoor
- Luxury, central heated holiday homes for hire • Full facilities for tourers, tents and motorhomes
- Village offers several pubs, restaurants and shops selling local produce
- Ideal base from which to explore Exmoor, whether walking, cycling or riding

Facilities on Site include: • Reception & Information Area • Free Showers and hot water • Hair dryer and shaver points • Disabled facilities • Dishwashing room • Laundry room and drying area • Microwave oven • Free freezer block facility • Electric hook-up • Grass or hardstanding pitches • Chemical waste disposal room • Dog exercise area • Calor gas exchange • Cars park beside units • WiFi

Phone for brochure 01643 862269 or e-mail: info@porlockcaravanpark.co.uk
www.porlockcaravanpark.co.uk

Ashe Farm
Touring Park

Thornfalcon, Taunton, Somerset TA3 5NW
Tel: 01823 443764
e-mail: info@ashefarm.co.uk
www.ashefarm.co.uk

Ashe Farm Touring Park is a quiet, informal family-run site, part of a working farm situated in the Vale of Taunton between the Quantock and Blackdown Hills. The six acre site has two sheltered meadows with lovely views of the hills and an atmosphere of peace and seclusion. Towing approach from the M5 motorway is easy and the site is easy to find at the end of your journey.

There are electric hook-ups in both fields. The first field has a new toilet block with showers, hot water, hair dryers and razor points. There are toilet facilities for the disabled and a laundry with tumble dryer and iron. Nearby is the information Room and a play area for small children. also wash up sinks and waste disposal points.

Somerset — **SOUTH WEST ENGLAND** 65
Taunton

Quantock Orchard Caravan Park

Award-winning, family-run campsite set amidst the stunning Somerset countryside.

Quantock Orchard is situated in an idyllic setting surrounded by picturesque views of the Quantocks, in an Area of Outstanding Natural Beauty. This peaceful park is close to Exmoor, the coast and the West Somerset Railway. Relax and unwind among these beautiful surroundings whilst enjoying our Five Star facilities.

- fully heated toilet and shower block • launderette • games room
- adventure playground • shop • outdoor heated pool • gym with jacuzzi, steam room and sauna • cycle hire • caravan storage

Tents, tourers and motorhomes welcome
Luxury static holiday homes for sale or hire
Open all year

Michael & Sara Barrett,
Quantock Orchard Caravan Park, Flaxpool,
Crowcombe, Near Taunton TA4 4AW
01984 618618
e-mail: qocp@flaxpool.freeserve.co.uk
www.quantock-orchard.co.uk

DE LUXE PARK

Looking for Holiday Accommodation?

FHG K·U·P·E·R·A·R·D

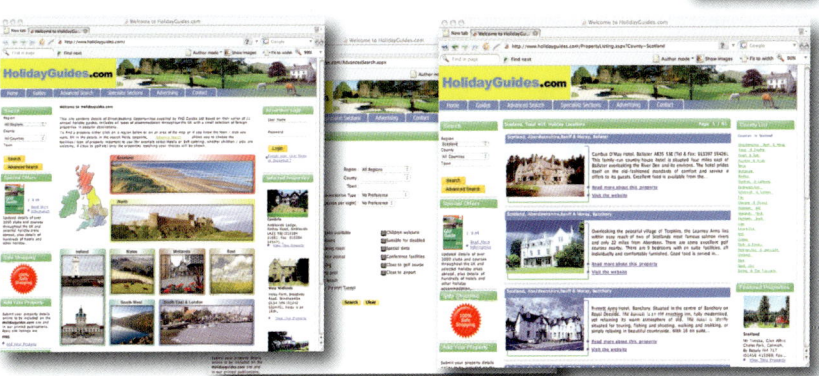

for details of hundreds of properties throughout the UK, visit our website

www.holidayguides.com

Wiltshire

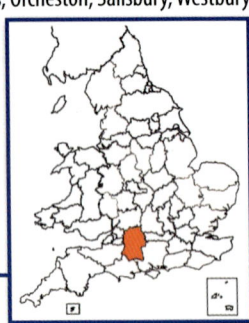

Devizes, Orchester, Salisbury, Westbury

Colin and Cynthia Fletcher
FOXHANGERS CANALSIDE FARM
Lower Foxhangers, Rowde, Devizes SN10 1SS
Tel & Fax: 01380 828254
e-mail: sales@foxhangers.co.uk
www.foxhangers.com

Small farm/marina with its many diverse attractions situated alongside the famous "Caen Hill" flights of 29 locks. Hear the near musical clatter of the windlass heralding the lock gate opening and the arrival of yet another colourful narrowboat. Relax on the patios of our rural retreats - 4 holiday mobile homes, all new models, sleeping 4/6. Ideally situated for fishing, cycling or walking. Pubs within easy walking distance. Short breaks when available. Secluded campsite nestling under the hedgerows, with electricity and facilities.
Also narrowboat hire for weekly or short breaks. Avebury, Stonehenge, Bath and Longleat all close by.

ORCHESTON. Stonehenge Touring Park, Orcheston, Near Shrewton, Salisbury SP3 4SH
Tel: 01980 620304 • www.stonehengetouringpark.com
Located on the edge of Salisbury Plain and just 4 miles from historic Stonehenge, this small site is maintained to the highest standards. Some hardstandings are available and there are 20 electric hook-ups. Open all year.

SALISBURY. Alderbury Caravan & Camping Park, Southampton Road, Whaddon, Salisbury SP5 3HB
Tel: 01722 710125 • www.alderburycaravanpark.co.uk
A small, friendly, family-run site, convenient for visiting Salisbury and just a short drive from the New Forest. A pub serving meals is located just opposite and the village shops are close by. Tourers and tents welcome.

WESTBURY. Brokerswood Country Park, Westbury BA13 4EJ
Tel: 01373 822238 • www.brokerswood.co.uk
Spacious pitches are available for tents and caravans in 80 acres of woodland just a few minutes from Longleat. Attractions include woodland walks, a fishing lake, and a cafe serving meals until 5pm. A pub is just a short walk away.

🔌	Electric hook-ups available	♿	Facilities for disabled visitors
🛝	Children's play area	🐕	Pets welcome
🧺	Laundry facilities	🛒	Shop on site
🍷	Licensed bar on site	W	Wifi access available

London & South East England

The Houses of Parliament as seen from the London Eye

The focus of the South East of England is the capital, London, a thriving metropolis, with shops, theatres, concerts, museums and sporting events attracting visitors from all over the world. Away from the city, the seaside resorts in Kent, Sussex and Hampshire provide traditional family fun and sandy beaches, as well as all kinds of water-based sports, while further inland both in these counties and in Oxfordshire, Buckinghamshire and Berkshire there are market towns, stately homes, country parks and nature reserves to explore and enjoy.

London has everything to offer! With a wide range of accommodation at prices to suit every pocket, it's easy to spend a weekend here or a take a longer break. Among the most popular places for visitors are the museums and art galleries. The National Gallery houses one of the largest art collections in the world, while the Tate Modern concentrates on the work of artists from the beginning of the 20th century. Except for some special exhibitions, entry to both is free, and this also applies to the Natural History Museum and the Victoria and Albert Museum. To see what's going on all over London, take a trip on the London Eye, the world's highest observation wheel, or meet celebrities (or at least their wax doubles) at Madame Tussauds.

Kent, a county of gentle, rolling downland, long known as the 'Garden of England', provides opportunities for all kinds of outdoor pursuits. The North Downs Way makes its way through an Area of Outstanding Natural Beauty stretching from Kent through Sussex to Surrey, starting at Dover, including a loop to Canterbury along the Pilgrim's Way. In the White Cliffs area there are a number of heritage walks and trails to follow, while a stay in the downland villages offers an excellent opportunity to explore the many local paths. With easy access from London, the shingle and sandy beaches at resorts such as Deal, Ramsgate, Margate, Broadstairs and Herne Bay have long been an attraction.

West and East Sussex share with neighbouring Kent an attractive coastline with cliffs and sandy beaches, and the countryside of the High Weald and the North Downs. There are endless possibilities for walking, cycling, horse riding, golf, and if you're looking for something more adventurous, hang gliding and paragliding! Don't forget the castles, like Bodiam near Hastings, and the historic ruins at Pevensey and Lewes, or Arundel, one of England's most important stately homes, in West Sussex. The best known resort is Brighton, with its pebble beach, classic pier, Royal Pavilion and Regency architecture. For a shopping day out visit the designer shops, art galleries and antique shops in The Lanes.

LONDON & SOUTH EAST ENGLAND

Whether you prefer an active break or a quiet country holiday, **Hampshire** offers plenty of choices. There are gardens and country parks, historic houses and wildlife parks, museums and castles, and with its location on the Channel coast, all the activities associated with the seaside. There's plenty to do outdoors in Hampshire: walking, cycling and horse riding on the heathland and ancient woodlands of the New Forest National Park, and for more thrills, paragliding and hang gliding at the Queen Elizabeth Country Park on the South Downs.

All kinds of watersports are available along the coast, but of course the **Isle of Wight**, only a short ferry ride away from the mainland, has award-winning beaches, water sports centres, seakayaking, diving, sailing and windsurfing. For land-based activities there are over 500 miles of interconnected footpaths, historic castles, dinosaur museums, theme parks and activity centres, while the resorts like Sandown, Shanklin, Ryde and Ventnor offer all that is associated with a traditional seaside holiday. There is a thriving arts community, and of course two internationally renowned music festivals held every year.

Less than an hour from London, **Surrey** is the most wooded county in the UK, and an extensive network of footpaths for walkers covers the chalk downs, woods and heathland of the Surrey Hills and North Downs. Alternatively wander through the traditional villages and historic market towns, and stop for lunch at a traditional pub or restaurant. Walk along the Thames towpath to Runnymeade Meadow where the Magna Carta was signed in 1215, or take a leisurely boat trip through the traditional English countryside. Families will enjoy a visit to a working farm, cycling or horse riding, or for more excitement, try the thrilling rides at one of the theme parks.

Whatever your interests, whether in the countryside or the town, **Berkshire** has much to offer. In the east of the county, just a short train ride away from central London, is Windsor Castle, the largest inhabited castle in the world. Racegoers will find plenty of action in Berkshire, with both Ascot and Royal Windsor in the east, and Newbury to the west, where you can also take a tour of the stables at Lambourn and watch the early morning gallops.

Oxford, the 'city of dreaming spires', has attracted visitors for centuries, and in contrast to lively city life, the **Oxfordshire** countryside is ideal for a relaxing break. Stretching from Oxford to the Cotswolds, the mysterious Vale of the White Horse is named after the oldest chalk figure in Britain, dating back over 3000 years. The historic market towns like Abingdon and Wantage make good shopping destinations, or visit the pretty villages, stopping for lunch in one of the many traditional English pubs. Follow the village trail at Kidlington, the largest village in England, or visit the nature reserve at Adderbury Lakes.

Only half an hour from London, the rolling hills and wooded valleys of the **Buckinghamshire** countryside provide a wonderful contrast to city life. There are fascinating historic towns and villages, including West Wycombe, owned by the National Trust, which also has many other interesting properties in the area. These include the stunning gardens at Cliveden, former home of the Astors and focus of the early 20th century social scene.

Photo courtesy Thanet District Council

London (Central & Greater) LONDON & SOUTH EAST ENGLAND 69

London

London
(Central & Greater)

Debden House Camp Site

15 miles north of London in Epping Forest, two miles north of Loughton. M25 to Junction 26 then A121 (Loughton). Left onto A1168 Rectory Lane, second left Pyrles Lane, over crossroads, right onto England's Lane, then second left. Epping Forest is 40 minutes from London (Underground nearby).
Site facilities include shop, café, launderette, showers, play area and much more.
Electric hook-ups. Terms £7.00 adult, £3.50 child; family ticket £25.00. Day ticket £3.50.
London Borough of Newham residents reduced rates.
Open May to September. Brochure available.

**Debden Green Loughton,
Essex IG10 2NZ
Tel: 020 8508 3008
Fax: 020 8508 0284
www.debdenhouse.com**

EDMONTON. Lee Valley Camping And Caravan Park, Meridian Way, Edmonton, London N9 0AS
Tel: 0208 803 6900 • Fax: 020 8884 4975 • www.leevalleypark.org
Set within Lee Valley Regional Park which stretches over 26 miles, this is a ideal base for experiencing the attractions of London from a peaceful and good value base (40 minutes by Tube). Open all year.

LONDON. Abbey Wood Caravan Club Site, Federation Road, Abbey Wood, London SE2 0LS
Tel: 0208 311 7708 • Fax: 0208 311 1465
With good rail connections to the city centre just a short walk away, this popular rural site welcomes caravans, motorhomes and tents. The atmosphere is very rural, with local wildlife and mature trees providing a peaceful haven at the end of a busy day. Open all year.

70 LONDON & SOUTH EAST ENGLAND
Berkshire
Maidenhead, Riseley

Berkshire

HURLEY RIVERSIDE PARK

Family-run park situated in the picturesque Thames Valley alongside the River Thames. Ideal location for visiting Legoland Windsor, Oxford, Henley and London.
- Multi-service and and hard standing pitches available
- Tourers, tents and motorhomes welcome • Launderette • Shop
- Shower blocks with all main services • Fully serviced caravan holiday homes and ready tents for hire • Disabled facilities • Slipway
- Riverside walks • Fishing in season • Discounted Legoland tickets available
- Open 1st March–31st October • Brochure on request.

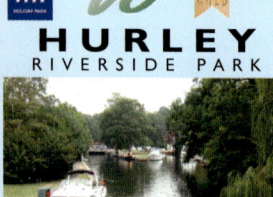

HURLEY RIVERSIDE PARK, HURLEY, MAIDENHEAD, BERKSHIRE SL6 5NE
TEL: 01628 824493/823501
www.hurleyriversidepark.co.uk • info@hurleyriversidepark.co.uk

---

Our Camping Caravan site lies within beautiful woodlands on the Hampshire/Berkshire border, near Reading. Facilities include toilets, free showers, shaving points, hairdryers and laundry.
Campers have 'FREE' access to Country Park facilities including adventure play/toddlers' area, sand pits, slides, crazy golf, miniature railway (£1 extra), nature trail maze, an assortment of play equipment to climb on, as well as four nature trails to experience the vast array of wildlife in their natural habitat, including our Red Deer herd.
Opening 2010 – our new 'Animal Farm'

Wellington Country Park
Odiham Road, Riseley, Near Reading, Berkshire, RG7 1SP
Tel: 0118 932 6444 • Fax 0118 932 6445
e-mail: info@wellington-country-park.co.uk
www.wellington-country-park.co.uk

---

symbols

- ☼ Holiday Parks & Centres
- 🚐 Caravans for Hire
- S Caravan Sites and Touring Parks
- ▲ Camping Sites

Berkshire
Wokingham

California Chalet & Touring Park

Small, family-run park alongside a lake. Secluded pitches in a wooded setting. Close to London, Windsor and Oxford. Also available, 10 self-catering holiday chalets. Terms on request.

California Chalet & Touring Park
Nine Mile Ride, Finchampstead, Wokingham, Berkshire RG40 4HU
Tel: 0118 973 3928 • Fax: 0118 932 8720
e-mail: enquiries@californiapark.co.uk
www.californiapark.co.uk

Other specialised holiday guides from FHG

PUBS & INNS OF BRITAIN
COUNTRY HOTELS OF BRITAIN
PETS WELCOME!
THE GOLF GUIDE WHERE TO PLAY, WHERE TO STAY
500 GREAT PLACES TO STAY
SELF-CATERING HOLIDAYS IN BRITAIN
BED & BREAKFAST STOPS IN BRITAIN
WEEKEND & SHORT BREAKS IN BRITAIN
FAMILY BREAKS IN BRITAIN

Published annually: available in all good bookshops or direct from the publisher:
FHG Guides, Abbey Mill Business Centre, Seedhill, Paisley PA1 1TJ
Tel: 0141 887 0428 • Fax: 0141 889 7204
e-mail: admin@fhguides.co.uk • www.holidayguides.com

72 LONDON & SOUTH EAST ENGLAND — **Buckinghamshire**

Beaconsfield, Milton Keynes, Newport Pagnell

Buckinghamshire

Quiet, level meadowland park. Ideal for touring London, train station one mile. 25 minutes to Marylebone, cheap day return fares available. Legoland 12 miles, with Windsor Castle and the Thames. Model village three miles, many local attractions, including rare breeds farm. Local inn for food quarter of a mile. Lots of walks, ideal for dogs. En suite accommodation available – room only. New shower block and tenting area. 65 pitches available. Open March to January.

Tourers from £15 to £19, tents from £10, motor homes £13 to £18, electric point £2.50

HIGHCLERE FARM

New Barn Lane, Seer Green, Near Beaconsfield, Bucks HP9 2QZ

Tel & Fax: 01494 874505
e-mail: highclerepark@aol.com
www.highclerefarmpark.co.uk

MILTON KEYNES. Old Dairy Farm, Orchard Mill Lane, Stoke Hammond, Milton Keynes MK17 9BF
Tel & Fax: 01908 274206
Picturesque farm site, with good walking nearby on Grand Union Canal towpath; Milton Keynes is just 5 miles away, with lots of shopping and leisure amenities. Ideal for anglers - River Ouzel adjacent. 10 caravan and 10 tent pitches.

NEWPORT PAGNELL. Lovat Meadow Caravan Park, London Road, Newport Pagnell MK16 0AE
Tel: 01908 610858 • Fax: 01908 617874
This gently sloping site has 40 grass pitches and is bordered by woodland and by the River Ouzel where fishing is available in season. No shower or toilet facilities. The site is open March to October.

Hampshire
Hayling Island

Hampshire

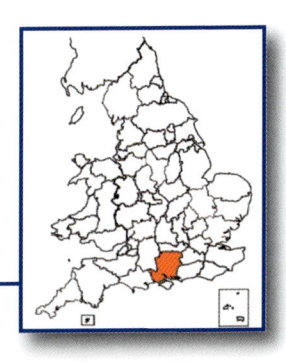

LONDON & SOUTH EAST ENGLAND 73

WELCOME TO HAYLING ISLAND FAMILY CAMP SITES

Hayling Island is an ideal touring base for Portsmouth, the Isle of Wight and the New Forest, with excellent motorway access.
We have safe, clean, award-winning beaches, and windsurfing, sailing, horse riding, golf, tennis and walking to be enjoyed locally.

Our campsite has children's play areas, electric hook-ups, toilets and hot water, heated swimming pool. Many other extras included.

The Oven Campsite

Tel: 023 9246 4695 • Mobile: 07758410020
e-mail: theovencampsite@talktalk.net
www.haylingcampsites.co.uk

symbols

- ☀ Holiday Parks & Centres
- 🚐 Caravans for Hire
- Ⓢ Caravan Sites and Touring Parks
- ▲ Camping Sites

Hampshire

DISCOVER RELAX EXPLORE UNWIND ENJOY

Have you heard about Shorefield Holidays?

All six of our holiday parks are set in peaceful, unspoilt parkland in the beautiful South Coast area.

We offer a choice of touring pitches or self-catering accommodation depending on which park you choose. There are comprehensive leisure facilities available and great entertainment for the whole family.

Pamper yourself in our 'Reflections' Day Spa at Shorefield Country Park, explore the New Forest National Park, or relax on Bournemouth's sandy beaches. For full details, ask for our brochure or browse online.

SHOREFIELD HOLIDAYS LIMITED

Tel 01590 648331
holidays@shorefield.co.uk
www.shorefield.co.uk

Ref: FHG

HAMPSHIRE
Shorefield Country Park
Milford on Sea, SO41 0LH

Lytton Lawn Touring Park
Milford on Sea, SO41 0TX

Oakdene Forest Park
St. Leonards, BH24 2RZ

Forest Edge Holiday Park
St. Leonards, BH24 2SD

DORSET
Merley Court Touring Park
Wimborne, BH21 3AA

Swanage Coastal Park
Swanage, BH19 2RS

Hampshire
Milford-on-Sea, Ringwood

Downton Holiday Park

Downton Holiday Park is a small, peaceful park on the edge of the New Forest and close to the sea. Green fields are across the country lane from us.

We let only 22 static caravans on our small park; each caravan has shower and colour TV.

A laundry and children's play equipment are on premises. Swimming, riding and sailing are all nearby. Bournemouth is about 25 minutes away by car. The Isle of Wight can be reached by ferry from Lymington.

We believe our prices which start at £130 per week Low Season are excellent value. Please telephone or write for a free brochure. **CARAVANS FOR SALE**

Downton Holiday Park, Shorefield Road, Milford-on-Sea SO41 0LH
Tel: 01425 476131 or 01590 642515
info@downtonholidaypark.co.uk
www.downtonholidaypark.co.uk

For a Happy, marvellous seaside holiday

Beautifully situated in the heart of the NEW FOREST, yet only half-an-hour's drive to Bournemouth and coast. Four acres of close mown meadow. Ideal centre for walking and touring and for nature lovers. Pets welcome.

Open 1st March to 31st October
- Approved site – tents, caravans and motor caravans • Amenities block recently upgraded to very high standard
- Facilities for disabled visitors
- Well stocked shop • Safe playground • Laundry room • Electric hook-ups • Forest Inn adjacent - families and dogs welcomed • Owner-managed to high standard.

Please send SAE for brochure. From east turn off M27 at Exit 1 and follow signs to Linwood. From west turn off A388 2 miles north of Ringwood and look for our sign.

Red Shoot Camping Park
Linwood, Near Ringwood BH24 3QT
Tel: 01425 473789 • Fax: 01425 471558
e-mail: enquiries@redshoot-campingpark.co.uk
www.redshoot-campingpark.com

Hampshire
Romsey

A friendly welcome awaits you from Tony and Jane at their family-run farm and campsite. All types of touring units are catered for. Cleanliness is top priority with our toilet facilities, and free hot showers are available. We have a toilet and shower for the disabled; washing machine and dryer; washing-up sinks; electric hook-ups; small shop; Calor and camping gas; payphone. Well-controlled dogs are welcome. Daytime kennels are available. Children love the space, where they can play in full view of the units (parents appreciate that too). 20 minutes' walk to local pub, serving good food. Fishing and golf nearby.

Tel: 023 8081 4444
e-mail: enquiries@greenpasturesfarm.com
www.greenpasturesfarm.com

Green Pastures Farm
Ower, Romsey, Hampshire SO51 6AJ

Looking for Holiday Accommodation?

for details of hundreds of properties throughout the UK, visit our website

www.holidayguides.com

Kent

Battle, Biddenden

LONDON & SOUTH EAST ENGLAND 77

Crazy Lane Tourist Park
Camping & Caravanning in Sedlescombe,
Near Battle, East Sussex ★★★

A small secluded family park situated in a sun trap valley in the heart of 1066 country, within easy reach of beaches and all historical sites. Sailing, horse riding, golf, tennis and fishing facilities are all in easy reach. First class luxury toilet facilities; launderette. All pitches individually numbered. 36 touring, 20 motor caravan, 36 electrical hook-up points. Directions - travelling south of A21 turn left 100 yards past Junction B2244 opposite Blackbrooks Garden Centre, into Crazy Lane, site 70 yards on right. Rates: From £13.00 per night; book seven nights, only pay for six!
- Hardstanding for disabled with own fully equipped toilet facility. • Dogs are welcome on lead.
- Open 1st March to 31st October.

Whydown Farm, Sedlescombe, Battle TN33 0QT
Tel: 01424 870147 • e-mail: info@crazylane.co.uk • www.crazylane.co.uk

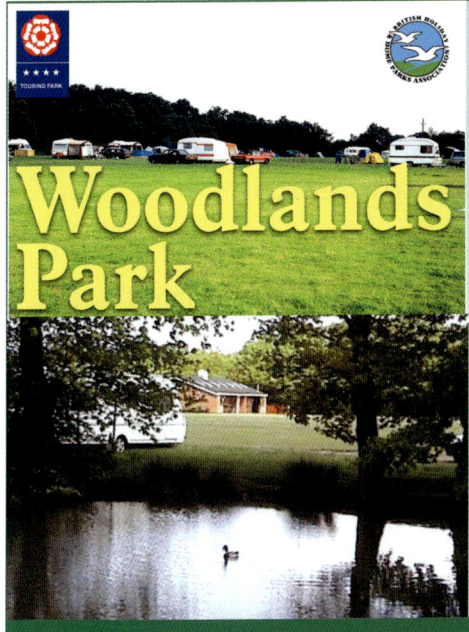

Woodlands Park

Situated in the heart of the beautiful Kent countryside, a quiet and tranquil environment to enjoy your holiday.
An ideal base for visiting the many historic Castles and other attractions throughout Kent and East Sussex.
Large open level grassland park with two ponds to enjoy a spot of fishing
Electric hook-ups available, modern toilet and shower block facility.
Plenty of space for children to run around and let off steam.
Small site shop where all essential items can be purchased from camping gaz to a bottle of milk. Friendly staff are on hand to answer any questions on the area and to provide tourist information.

Tenterden Road,
Biddenden, Kent TN27 8BT
Tel: 01580 291216
e-mail: woodlandspark@
overlinebroadband.com
www.campingsite.co.uk

Residential Park Homes, Leisure Homes and Tourist Park

Kent

Birchington

Two Chimneys Caravan Park

www.twochimneys.co.uk

Two Chimneys is a family-run, five star holiday park set in 40 acres of Kent countryside. We are just a few minutes' drive from the coast, which boasts miles of golden sandy beaches and calm seas of the English Channel. In recent years Two Chimneys Caravan Park has undergone a large amount of expansion and improvement providing more modern facilities, Toilets, Showers, Launderette and a Telescopic Swimming Pool Enclosure, so the pool can still be enjoyed on those not so warm days. **Licensed Club House, on-site Shop, Take Away Food, Tennis Court, Children's Play Areas. Holiday hire also available.** Two Chimneys has over 200 tent and touring pitches available on level grass fields. Open from March to October. Sorry no dogs.

Telephone: 01843 841068 / 843157
Fax: 01843 848099
Two Chimneys Caravan Park,
Shottendane Road, Birchington,
Kent CT7 0HD

Visit the FHG website
www.holidayguides.com
for details of the wide choice of accommodation featured in the full range of FHG titles

---

Please note

All the information in this book is given in good faith in the belief that it is correct. However, the publishers cannot guarantee the facts given in these pages, neither are they responsible for changes in policy, ownership or terms that may take place after the date of going to press. Readers should always satisfy themselves that the facilities they require are available and that the terms, if quoted, still apply.

East Sussex
Bodiam

East Sussex

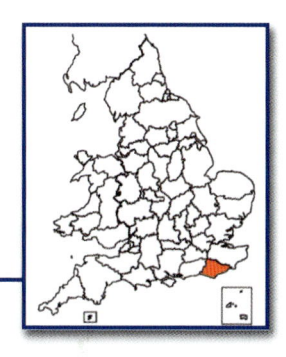

Lordine Court Holiday Park,
Ewhurst Green,
Robertsbridge TN32 5TS
01580 830209
Bookings Direct: 01580 831792
e-mail: enq@lordine-court.co.uk
www.lordine-court.co.uk

A well known and established caravan and camping park, situated in the heart of the Sussex countryside, approximately 10 miles from the ancient historic towns of Hastings, Battle and Rye, on the doorstep of Bodiam Castle and a short drive from Battle Abbey.

The Park's facilities include: outdoor swimming pool, restaurant and cafe with take-away service, clubhouse with two bars (one child-friendly), mini-shop and children's play area.
Dogs are permitted in designated areas. Woodland walks. Brochure on request.

Touring park with electric hook-ups • Holiday caravans for hire and purchase • Holiday homes and lodges

Park Farm Caravan and Camping Site

Relaxed rural site in beautiful setting. Hot showers; children's play area. Small camp fires and barbecues permitted. Riverside walk to Bodiam Castle and Castle Inn Pub. Free fishing in River Rother. Off B2244, signposted. Open Easter to November. Dogs allowed.

Park Farm, Bodiam, East Sussex TN32 5XA
Tel: 01580 831982 • e-mail: info@parkfarmcamping.co.uk • www.parkfarmcamping.co.uk

LONDON & SOUTH EAST ENGLAND — East Sussex
Eastbourne

Fairfields Farm & Caravan and Camping Park
Eastbourne Road, Westham, Pevensey BN24 5NG • Tel: 01323 763165 • Fax: 01323 469315

Quiet country touring site on a working family-run farm. Close to the beautiful resort of Eastbourne, we offer an excellent base from which to explore the stunning scenery and diverse attractions of South East England.

- drinking water taps • wash basins and showers • flush toilets • washing-up area
- laundry sinks • washing machine and tumble dryer • chemical sluice disposal

Our farm spans an area of almost 200 acres, and alongside the extensive views you will find a duck pond, numerous farm animals and pets, a recreational walk and a fishing lake.

Site open from 1st April to 31st October.

e-mail: enquiries@fairfieldsfarm.com • www.fairfieldsfarm.com

symbols

- ☼ Holiday Parks & Centres
- 🚐 Caravans for Hire
- Ⓢ Caravan Sites and Touring Parks
- ⛺ Camping Sites

Looking for Holiday Accommodation?

FHG KUPERARD

for details of hundreds of properties throughout the UK, visit our website

www.holidayguides.com

East Sussex

LONDON & SOUTH EAST ENGLAND 81

Hastings

Hastings
Touring Park

Welcome to Hastings....

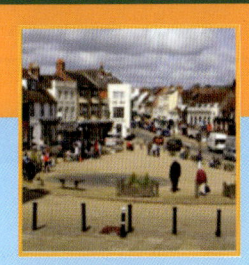

If it's the very best in camping, caravan or motor home holidays you're looking for then look no further. An ideal, easy to access location, thoughtfully placed pitches, and great facilities all add up to the perfect place to spend valuable holiday time, and that's before you begin to explore the stunning countryside!

Shearbarn

Set in the rolling hills above the historic town of Hastings, Shearbarn's location offers the best of so many worlds.
Literally on the doorstep there's the rural beauty of the 660 acres of the Hastings Country Park to explore; then there's mile upon mile of unspoilt beaches stretching into the distance, and the charming town of Hastings itself, with its enviable selection of restaurants and bars as well as museums, galleries and interesting shops to browse in.

Facilities

With 131 pitches, over 100 of which have electrical hook-ups, we have plenty of room for you and your friends.
As a customer of Hastings Touring Park, you'll be able to use the neighbouring bar and restaurant at 'Shearbarn'. The restaurant offers a varied menu with regular specials. There's nothing better at the end of a long and enjoyable day.
A smart casual dress code operates in the Bar and Restaurant complex. And if you'd rather cook for yourselves and eat in, there is a small shop just perfect for daily essentials. For more choice, there is a wide range of shops a short drive away. And don't forget the kids, at Hastings Touring Park we have indoor soft play and outdoor play areas.

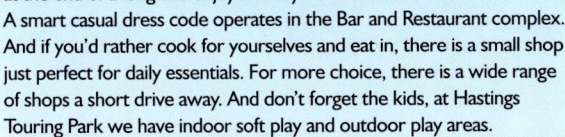

Hastings Touring Park
Barley Lane, Hastings, East Sussex TN35 5DX
Telephone: 01424 423583 • Fax: 01424 718740
e-mail: info@hastingstouring.co.uk
www.hastingstouring.co.uk

A superb sea view location for your perfect holiday...

West Sussex

Chichester, Dial Post

CARAVAN SITES & TOURING PARKS

CHICHESTER. Bell Caravan Park, Bell Lane, Birdham PO20 7HY (01243 512264). Holiday home (owner-occupied only) and small touring park with electric hook-ups, toilet blocks with showers. Local shop within walking distance. We are approximately within one/two miles from the beach and Chichester Harbour and Marina are a short drive away. The Roman city of Chichester is about five miles away and there are many places to visit in the area including Goodwood House and racecourse, Petworth House and Arundel Castle. Chichester is also ideal for visiting the historic town of Portsmouth. For prices please telephone or send a SAE.
- Children and dogs welcome.

Honeybridge Park

A picturesque 15-acre touring, camping and caravan park set in an Area of Outstanding Natural Beauty, convenient for London, Gatwick & South Coast.

Large hardstanding and grass pitches, electric hook-ups, heated amenity blocks, licensed shop, laundry, games room and play area. Seasonal pitches and storage available. Luxury lodges and static caravans for sale on 11-month holiday licences. Dogs welcome. Open all year.

Tel: 01403 710923
web: www.honeybridgepark.co.uk
e-mail: enquiries@honeybridgepark.co.uk
Honeybridge Lane, Dial Post, West Sussex, RH13 8NX

East of England

Leighton Buzzard Railway, Bedfordshire

Stretching inland from the North Sea, a peaceful rural landscape of downland, fens, ancient forest and heathland covers the counties of Norfolk, Suffolk, Essex, Cambridgeshire, Hertfordshire and Bedfordshire, while along the coast there are sandy beaches, cliffs and rockpools, sleepy villages, quiet seaside towns and busy family resorts. This is the area to visit for anyone who loves the outdoors. Long subject to the influence of Europe, remains exist from the times of the Romans, Anglo-Saxons and Normans and the countryside is dotted with medieval towns and villages.

Along the **Norfolk** coast from King's Lynn to Great Yarmouth the broad, sandy beaches, grassy dunes, nature reserves, windmills, and pretty little fishing villages are inviting at all times of year. Following the routes of the Norfolk Coastal Path and Norfolk Coast Cycle Way, walk or cycle between the picturesque villages, stopping to visit the interesting shops and galleries, or to enjoy the seafood at a traditional pub or a restaurant. An important trade and fishing port from medieval times, the historic centre of King's Lynn is well worth a visit, and take a break at Great Yarmouth for family entertainment, 15 miles of sandy beaches, traditional piers, a sea life centre and nightlife with clubs and a casino. On the low-lying Fens, the Norfolk Broads or through the ancient pine forests and heathland of The Breck there are walking, cycling and horse riding trails, and market towns and villages to explore. In contrast to the quiet and calm of coast and country, in the medieval city of Norwich with its historic streets and half-timbered houses, cathedral, Norman castle and museums you'll find not only history, but opera, ballet, theatre, music and restaurants.

Suffolk's 40 miles of unspoilt World Heritage coastline is perfect for a seaside holiday. Wander through the coastal forests or along the shingle and sandy beaches admiring the scenery, or hire bicycles for a family bike ride. Eat oysters at Orford or follow the Suffolk Coastal Churches Trail. Fishing is particularly popular on the Waveney as well as many on other rivers and golfers have a choice of short local courses and some of championship standard. Horse racing enthusiasts can't miss Newmarket, whether for a fun day out, to visit the National Horseracing Museum or to take a guided tour round the National Stud. However you choose to spend the day, the wonderful choice of locally produced food served in one of the many pubs, restaurants and cafes will provide the perfect end to your stay.

EAST OF ENGLAND

From the historic port of Harwich in the north to the Thames estuary in the south, the 300 miles of coastline and dry climate of maritime **Essex** have attracted holiday makers since early Victorian times. There are fun family resorts with plenty of action like Clacton, on the Essex sunshine coast, and Southend-on-Sea, with over six miles of clean safe sand and the world's longest pleasure pier. Along the coast there are quiet clifftop walks, sheltered coves, long beaches, mudflats, saltmarshes and creeks. Previously the haunt of smugglers, these are now a great attraction for birdwatchers, particularly for viewing winter wildfowl. Walkers and cyclists will enjoy the gently rolling landscape of the Essex countryside. Explore the medieval towns and villages like Thaxted and Saffron Walden, where long ago saffron was produced for the textile industry, the Norman keep at Colchester, England's oldest town and the grand stately homes like Ingatestone Hall and Audley End. All this within an hour of London!

Cambridgeshire immediately brings to mind the ancient university city of Cambridge, lazy hours punting on the river past the imposing college buildings, students on bicycles, museums and bookshops. This cosmopolitan centre has so much to offer, with theatres, concerts varying from classical to jazz, an annual music festival, cinemas, botanic gardens, exciting shops and to round it all off, restaurants, pubs and cafes serving high quality food. In the surrounding countryside historic market towns, pretty villages and stately homes wait to be explored. Visit Ely with its magnificent cathedral and museum exhibiting the national collection of stained glass, antique shops and cafes. Elizabethan Burghley House and Elton Hall with its beautifully restored rose garden are among the stately homes and historic houses in the county, and there's a wide choice of art galleries to visit too.

Hertfordshire's situation just north of London means that visitors based here have the advantage of easy access to all the city's facilities while staying in a pleasant rural environment. This is a county of small, historic market towns and villages with interesting shops, pubs and restaurants serving wonderful food, art galleries and museums. Despite its magnificent Gothic appearance Knebworth hides an original Tudor mansion, and is well worth a visit both for the exterior architecture and the treasures it contains. Perhaps it is best known now as the 'Stately Home of Rock' and is famous worldwide for the concerts held in the grounds. Hatfield House too has Tudor origins and a wing still survives of the Royal Palace of Hatfield where Elizabeth I spent her childhood. The present Jacobean mansion is surrounded by 1000 acres of parkland with trails marked out for pleasant country walks.

Whatever the weather, in **Bedfordshire** there's a wide choice of activities and places to visit. For a family day out, go on safari to find the 'big five' at ZSL Whipsnade, near Dunstable, one of Europe's biggest wildlife conservation parks or at Woburn Safari Park. Visitors interested in gardening history will enjoy the formal gardens modelled on Versailles laid out in the early 18th century at Wrest Park near Bedford and a later Regency design at the Swiss Garden at Biggleswade, and everyone will have fun finding the way round the Hoo Hill Maze at Shefford.

Maldon, Essex

Photo courtesy Essex County Council

Cambridgeshire

Comberton, Ely, Pidley

Cambridgeshire

EAST OF ENGLAND 85

COMBERTON. Highfield Farm Touring Park, Long Road, Comberton CB3 7DG
Tel: 01223 262308 • Fax: 01223 262308 • www.highfieldfarmtouringpark.co.uk
Five miles from Cambridge, the park is set in 8 acres of secluded countryside, with outstanding views. The careful layout, with a central open area, gives a great feeling of space. 60 touring pitches available. Caravans, motorhomes and tents welcome. Open from April/Easter to October.

ELY. Riverside Camping & Caravan Park, 21 New River Bank, Ely CB7 4TA
Tel: 01353 860205 • www.riversideccp.co.uk/
The ideal fisherman's escape, this adults-only site is situated on 4 acres of well laid out parkland, with pleasant paths leading along the riverside to the local marina and pub and into town. Open all year round. 37 touring pitches, 37 tent pitches available. Caravans, motorhomes and tents welcome.

Stroud Hill Park
Touring Caravans & Camping

Fen Road, Pidley, Cambridgeshire PE28 3DE

Stroud Hill Park is a privately owned, exclusively adult, touring caravan site in Pidley, Cambridgeshire.

The quiet, attractive, rural site provides a central Cambridgeshire location for touring caravans and campers.

At the heart of the site is a green oak timber-framed building which houses reception, a shop, café, bar and award-winning restaurant, along with the excellent toilets and showers.

There are 60 pitches (44 hard standing and 16 grass pitches), all with electric hook up, drinking water and an individual ground level drain to accept grey water. The site is built to accommodate the disabled.

Stroud Hill Park is open all year round and advance booking is advisable. Well-behaved dogs are welcome.

Please note that this is a non-family site and therefore children under the age of 16 are not allowed.
Tel: 01487 741 333 • Fax: 01487 741 365 • e-mail: stroudhillpark@btconnect.com
www.stroudhillpark.co.uk

Overall Winner
AA Campsite of the Year 2008

LOO OF THE YEAR Awards WINNER

Essex

Clacton-on-Sea, Colchester, Maldon, Southminster

CLACTON-ON-SEA. Highfield Grange Holiday Park, London Road, Clacton-on-Sea CO16 9QY
Tel: 0871 664 9746 • Fax: 01255 689805 • www.park-resorts.com
Highfield Grange is situated by Clacton's charming beaches and Victorian pier. This is the ideal getaway for the whole family, with plenty of amusements as well as activities to suit the mature traveller. The facilities include a bar and restaurant, and indoor swimming pool with a 200ft chute! 43 touring pitches available. Caravans and motorhomes welcome. Open from March to October.

CLACTON-ON-SEA. Martello Beach Holiday Park, Belsize Avenue, Jaywick, Clacton-on-Sea CO15 2LF
Tel: 01255 820372 • Fax: 01255 820060 • www.park-resorts.com
Sandy beaches and countryside to explore are among the attractions of this seaside site. There are facilities for all the family, including walking paths for those seeking peace and quiet. Open from March to October. 70 touring pitches, 100 tent pitches available. Caravans, motorhomes and tents welcome.

COLCHESTER. Colchester Camping & Caravan Park, Cymbeline Way, Colchester CO3 4AG
Tel: 01206 545551 • Fax: 01206 710443 • www.colchestercamping.co.uk
Surrounded by wildlife and idyllic landscapes and offering modern facilities, including free showers with hot water. There is easy access to the nearby town centre. Open all year round. 120 electric hook-ups available. 168 touring pitches, 40 tent pitches. Caravans, motorhomes and tents welcome.

COLCHESTER. Fen Farm Caravan Site, Moore Lane, East Mersea, Colchester CO5 8UA
Tel: 01206 383275
The perfect escape for those with an interest in wildlife, with Fingringhoe Wick nature reserve only 6 miles way. Open from March to September. 95 touring pitches. Caravans, motorhomes, tents welcome.

COLCHESTER. Waldegraves Holiday Park, Mersea Island, Colchester CO5 8SE
Tel: 01206 382898 • Fax: 01206 385359 • www.waldegraves.co.uk
Waldegraves provides entertainment for the whole family including a designated play area for children. Many attractions nearby including Colchester Zoo and museums. Open from March to November. 60 touring pitches. Caravans, motorhomes and tents welcome.

MALDON. Mundon Caravan Site, Hook Farm Nursery, Mundon Road, Maldon CM9 6PN
Tel: 0785 093 5540 • www.mundoncaravansite.com
Quiet site with views of the River Blackwater. Nearby attractions include golf, theatre and Colchester Zoo. Open all year round. Caravans, motorhomes and tents welcome.

SOUTHMINSTER. Steeple Bay Holiday Park, Steeple, Southminster CM0 7RS
Tel: 0845 815 9766 • Fax: 01621 773967 • www.parkholidaysuk.com
This coastal family retreat in Southminster offers great facilities including a leisure pool, paddling pool, and nightly entertainment. Open March – November. 55 touring pitches available. Caravans, motorhomes and tents welcome.

Essex / Hertfordshire — EAST OF ENGLAND

Southminster, Walton-on-the-Naze, Weeley

SOUTHMINSTER. Waterside at St Lawrence Bay, Main Road St Lawrence Bay, Southminster CM0 7LY
Tel: 0871 664 9794 • Fax: 01621 778 106 • www.park-resorts.com
A coastal getaway perfect for the whole family, offering plenty of facilities including a small indoor pool, and activities including crabbing in the estuary. 70 touring pitches, 8 tent pitches available. Caravans, motorhomes and tents welcome. Open from March to October.

WALTON-ON-THE-NAZE. Naze Marine Holiday Park, Hall Lane, Walton-on-the-Naze CO14 8HL
Tel: 0871 664 9754 • Fax: 01255 682 427 • www.park-resorts.com
A park with a difference offering a great variety of facilities, including nature reserves, walking paths, beaches and a wonderful pier, as well as a pool and poolside café. Nightly entertainment. 44 touring pitches available. Caravans and motorhomes welcome. Open from March to October.

WEELEY. Homestead Lake Caravan Park, Thorpe Road, Weeley CO16 9JN
Tel: 0800 093 1966 • Fax: 01255 830031
This quiet site is situated in 25 acres of lovely countryside near Clacton. There is a well established fishing lake on site. Open from March to January. 50 pitches available. Caravans, motorhomes and tents welcome.

Hertfordshire

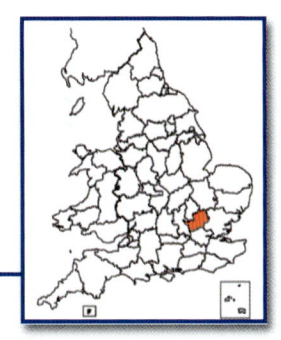

Hertford, Royston, Waltham Cross

HERTFORD. Hertford Camping and Caravanning Club Site, Mangrove Road, Hertford SG13 8AJ
Tel: 01992 586696
Surrounded by parkland, this well equipped site has two large camping fields, a tent field and a children's playing field. There are good public transport links to London. Open all year. Caravans, motorhomes and tents welcome.

ROYSTON. Highfields Farm, Old North Road, Bassingbourn, Royston SG8 5JT
Tel: 01763 248570
Small level site just outside the town of Royston, with generously spaced pitches and a large flat rally field. Tourers and motorhomes welcome. Open all year.

WALTHAM CROSS. Theobalds Park Camping & Caravanning Site, Waltham Cross EN7 5HS
Tel: 01992 620604 / 0870 243 3331
Set in Hertfordshire just outside London, this friendly country park provides exciting wildlife views and activities including boating, sailing and swimming. Non-members welcome. 90 pitches available.

Norfolk

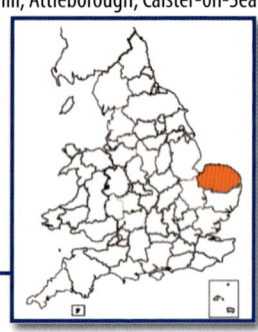

Ashill, Attleborough, Caister-on-Sea

ASHILL. Brick Kiln Farm Caravan Park, Swaffham Road, Ashill, Thetford IP25 7BT
Tel: 01760 441300
This family-run park is set on 15 acres of meadow and woodland on the Norfolk/Suffolk border. 90 pitches available. Caravans, motorhome and tents welcome. Open all year round.

ATTLEBOROUGH. Moat Farm Caravan Park & Campsite, Low Road, Breckles, Attleborough NR17 1EP
Tel: 01953 498510 • Fax: 08714 336468 • www.moatfarm-cp.co.uk
Set within undisturbed fields, with a number of local attractions nearby, including Thetford Forest. Excellent facilities. Open all year round. Caravans, motorhomes and tents welcome.

Elm Beach Caravan Park

Manor Road, Caister-on-Sea, Norfolk NR30 5HG
Freephone: 08000 199 360
www.elmbeachcaravanpark.com
e-mail: enquiries@elmbeachcaravanpark.com

Elm Beach is a small, select, 4-star Caravan Park with unique, uninterrupted views of the Sea and Caister's golden, sandy beaches.
We offer a range of 4-6 berth, fully equipped Heated Caravans, many of which overlook the sea or have sea views. We are a quiet, privately-run park with no entertainment facilities, but enjoy, free of charge, entertainment supplied by neighbouring parks, both within easy walking distance.
Pets very welcome.

NOW OPEN MARCH TO JANUARY

A useful index of towns/counties appears at the back of this book

Norfolk
Cromer, Diss, Great Yarmouth

EAST OF ENGLAND 89

CROMER. Ivy Farm Holiday Park, High Street, Cromer NR27 0PS
Tel: 01263 579239 • www.ivy-farm.co.uk
An award-winning park set in a delightful area offering genuine peace and quiet. Minutes from sandy beaches; lots of country walks over farm meadows and lanes. 22 touring pitches; caravans, motorhomes and tents welcome.

CROMER. Laburnum Caravan Park, Water Lane, West Runton, Cromer NR27 9QP
Tel: 01263 837473
The park's cliff top position means visitors are guaranteed superb views of the beach. Children are welcome at Laburnum Park, with excellent facilities. Open from March to October. 6 touring pitches. Caravans and motorhomes welcome.

WAVENEY VALLEY HOLIDAY PARK

★ Touring Caravan and Camping Site ★ Licensed Bar ★ Electric Hook-ups
★ Restaurant, Shop, Laundry ★ Self-Catering Mobile Homes
★ Outdoor Swimming Pool ★ Horse Riding on Site ★ Good Fishing in Locality

Good access to large, level site, two miles east of Dickleburgh.
Midway between Norwich and Ipswich off A140.

Airstation Lane, Rushall, Diss,
Norfolk IP21 4QF
Telephone: 01379 741228/741690
Fax: 01379 741228
e-mail: waveneyvalleyhp@aol.com
www.caravanparksnorfolk.co.uk

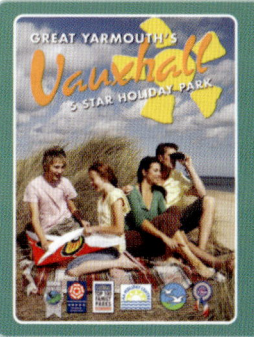

GREAT FUN, GREAT VALUE, GREAT TOURING
GREAT YARMOUTH

GREAT YARMOUTH'S Vauxhall 5 STAR HOLIDAY PARK

5 STAR TOURING FACILITIES
• Over 220 all electric sites • Free car parking
• Grass & hard standings • Baby changing facilities
• Gas cylinder refills on site • Hair dryers
• Heated shower & toilet blocks • Awnings FREE
• Night security for late arrivals
SUPER PITCH: Full mains service pitch with hedged, landscaped and awning areas

FREE WITH YOUR HOLIDAY
• Star Studded Entertainment • Electricity
• Kid's Club • Indoor Tropical Waterworld
• Satellite T.V. (super pitch only)
• Louie's Adventure Playground
• Sport & Fitness Fun

KIDS WILL LOVE IT!

Call Now For a Free Colour Brochure
01493 857231
Vauxhall Holiday Park, 91 Acle New Road, Great Yarmouth, Norfolk NR30 1TB Ref: 91
visit the web site for great touring savers www.vauxhalltouring.co.uk

90 EAST OF ENGLAND   Norfolk
                                                  Hunstanton, Lyng

Searles LEISURE RESORT • HUNSTANTON

Creating Happiness for all ages

On the west Norfolk Coast

Luxury Accommodation • Relaxation • Touring • Swimming Pools • Golf • Entertainment

Call our friendly booking team today!
Searles Leisure Group, Hunstanton, PE36 5BB

Caravan Club rally groups are more than welcome, special rates on enquiry.

Quote Ref: CC

www.searles.co.uk   01485 534211

UTOPIA PARADISE CARAVAN PARK   LYNG, NORFOLK

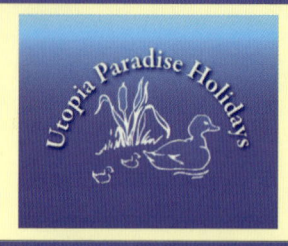

ADULTS ONLY • Prices £9.00 per night

For SatNav users NR9 5RF

♦ Fishing on site ♦ Electric hook ups, (by meter) ♦ Pets welcome ♦ Good cycling & walking ♦ No Tents ♦ Touring caravans only (all pitches are around the edge of the lake) ♦ Toilets and shower

Utopia Paradise Caravan Park is a small 15-pitch family-run park which nestles beside a naturally attractive willow-clad mixed coarse fishing lake in the picturesque village of Lyng, in Wensum Valley, which is steeped in history and legends. Lyng is situated 13 miles from Norwich and is ideally positioned to visit the North Norfolk coast. Shop, post office, pub, garage, public telephone, riding stables and a nature reserve are all within a 5 minute walk. Places to visit include, steam railways, stately homes, garden and craft centres, the Norfolk Broads, mediaeval city of Norwich, Pensthorpe Waterfowl Park, and Wensum Valley and Barnham Broom Golf Clubs.

Free brochure available • Contact Suzan Jarvis • Tel: 0044(0)1603 870812
The Mallards, Farman Close, Lyng, Norwich, Norfolk NR9 5RD
e-mail: info@utopia-paradise.co.uk • www.utopia-paradise.co.uk

Norfolk
Mundesley, Sea Palling

EAST OF ENGLAND 91

Sandy Gulls Caravan Park Ltd
Cromer Road, Mundesley, Norfolk NR11 8DF

Found on the Mundesley cliff tops, this quiet private park, managed by the owning family for over 30 years, offers a warm welcome to all visitors. The touring park has grass and non-turf pitches, all have uninterrupted sea views, electric/TV hook-ups and beautifully refurbished shower rooms. Holiday caravans for sale or hire, which are always the latest models.

Our charges include gas and electricity.
Superbly situated for exploring the beauty of North Norfolk including The Broads National Park.

Sandy Gulls does not cater for children or teenagers.

Mr Shreeve
01263 720513

GOLDEN BEACH
HOLIDAY CARAVAN PARK

Golden Beach is a lovely quiet park situated in the small unspoiled village of Sea Palling on the Norfolk coast, just behind sand dunes which border miles of golden beaches with excellent sea fishing. Luxury caravans for sale and for hire.

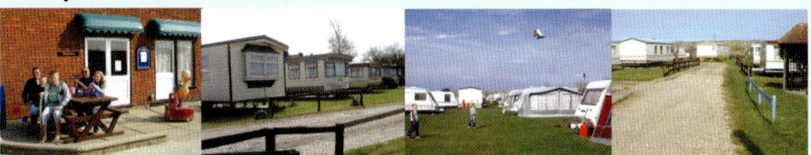

Golden Beach Holiday Centre
Beach Road, Sea Palling, Norfolk NR12 0AL
Tel: 01692 598269
e-mail: goldenbeach@keme.co.uk   www.goldenbeachpark.co.uk

EAST OF ENGLAND

Suffolk
Bungay, Lowestoft

Suffolk

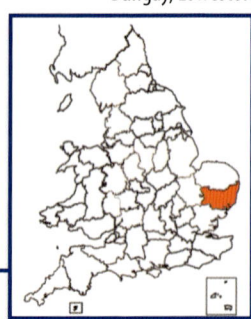

Outney Meadow Caravan Park

This caravan and camping site in Suffolk is in a beautiful location, set in eight acres of ground on pleasant grassy areas beside the River Waveney, with screened pitches for tents, motor homes and caravans.

Toilets and shower block with hot showers and shaver points. Shop and launderette on site.

45 touring pitches and five hardstandings for motor caravans; some electric hook-ups.

Fishing, boat, canoe and bike hire. Barbecues are allowed; picnic tables. Pets welcome, special dog-walking area; dogs must be kept on leads.

The site is quiet day and night.

Please telephone or see our website for further details.

**Outney Meadow,
Bungay, Suffolk NR35 1HG
Tel: 01986 892338
www.outneymeadow.co.uk**

Beach Farm Residential & Holiday Park Ltd

1 Arbor Lane, Pakefield, Lowestoft, Suffolk NR33 7BD
Tel: 01502 572794 • Mobile: 07795 001449
e-mail: beachfarmpark@aol.com • www.beachfarmpark.co.uk

A friendly, peaceful family-run park set in six acres of attractive, sheltered surroundings only 500 yards from Pakefield beach and supermarket, two miles from the town centre.
- De luxe caravan holiday homes with central heating
- Deluxe Country Lodges (3-bed)
- Luxury residential Park homes for sale
- Limited spaces for touring / camping inc. hook-ups
- Licensed bar / beer garden with children's play area
- Seasonal entertainment • Outdoor heated swimming pool
- Launderette • Restaurant adjacent

The park is very close to many local attractions including Pleasurewood Hills Theme Park and Africa Alive.

Suffolk
Leiston, Lowestoft

EAST OF ENGLAND

LEISTON. Cliff House Park, Sizewell Common, Leiston IP16 4TU
Tel: 01728 830724 • www.cliffhousepark.co.uk/
With a frontage on the Suffolk coast, this site is ideal for active holidays, with cycle trails nearby, and the possibility of walking to Dunwich, Southwold or Thorpeness. There is also access to a private beach, and a games room. 60 touring and seasonal pitches available. Caravans and tents welcome. Open from March to November.

LOWESTOFT. Heathland Beach Caravan Park, London Road, Kessingland, Lowestoft NR33 7PJ
Tel: 01502 740337 • Fax: 01502 742355 • www.heathlandbeach.co.uk
This friendly resort overlooks Kessingland's fabulous sandy beach. The park has achieved a David Bellamy Gold Award. Open from March to October. 63 touring pitches available. Caravans, motorhomes and tents welcome.

LOWESTOFT. Kessingland Beach Holiday Park, Kessingland, Near Lowestoft NR33 7RN
Tel: 0871 664 9748 • Fax: 01502 740907 • www.park-resorts.com
Kessingland provides a tranquil base by the beach for the whole family, with a number of exciting attractions nearby. Lowestoft Blue Flag beach is only 5 miles from the park. Open from March to October. 93 touring pitches available. Caravans, motorhomes and tents welcome.

Pakefield Caravan Park

Pakefield Caravan Park occupies a cliff top setting overlooking Pakefield Beach and enjoys easy access on to the Suffolk coast and the nearby Norfolk Broads. The Park is perfectly located for enjoying the natural coastal beauty and tourist attractions at pretty Southwold, Walberswick and Dunwich, while the Norfolk Broads, Lowestoft and Great Yarmouth are also within easy reach.

The Park offers good quality holiday caravans for sale (some with sea views), holiday caravans for hire, short breaks and late availability deals.

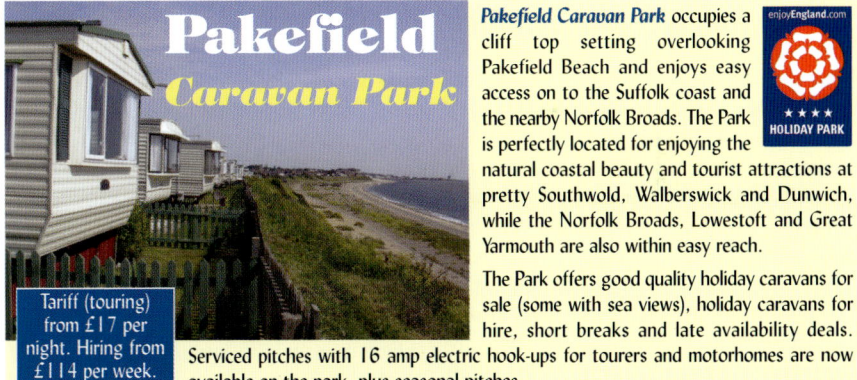

Tariff (touring) from £17 per night. Hiring from £114 per week.

Serviced pitches with 16 amp electric hook-ups for tourers and motorhomes are now available on the park, plus seasonal pitches.

Facilities on this well maintained caravan park include a modern children's playground, refurbished toilet and shower block, modern launderette, club and bar (with seasonal entertainment), well stocked shop and outdoor pool.
• Dogs are welcome on this pet-friendly park.
• Wi-fi is now available.
• Season open from 1st March until 30th November

Pakefield Caravan Park, Arbor Lane, Pakefield, Lowestoft, Suffolk NR33 7BQ
Tel: 01502 561136
info@pakefieldcaravanpark.co.uk
www.pakefieldpark.co.uk

🔌	Electric hook-ups available	♿	Facilities for disabled visitors
🛝	Children's play area	🐕	Pets welcome
🧺	Laundry facilities	🛒	Shop on site
🍷	Licensed bar on site	W	Wifi access available

The Midlands

Photo courtesy Herefordshire Tourism

View towards Scotland Bank, Herefordshire

Extending eastwards across the centre of England from the Welsh borders to the North Sea coast and the Wash, the Midlands includes Derbyshire, Herefordshire, Leicestershire and Rutland, Lincolnshire, Northamptonshire, Nottinghamshire, Shropshire, Staffordshire, Warwickshire, West Midlands and Worcestershire. The heart of England and birthplace of the industrial revolution, the landscape varies between quiet farmland, dramatic, windswept moors and tors and gently rolling hills. For outdoor lovers there's a tremendous variety of activities, from watching the seals on the Lincolnshire coast to rock climbing in the Peak District. There are magnificent stately homes to visit, castles steeped in history, beautiful gardens and of course, endless shopping of every kind. The towns and cities offer a wide choice of nightlife, theatres and concerts.

The **West Midlands**, with Birmingham its hub, is the focus of all transport networks in central England so that access is easy by road, rail and air. In Birmingham's vibrant centre there's plenty to do. Shopping has to be high on the agenda and there are art galleries, and art, dance and music festivals to go to, as well as major international events and exhibitions to appeal to everyone.

Herefordshire, on the on the border with Wales, will appeal equally to outdoor lovers and enthusiasts for the arts, crafts and literature, as well as to all food lovers! There are endless opportunities for all kinds of outdoor activities, with footpaths and bridleways through countryside rich in wildlife. The Black and White Village Trail takes visitors through beautiful countryside to pretty little villages and towns, each with its own individual characteristics and shops. The climate and fertile soil has resulted in wonderful local produce, particularly fruit and vegetables, beef and dairy products.

If you're looking for a break from the pace of life today, but with plenty to do and see, and with a choice of superb food to round off your day, Ludlow in South **Shropshire** is the place to visit. The annual Ludlow Festival, with classical music and jazz, Shakespeare performances, dance and fireworks is just one major event in the town's calendar. There are over 30 castles all over Shropshire, as well as stately homes and all kinds of gardens. For more recent events visit the ten museums at the Ironbridge Gorge where you can learn all about the early inventions leading to the start of the Industrial Revolution.

Worcestershire, stretching south-east from the fringes of Birmingham, is a county of Georgian towns, Cotswold stone villages, Victorian spas, former industrial centres and wonderful walking country. In the Malvern Hills choose between gentle and more strenuous exercise to appreciate the superb views of the surrounding countryside, or take a more restful look at the countryside on a ride on the Severn Valley Railway between Bromsgrove and Kidderminster.

Think of **Warwickshire**, and Shakespeare and Stratford-on-Avon immediately come to mind. A great way to see round this interesting town of black and white, half-timbered buildings is to take a guided walking tour, or better still, hire a bike. Round off the day at the newly rebuilt Royal Shakespeare Theatre next to the river. As well as Sir Basil Spence's Coventry Cathedral and two other churches designed by him, Coventry is home to Warwick Arts Centre, the largest in the Midlands, and there's an Art Trail to follow alongside Coventry Canal.

Northamptonshire may appear a quiet, rural county, but it's very much a place for action and family fun. Everything you would expect to find in the countryside is here – walking, cycling, fishing, wildlife, beautiful villages and traditional inns and pubs. Motorsports enthusiasts will be more than satisfied, with stock car racing at the Northampton International Raceway, Santa Pod, the home of European Drag Racing.

Coast or country, the choice is yours for a holiday in **Lincolnshire**. With award-winning beaches, miles of clean sand, theme parks, kite surfing, wake boarding and water skiing, there's action and excitement for everyone along the Fun Coast and at Cleethorpes on the Humber estuary. At Skegness, as well as all the fun on the beach, children will love watching the seals being fed at the seal sanctuary. In Lincoln walk round the battlements at the Castle, explore the cobbled streets lined with medieval buildings and visit the imposing Gothic cathedral, one of the finest in Europe.

Set in the centre of the Midlands, the rolling countryside, canals, forests, beautiful villages, interesting market towns and history make **Leicestershire and Rutland** well worth a visit. Spend a peaceful hour or two cruising along the Ashby Canal in a narrowboat past Bosworth Battlefield where the Wars of the Roses ended in 1485. With over 1000 different species there's plenty to see at Twycross Zoo at Hinckley, or take a walk through Burbage Wood to see the native fauna. Rutland is England's smallest county with the largest man-made lake in Europe. Cycle round the shoreline, cruise on the water, walk round the lake, while the really energetic can take the walkers' route, Round Rutland, all of 65 miles long.

Nottinghamshire's historic and literary connections make it a highly interesting area to spend a short break or longer holiday. Whether you prefer taking part in sport or just enjoy watching, there's a great variety available. Watch cricket at Trent Bridge, horse racing at Nottingham and the all-weather course at Southwell, and ice hockey at Nottingham's National Ice Centre, or try ice skating yourself. The city of Nottingham, with its links to the legend of Robin Hood, is also a wonderful place to shop - don't miss the traditional Lace Market.

For walking, climbing, mountain biking and caving visit **Derbyshire**. There are activities available at every level and courses to suit everyone. From the gently rolling farmland and National Forest in the south to the rugged demanding landscape of the Dark Peak in the north there are trails for cyclists and walkers to follow, many along old railway lines. Buxton was a spa from Roman times, but the main attractions now are concerts, theatre and the annual literary and music festival. Visit the market town of Chesterfield to see the church with the crooked spire, and for a step back in time go to Crich Tramway Village.

Situated right in the middle of England, **Staffordshire** is a county of open spaces and ancient woodlands, exciting theme parks, stately homes and castles, miles of canals and the largest street-style skate park in Europe at Stoke-on-Trent. There are thrills and fun for every age group at the theme parks. As well as the heart-stopping rides, walk through the Ocean Tank Tunnel at Alton Towers to watch the sea creatures from all the world's oceans and make a big splash in the Waterpark.

Derbyshire

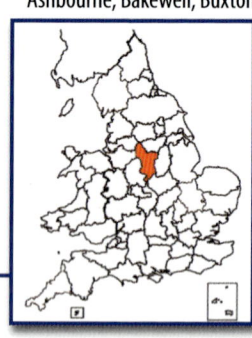

Ashbourne, Bakewell, Buxton

ASHBOURNE. Callow Top Holiday Park, Buxton Road, Ashbourne DE6 2AQ
Tel: 01335 344020 • Fax: 01335 343726 • www.callowtop.co.uk
Visitors can take part in numerous activities in and around Callow Top. Enjoy the trails, fishing, swimming and hilltop climbing in this beautiful part of the Peak District. 150 touring pitches, 150 tent pitches.

BAKEWELL. Bakewell Camping & Caravan Club Site, c/o Hopping Farm, Youlgreave, Bakewell DE45 1NA
Tel: 01629 636555
This peaceful camp site is located near the little town of Bakewell, with easy access to the Peak District National Park. Motorhomes, caravans and tents welcome. 100 touring pitches available. Open March to November.

NEWHAVEN Caravan & Camping PARK

Delightful site in the heart of the Peak District providing an ideal centre for touring the Derbyshire Dales, walking, climbing, potholing, etc. Convenient for visiting Chatsworth, Haddon Hall, Hardwick Hall, Alton Towers, Matlock and the Dams. Two first class toilet blocks providing FREE hot water; electric hook-ups. Children's playground, playroom, fully-stocked shop supplying Calor and Camping gas, fresh groceries, etc. Laundry. Ice pack freezing facilities. Restaurant adjacent. Tents, motor vans, caravans. Pets and children welcome.

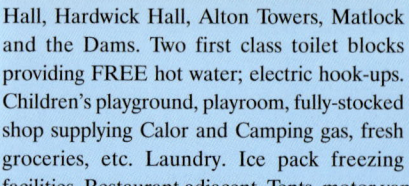

Terms from £11.25 per night – includes car and up to four people, discount for seven nights or more. SAE for brochure. Seasonal tourers welcome.

Newhaven Caravan and Camping Park, Newhaven, Near Buxton, Derbyshire SK17 0DT • 01298 84300 • www.newhavencaravanpark.co.uk

Derbyshire
Ripley

Golden Valley
Caravan & Camping Park

Coach Road, Golden Valley, Ripley, Derbyshire DE55 4ES
Tel: 01773 513881 • Fax: 01773 746786
e-mail: enquiries@goldenvalleycaravanpark.co.uk
www.goldenvalleycaravanpark.co.uk

Golden Valley Caravan and Camping Park is located in the beautiful hamlet of Golden Valley, in Amber Valley, the heart of Derbyshire. Next to Butterley Railway. Set within 26 acres of secluded woodland and contains 40 super pitches for motor homes/caravans each having its own independent water supply, electric hook-up point and mains drainage set in spacious bays within selected areas. There is also ample room for camping/tents with hook-ups.

The site has two independent toilet / shower blocks, laundry room, Jacuzzi, gym, children's play room, outside play area, cafe, bar and fishing pond.

Amber Valley has many tranquil villages and bustling market towns nestled amongst some of the most beautiful scenery around. From historic houses and heritage sites, steam trains to walking routes there's something for you.

Herefordshire

Leominster

Arrow Bank Holiday Park

**Nun House Farm, Eardisland
Near Leominster, Herefordshire HR6 9BG**

Arrow Bank Holiday Park is a family-run park enjoying peace and tranquillity in a spacious landscaped setting in the picturesque Tudor village of Eardisland. Touring caravans and motor homes are well catered for on a flat, level field with electric hook-up points.

Heated amenity block and Wi-Fi access. • Hardstanding seasonal pitches with hook-up available 1st March to 7th January.

Arrow Bank Holiday Park offers a superb opportunity to own your dream holiday Home from Home or to hire one of our double glazed 2008 holiday homes with central heating. (Short breaks available).

An ideal touring base with many historic market towns and cathedral cities close by. The beautiful Elan Valley, Brecon Beacons and Shropshire Hills, perfect for walking, bird watching and fishing are easily accessible. From Leominster, follow the A44 west towards Rhayader for approx. 1 mile. As you pass Morrison's, bear right towards Eardisland (approx 4 miles).

**Tel & Fax: 01544 388312 • e-mail: enquiries@arrowbankholidaypark.co.uk
www.arrowbankholidaypark.co.uk**

Leicestershire & Rutland

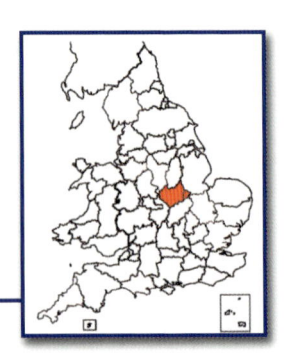

Wolvey

CARAVAN SITES & TOURING PARKS

WOLVEY. Wolvey Caravan Park, Villa Farm, Wolvey, Near Hinckley LE10 3HF (01455 220493/220630).
A quiet site situated on the borders of Warwickshire and Leicestershire, ideally located to explore the many places of interest in the Midlands. Site facilities include shop (licensed), toilets, showers, washrooms, launderette, TV room, 9 hole putting green, fishing. Tariff and brochure available on request. Registered with the Caravan and Camping Club of Great Britain.
Rates: Tents £10.00 per night, two persons; car, caravan and two persons with hook-up £13.00 per night (extra person £1.50); dogs 50p per night; disabled unit, hook-ups £3.00.
• Dogs welcome
AA ★★★
www.wolveycaravanpark.itgo.com

Lincolnshire

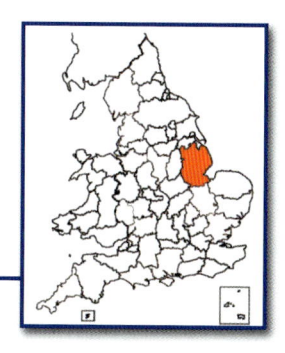

Boston, Grantham

Lincolnshire

MIDLANDS 99

---

perfect for fishing..walking.. sightseeing.. shopping.. touring..cycling.....or simply relaxing!

Nestling quietly in some 36 acres of delightfully landscaped parkland, Orchard Holiday Park is one of Lincolnshire's hidden jewels, where you can be as active or relaxed as you wish. Five-acre fishing lake. First-class amenities and services including licensed bar and new restaurant, shop, launderette, shower blocks etc.

120 luxury Holiday Homes, all with mains electricity, water and drainage. Separate area for touring caravans with mains electricity and water. Over 18s only.

ORCHARD HOLIDAY PARK

Frampton Lane, Hubbert's Bridge, Boston, Lincs
PE20 3QU
01205 290328/290368
Fax: 01205 290247

The park of 3½ acres is situated in quiet, rural surroundings and can be found 8 miles outside Boston on the A52 Skegness road; turn right opposite the B1184 Sibsey road, the park is 300 yards on the left. Flush toilets, handbasins, H&C, chemical disposal point, free showers, washroom, razor points, electric hook-ups, site shop and children's swings. Public houses and restaurants nearby. Ideal for touring and local fishing. Further details on request. Dogs allowed. Open April to October.

£11 per night for low season rising to £19 high season - these pitch prices include electric hook-up. Six-berth caravans for hire from £195 per week or nightly rate, min. two nights.

The White Cat Caravan & Camping Park,
Shaw Lane, Old Leake, Boston PE22 9LQ
Tel & Fax: 01205 870121 *(Mr & Mrs Lannen)*
e-mail: kevin@klannen.freeserve.co.uk
www.whitecatpark.com

WOODLAND WATERS Willoughby Road, Ancaster, Grantham NG32 3RT
Tel & Fax: 01400 230888
e-mail: info@woodlandwaters.co.uk
www.woodlandwaters.co.uk

Set in 72 acres of parkland. Five fishing lakes. Large touring and camping site with electric hook-ups. Luxury holiday lodges from £435 weekly. Excellent toilets, shower block with disabled facilities. Bar/restaurant on site. Children's play area. Dogs welcome. Four Golf Courses nearby. Rallies welcome. New function room " Malden Suite" available for weddings, events and conferences. Short Breaks available. Open all year.

100 MIDLANDS   Lincolnshire
                                                Alford

WOODTHORPE HALL
CARAVAN & LEISURE PARK

ETC ★★★★
COTTAGES

Ideally Situated to Make Your Holiday Special

- Tourers • Static Van Lettings • Static Van Sales
- Holiday Cottages • Leisure Activities • Bar & Restaurant
- Aquatics Centre • Garden Centre • Family Camping

Woodthorpe Hall Leisure Park is ideally situated, nestled between the rolling hills of the Lincolnshire Wolds and the wide open spaces of the marshes leading down to the sea, close to the seaside resorts of Skegness, Sutton on Sea and Mablethorpe.
The historic city of Lincoln with its 1200 year old cathedral and castle is only 40 minutes' drive.

We have about twenty static vans for letting along with plenty of room for tourers, motor homes and family tents.

The caravans are of the highest standard and equipped with all bedding, cookery utensils, crockery and cutlery. Letting charges are fully inclusive of gas, electricity TV and water.

Touring field, fully equipped with electricity hook-ups, shower, water, waste and chemical waste facilities.

Car parking is adjacent to your caravan or tent, there is a shop, and full disabled access and golf and fishing on site.

The park is in a quiet, secure location with groups and rallies also catered for. Don't forget to visit Woody's Bar and Restaurant where you can relax and a meal and drink can be enjoyed.

Also available, very well appointed one and three bedroom cottages overlooking the golf course. All have central heating, colour TV, microwave, washer, dryer, dishwasher and fridge freezer. Hot tubs new for 2010.

Leisure Park: 01507 450294 • Golf Club: 01507 450000
Woody's Bar: 01507 450079 • Garden Centre: 01507 450509
Aquatics Centre: 01507 451000

www.woodthorpehallleisure.co.uk
e-mail: enquiries@woodthorpehallleisure.co.uk

Woodthorpe Hall • Woodthorpe • Near Alford • Lincolnshire LN13 0DD

Nottinghamshire — MIDLANDS 101
Tuxford

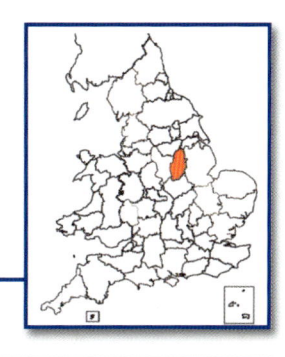

Nottinghamshire

Orchard Park

Quiet, sheltered Park set in an old orchard. Ideal for Sherwood Forest and many attractions, all pitches with electric hook-up, children's play trail, dog walk, excellent heated facilities with free hot showers and facilities for disabled. Brochure available on request.

Orchard Park Touring Caravan and Camping Park
Marnham Road, Tuxford NG22 0PY
Tel: 01777 870228 • Fax: 01777 870320

www.orchardcaravanpark.co.uk

Greenacres caravan park

Lincoln Road, Tuxford
Nottinghamshire NG22 0JN

Greenacres is a family-owned and run holiday park in North Nottinghamshire, often referred to as a 'gem set in the heart of Robin Hood Country'. Facilities available for tourers, motorhomes, small tents etc.
Static holiday homes for sale and hire.
Seasonal touring caravan pitches available.
Open mid March to end of October.

Tel & Fax: 01777 870264

e: stay@greenacres-tuxford.co.uk
www.greenacres-tuxford.co.uk

Shropshire

Craven Arms, Prees, Shrewsbury, Telford

The Anchorage

Two well-equipped modern caravan holiday homes situated at the head of the Clun valley in South Shropshire's Area of Outstanding Natural Beauty. Perfect for walking, cycling, riding, or just unwinding! Each caravan has three bedrooms, TV, shower room with flush toilet, and kitchen with fridge and microwave. Further shower room and laundry/drying room on site. Well behaved pets and children welcome, horses also accommodated. Open April to September. From £160 per week incl. gas, electricity, bed linen and towels.

www.adamsanchor.co.uk
nancynewcwm@btinternet.com
Anchor, Newcastle on Clun, Craven Arms, Shropshire SY7 8PR • 01686 670737

PREES. Green Lane Farm, Green Lane Farm, Prees SY13 2AH
Tel: 01948 840 460
Set in North Shropshire's rolling hills, this spacious campsite is ideal for children. 20 pitches for motor caravans and tents. Open all year round.

SHREWSBURY. Beaconsfield Farm, Battlefield, Shrewsbury SY4 4AA
Tel: 01939 210370 • Fax: 01939 210349 • www.beaconsfield-farm.co.uk
Caravan in luxury at this adults-only farm situated north of Shrewsbury. Close by are museums, parks and a shopping centre. 20 tent pitches, 60 touring pitches available. Motorhomes, caravans and tents welcome. Open all year round.

TELFORD. Severn Gorge Park, Bridgnorth Road, Tweedale, Telford TF7 4JB
Tel: 01952 684789
This adults-only park is located in the pretty Shropshire town of Tweedale just ten minutes from Telford. Open all year round. 10 touring pitches available. Caravans and motorhomes welcome.

TELFORD. Church Farm, Rowton, Near Wellington, Telford TF6 6QY
Tel: 01952 770381 • Fax: 01952 77038 • www.churchfarmshropshire.co.uk
Good modern facilities are provided on this small farm site with uninterrupted views of Wrekin Hill. Breakfast is available at the farmhouse. 5 touring pitches, 20 tent pitches available. Caravans, campervans and tents welcome.

A useful index of towns/counties appears at the back of this book

Staffordshire

Alton, Uttoxeter, Weston-under-Lizard

Staffordshire

MIDLANDS 103

The ★STAR★ Caravan & Camping Park

Bookings: Tel 01538 702219

Cotton, near Alton Towers ★ www.starcaravanpark.co.uk

With Alton Towers so near – just over a mile away from our main gates – we are the No.1 choice for visitors who are looking for a great family-friendly camping and caravanning experience, that offers not only value for money, but also excellent facilities in one of the best locations near to Alton Towers.

Site amenities include large children's play area, toilet block with free showers, etc., laundry room with drying and ironing facilities, electric hook-ups, etc. Full disabled toilet and shower. Dogs welcome. Parent and baby toilet.

Park opens from the end of March to November.
From £14 per night for two persons.

Modern static caravans for hire.
Brochure and further details available

UTTOXETER. Uttoxeter Racecourse Caravan Club Site, Wood Lane, Uttoxeter ST14 8BD
Tel: 01889 564171
This friendly park at Uttoxeter racecourse is surrounded by 60 acres of dog-walking terrain. Beside the scenic Weaver Hills and with a golf course nearby; easy access to Alton Towers and Lichfield Cathedral. 76 touring pitches. Motorhomes, caravans and tents welcome. Open March to November.

WESTON-UNDER-LIZARD. White Pump Farm, Ivetsey Bank, Near Weston-under-Lizard ST19 9QU
Tel: 01785 841153/ 07990 607125 • www.whitepumpfarm.com
Situated in the depths of the Lincolnshire countryside, White Pump Farm is open all year round. There is easy access to events at Weston Park. Home produce for sale in the farm shop. 5 motorhome pitches, 100 tent pitches, 5 touring pitches available.

Warwickshire

Aston Cantlow, Market Bosworth, Rugby, Warwick

ASTON CANTLOW. Island Meadow Caravan Park, Aston Cantlow, Henley-in-Arden B95 6JP
Tel/Fax: 01789 488273 • www.islandmeadowcaravanpark.co.uk/
7 acres of flat Warwickshire countryside – with a weir for fishing and ideal terrain for cycling, walking or simply taking a break from it all. 24 touring pitches and 10 tent pitches available. Motorhomes, caravans and tents.

MARKET BOSWORTH. Bosworth Caravan Park, Cadeby Lane, Cadeby, Market Bosworth CV13 0BA
Tel: 01455 292259 • Fax: 01455 292922 • www.bosworthcaravanpark.co.uk
An ideal venue for rallies, the facilities at this 5-acre site include a large free car park, licensed restaurant, tearooms, bed and breakfast or self-catering accommodation. Caravans and motor homes welcome.

RUGBY. Lodge Farm, Bilton Lane, Rugby CV23 9DU
Tel: 01788 560193 • www.lodgefarm.com
Pets are welcome at this environmentally aware camp site. Lodge Farm offers level pitches in peaceful, countryside with a range of modern facilities. Open from February to October. Caravans, motorhomes and tents welcome.

WARWICK. Warwick Racecourse Caravan Club Site, Hampton Street, Warwick CV34 6HN
Tel: 01926 495448
The site is only six minutes from Warwick town, with a nearby golf course and numerous walking routes. Medieval Warwick Castle nearby provides an interesting day out for all the family. 55 touring pitches available. Caravans welcome. Open from March to January.

Symbol	Meaning
	Electric hook-ups available
	Facilities for disabled visitors
	Children's play area
	Pets welcome
	Laundry facilities
	Shop on site
	Licensed bar on site
W	Wifi access available

Warwickshire
Stratford-Upon-Avon

MIDLANDS 105

dodwell park

A small touring park, very clean and quiet, set in the countryside two miles south west of Stratford-upon-Avon. An ideal location from which to visit Shakespeare's birthplace, Anne Hathaway's Cottage, Warwick Castle and the Cotswolds. There are country walks to the River Avon and the village of Luddington. From Stratford-upon-Avon take B439 (formerly A439) towards Bidford-on-Avon for two miles. The park lies on the left, signposted. Free brochure on request.

From £14.50 to £19.00 including electricity • Open all year.
Over 50 years as a family business.

A warm welcome awaits!

Dodwell Park is very well equipped to make your camping stay homely and comfortable. These are some of our facilities: -
Toilets • Free hot showers • Washhand basins with hot water
Hand and hair dryers • Shaving points
Calor and Camping Gaz • Dishwashing facilities
Shop and off-licence • Hard standings • Electric hook-ups
Public telephone and post box • Dogs are welcome

Evesham Road (B439)
Stratford-upon-Avon
Warwickshire
CV37 9SR

Tel: 01789 204957
enquiries@dodwellpark.co.uk
www.dodwellpark.co.uk

Stratford-upon-Avon

RIVERSIDE LOCATION – ONLY ONE MILE FROM THE TOWN CENTRE

LUXURY HOLIDAY HOMES FOR HIRE • TOURING CARAVANS AND MOTORHOME PITCHES • RIVERFRONT COTTAGES TO RENT

Short Stay Bookings Welcome & 3-day Long Weekend Deals

Set in the heart of the lovely Warwickshire countryside and right on the banks of the beautiful River Avon, is Riverside Caravan Park, the perfect location for exploring Shakespeare Country and the Cotswolds. Holiday Home units accommodate 6 persons and Riverford Cottages 4 persons comfortably.

RIVER TAXIS TO AND FROM TOWN • ADJACENT LOCAL VILLAGE • FREE FISHING • RIVERSIDE WALKS ON SITE SHOP & CAFE • CLUB HOUSE • KIDS PLAYGROUND

Riverside Caravan Park

Tiddington Road
Stratford-upon-Avon
Warwickshire CV37 7AB

01789 292312

www.stratfordcaravans.co.uk

West Midlands

Marston, Meriden, Sutton Coldfield

West Midlands

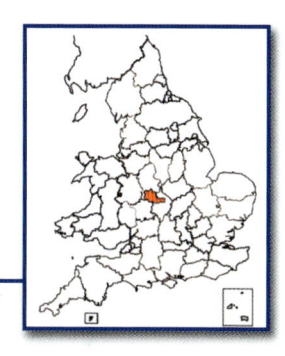

MARSTON CAMPING AND CARAVAN PARK
KINGSBURY ROAD, MARSTON B76 0DP
NEAR SUTTON COLDFIELD AND BIRMINGHAM
Tel: 01675 470902 or 01299 400787

One mile off Junction nine of the M42, towards Kingsbury on the left hand side. Brand new park for 120 caravans, tents and motor homes. Site is open all year round. All pitches have electricity and fully hard standings. Brand new toilet/shower block, laundry room. Play area. Pets welcome.

Kingsbury Water Park • Hams Hall • Drayton Manor Park • Belfry Golf Course National Exhibition Centre • Tamworth Ski Slope • Lee Manor Leisure Complex.

MERIDEN. Somers Wood Caravan Park, Somers Road, Meriden CV7 7PL
Tel: 01676 522978 • Fax: 01676 522978 • www.somerswood.co.uk
This adults-only caravan park is set in beautiful North Warwickshire, overlooking a golf course and only 3 miles from Birmingham NEC. Open February to December. 48 pitches available. Caravans and motorhomes welcome. No tents.

SUTTON COLDFIELD. Kingsbury Water Park, Bodymoor Heath Lane, Sutton Coldfield B76 0DY
Tel: 01827 874101
There are at least 200 species of birds to see in this peaceful area of natural beauty. Discover the 600-acre Tame Valley Water Park or have a day out to Staffordshire's best loved theme park, Drayton Manor. 120 touring pitches available. Caravans, motorhomes, tents and trailer tents welcome. Open January to December.

⚡	Electric hook-ups available	♿	Facilities for disabled visitors
⛺	Children's play area	🐕	Pets welcome
🧺	Laundry facilities	🛒	Shop on site
🍷	Licensed bar on site	W	Wifi access available

The FHG Directory of Website Addresses
on pages 195-210 is a useful quick reference guide for holiday accommodation with e-mail and/or website details

Yorkshire

Photo courtesy Scarborough Borough Council

South Bay, Scarborough, North Yorkshire

Seaside with cliffs and golden beaches, wild moorland, rolling hills and dales, castles and abbeys, museums, wildlife, lively cities, busy market towns, wonderful food, great shopping, Yorkshire has it all! From gliding to wind surfing to steam trains, there's an activity for everyone. Situated in north east England, and historically divided into North, West and East Ridings, each of the regions in this guide, North, South, East and West, has its own characteristics, but together they still have much in common.

East Yorkshire is all about fun and action outdoors. From building sandcastles on the award-winning beaches along the North Sea coast in the east to walking in the Wolds inland, all the family will find an activity to enjoy. The Blue Flag beaches at Bridlington and Hornsea are ideal for children and if they tire of the sun and sand there's plenty of traditional entertainment too. Water sports aren't confined to the seaside, with windsurfing at Dacre Lakeside Park and jet skiing at Fossehill near Driffield, an ideal centre from which to explore both coast and country, and for golfers there's a choice of clifftop links and parkland courses inland and on the coast. For a taste of city life visit Hull, with its lovely waterfront, explore the Old Town while following the sculptures of the Seven Seas Fish Trail, enjoy modern drama at the Truck Theatre, and jazz, sea shanty and literature festivals, or watch football and rugby at the KC Stadium. Wherever you go, countryside, seaside or city, you're sure of an interesting and fun time.

Not only does **South Yorkshire** have a considerable industrial heritage to offer, but its situation at the eastern gateway to the Peak District National Park makes it an ideal destination for anyone looking for an outdoor break. Have fun and learn at the same time at the Magna Science Adventure at Rotherham, where the interactive displays are based on the four elements, air, earth, fire and water, or for a day outdoors picnic in the peaceful grounds of the nearby historic Roche Abbey in the beautifully landscaped valley of Maltby Beck, while listening to the birdsong. As well as the abbey ruins, there are interesting churches and chapels to visit, and Doncaster has fine examples of Georgian architecture. Children will love getting really close to wild and farm animals from all over the world at the nearby Yorkshire Wildlife Park, or if the weather isn't so good, there's swimming, ice skating and a climbing wall at Doncaster Dome.

West Yorkshire is a mix of wild moorland and towns and cities with a long industrial heritage. Spend time in one of the many fascinating museums of past working life, then stride out over the moors, taking in the dramatic scenery, before a shopping spree or a wonderful afternoon tea. There's a model Victorian village for mill workers at nearby Saltaire, where Salts Mill has been transformed into the Hockney Gallery, with a restaurant and everything from musical instruments to carpets for shoppers to browse and buy. From there, wander along the banks of the Leeds-Liverpool Canal, so vital for trade in a past age, and perhaps watch the Five Rise Locks in action. Leeds is the destination for a lively city break. Theatres, ballet, opera, festivals, restaurants, clubs, and of course, one of the best shopping experiences in the country, all are here to provide entertainment and a memorable stay. Visit the exclusive shops in the Victoria Quarter and find sought after brands in the new developments at The Light and Clarence Dock on the waterside. If all this is too much for some family members, Harewood House with its wonderful interior, gardens, and adventure playground is nearby, as well as the Yorkshire Planetarium.

The city of York in **North Yorkshire** is full of attractions for the visitor. View it gently floating through the air on a balloon trip, or if you prefer to keep your feet on the ground take a walk round the ancient walls, to get a first glimpse of the compact urban centre dominated by the magnificent York Minster, the largest medieval Gothic cathedral in northern Europe. Have fun finding your way through the the Snickelways, the maze of hidden alleyways, and enjoy a morning – or longer – in the interesting independent little shops and boutiques as well as all the top high street stores. Explore York's long past at Jorvik, the recreation of the original Viking city from 1000 years ago or become an archaeologist for the day at Dig! and excavate for yourself items from Viking, Roman, medieval and Victorian times. Outside the city the vast open stretches of the North York Moors and the Yorkshire Dales National Parks and the golden sandy beaches of the coast are perfect for an active holiday. Walking, riding, cycling, horse riding, or just enjoying the great outdoors, North Yorkshire provides an ideal destination. Every standard of fitness and ability is catered for, whatever the sport or activity. Walkers will find gentle short circular routes centred on interesting, historic stone villages and busy market towns, and more arduous long distance trails, like the Cleveland Way, the Pennine Trail and the Dales Way, or the really challenging Yorkshire Three Peaks in Ribblesdale.

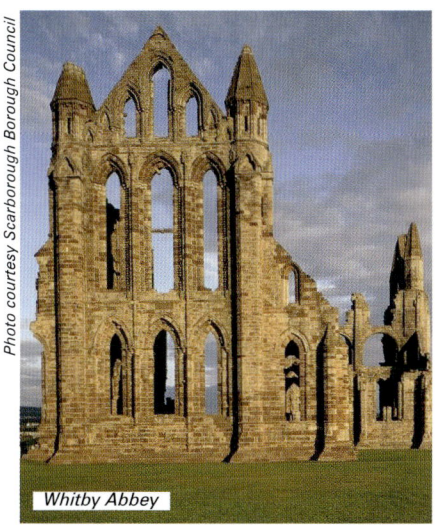

Photo courtesy Scarborough Borough Council

Whitby Abbey

Photo courtesy National Railway Museum

All aboard at the National Railway Museum

110 **YORKSHIRE**   **East Yorkshire**

Flamborough, Sproatley, Withernsea

East Yorkshire

Thornwick & Sea Farm Holiday Centre

THE place for ALL the Family

Set on the spectacular Heritage coast with unrivalled coastal scenery. Within easy reach of the north east coast holiday resorts.

- Six-berth extra wide caravans and fully equipped two-bedroom chalets for hire. • Tents and tourers welcome.
- Caravan Holiday Homes available.
- Bars, entertainment, shop. • Coarse fishing lake
- Health Suite with pool, sauna, gym and steam room on site.

Thornwick & Sea Farm Holiday Centre, Flamborough, East Yorkshire YO15 1AU
Tel: 01262 850369 • e-mail: enquiries@thornwickbay.co.uk • www.thornwickbay.co.uk

SPROATLEY. Burton Constable Holiday Park, The Old Lodges, Sproatley HU11 4LN
Tel:01964 562 508 • Fax: 01964 563 420 • www.burtonconstable.co.uk
Winner of a White Rose Award for Tourism. In a peaceful setting with stunning views and an adventure play area for children. Open from March to October. 170 touring pitches. 50 tent pitches. Motorhomes welcome.

WITHERNSEA. Withernsea Sands Holiday Park, North Road, Withernsea HU19 2BS
Tel: 01964 611161 • Fax: 01964 612411 • www.withernseaholidays.com
Lively park with an indoor swimming pool and children's splash bath, the Boathouse Tavern for excellent meals, entertainment and to top it all off – a beach just minutes away! Open from March to October. 100 touring pitches. 8 tent pitches. Caravans, motorhomes and tents welcome.

North Yorkshire

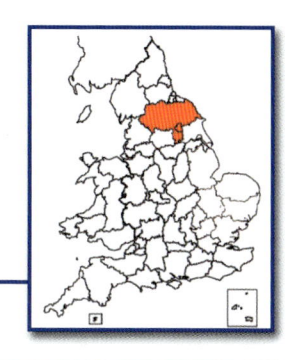

Brompton-on-Swale, Easingwold, Filey

BROMPTON-ON-SWALE. Brompton-on-Swale Caravan & Camping Park, Brompton-on-Swale DL10 7EZ
Tel: 01748 824629 • www.bromptoncaravanpark.co.uk
Standing on the banks of the River Swale only two miles from Richmond, the Gateway to the Yorkshire Dales. Excellent on-site fishing. Open all year round. 170 touring pitches. Caravans, motorhomes and tents welcome.

EASINGWOLD. Holly Brook Adults Only Caravan Park, Penny Carr Lane, Easingwold YO61 3EU
Tel: 01347 821906
Adults-only caravan park situated next to Easingwold Golf Club. Quiet, secluded and the ideal getaway for a relaxing break. 30 touring pitches. Caravans and tents welcome.

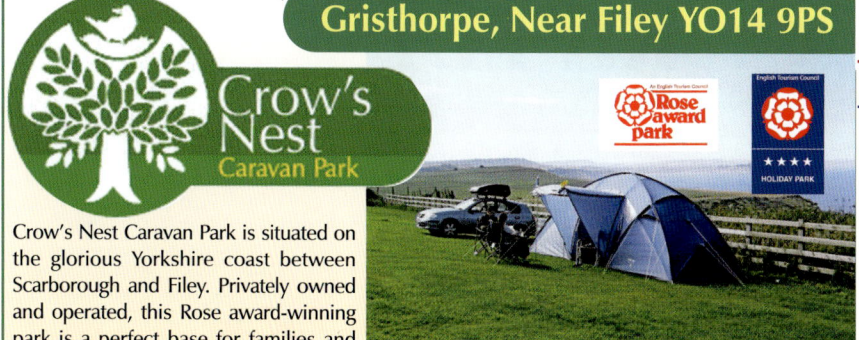

Gristhorpe, Near Filey YO14 9PS

Crow's Nest Caravan Park

Crow's Nest Caravan Park is situated on the glorious Yorkshire coast between Scarborough and Filey. Privately owned and operated, this Rose award-winning park is a perfect base for families and couples wishing to make the most of these two great seaside towns and their glorious sandy beaches.

The facilities at Crow's Nest are of a very high standard. The heated indoor swimming pool with waterslide provides fun for all ages, and together with the safe children's play area and games room, ensures that there is always something to do. Our well stocked supermarket will supply your every need. The family bar welcomes children, and our relaxing lounge bar features evening entertainment. Our non-smoking conservatory is ideal for a peaceful evening of relaxation after your day's excitement. Touring caravans, motor homes and tents welcome. Hard-standing pitches with electric hook-up are standard. Calor Gas and Camping Gaz stocked.

Telephone: 01723 582206
e-mail: enquiries@crowsnestcaravanpark.com
www.crowsnestcaravanpark.com

112 YORKSHIRE | North Yorkshire
Glaisdale, Harrogate

Hollins Farm

Small farm camp site (TENTS ONLY) in the valley of Glaisdale in the North Yorkshire Moors, nine miles from Whitby. Good walking country. Handy for Whitby, the coastal villages and steam railway. Pony trekking and fishing available. Village amenities include good store and butchers, pub which serves meals, tennis court. On-site amenities include flush toilet, showers, fridge/freezer, shaver point and washing up facilities. Slide and swing for small children. Children and pets welcome. Please write with SAE, or telephone for further details. Also good B&B, some rooms en suite.

Glaisdale, Whitby, North Yorkshire YO21 2PZ
✦ **01947 897516** ✦

RIPLEY
CARAVAN PARK

Situated adjacent to the delightfully quiet village of Ripley, dominated by its castle which has been occupied by the same family for over 600 years. Conveniently placed for the superb holiday and conference town of Harrogate and for historic Knaresborough; an ideal touring base with the Yorkshire Dales close by.

The site facilities include a leisure block with games room with colour TV, nursery playroom, telephone, shop and heated indoor swimming pool and sauna; toilet block with showers, ample washbasins, razor points and baby bath. There is a room for our disabled guests with its own specialised facilities. Laundry room, chemical toilet disposal. Electric hook-up points and hard standing for some pitches. Pets welcome by arrangement. Brochure and tariff available on request.

Ripley, Harrogate HG3 3AU
Tel: 01423 770050

North Yorkshire
Harrogate, Hawes, Helmsley

YORKSHIRE 113

The Yorkshire Hussar Inn Holiday Park

Secluded family site nestling deep in the heart of picturesque Yorkshire, midway between Ripon and Harrogate, which is noted for its splendid flower gardens and shops. The park is situated behind the 'olde worlde'

Further details on request from Mrs Denton

inn, in a peaceful garden setting, and is licensed for 75 caravans, plus space for some tourers and tents.

Five luxury six-berth caravans for hire on a weekly basis; nightly lets allowed if available. Each caravan has a double and a twin bedroom, plus sofa bed in the lounge; bathroom/shower room. The caravans are connected to all services, and TV, cooking utensils, crockery, cutlery, duvets and pillows are supplied. Guests must supply own bed linen and towels. Children's play area. Village shop and Post Office.

Markington, Near Harrogate HG3 3NR
Tel: 01765 677327
e-mail: yorkshirehussar@yahoo.co.uk
www.yorkshire-hussar-inn.co.uk

CAMPING SITES

HAWES. Mr and Mrs Facer, Bainbridge Ings Caravan and Camping Site, Hawes DL8 3NU (01969 667354).
A quiet, clean, family-run site with beautiful views and only half-a-mile from Hawes. Good centre for walking and touring the Dales. You can be assured of a warm welcome.
Rates: from £13.00 per day.
• Pets welcome. • Children welcome.
ETC ★★★
e-mail: janet@bainbridge-ings.co.uk   www.bainbridge-ings.co.uk

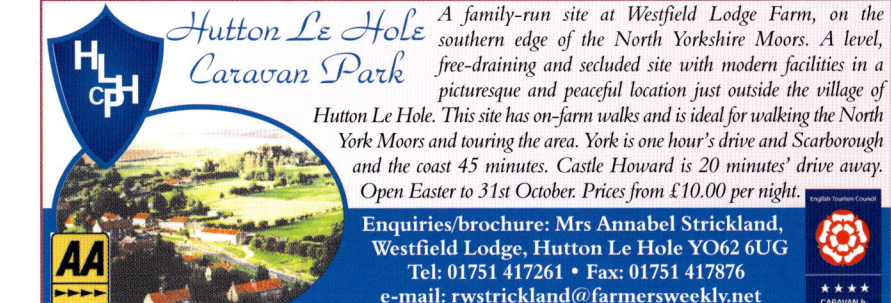

Hutton Le Hole Caravan Park

A family-run site at Westfield Lodge Farm, on the southern edge of the North Yorkshire Moors. A level, free-draining and secluded site with modern facilities in a picturesque and peaceful location just outside the village of Hutton Le Hole. This site has on-farm walks and is ideal for walking the North York Moors and touring the area. York is one hour's drive and Scarborough and the coast 45 minutes. Castle Howard is 20 minutes' drive away. Open Easter to 31st October. Prices from £10.00 per night.

Enquiries/brochure: Mrs Annabel Strickland,
Westfield Lodge, Hutton Le Hole YO62 6UG
Tel: 01751 417261 • Fax: 01751 417876
e-mail: rwstrickland@farmersweekly.net
www.westfieldlodge.co.uk

A useful index of towns/counties appears at the back of this book

114 YORKSHIRE
North Yorkshire
Kirkbymoorside, Leyburn, Northallerton

Welcome To Wombleton Caravan & Camping Park

The Willoughby family welcome you to a quiet retreat set in the middle of rural Ryedale. Wombleton is a five star touring park located halfway between Helmsley and Kirkbymoorside south of the A170. A good base to explore the North Yorkshire Moors and York and twenty miles from the east coast.

Wombleton Caravan & Camping Park
Moorfield Lane, Wombleton,
Kirkbymoorside, North Yorkshire Y062 7RY
Tel/Fax: 01751 431684

e-mail: info@wombletoncaravanpark.co.uk • www.wombletoncaravanpark.co.uk

---

LEYBURN. Akebar Caravan Park , Wensleydale, Near Leyburn DL8 5LY
Tel: 01677 450201 • Fax:01677 450046 • www.akebarpark.com
Akebar in the Yorkshire Dales is ideally placed between two National Parks, offering ample opportunites to enjoy outdoor pursuits. Amenities include a 27 hole floodlit golf course, pub and restaurant, and croquet/bowling green. Open from March-January. 200 touring pitches. 25 seasonal pitches. 50 tent pitches. 5 motorhome pitches.

Otterington Park

Situated in the Vale of York on a family-run farm, Otterington Park is a quality, purpose built 5-acre site designed to cater for up to 40 touring units. Electricity and luxury heated amenity block complete with individual bath/shower rooms, disabled facilities and laundry facilities available. Coarse fishing on site. Children and dogs welcome!
There is also a brand new development, adjoining the Touring Caravan site, ready for 40 Luxury Holiday Lodges and Static Caravans. Full details on request.
This is an ideal base for visiting the moors and dales of Yorkshire including locations from TV favourites such as *Heartbeat*, *Brideshead Revisited* and *Emmerdale*, market towns, leisure centres, golf courses, theme parks and other tourist attractions.

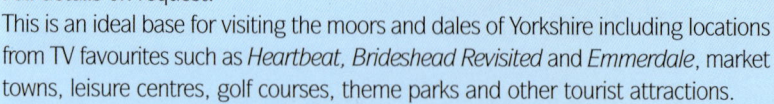

Otterington Park, Station Farm,
South Otterington, Northallerton DL7 9JB
Tel: 01609 780656
www.otteringtonpark.com • info@otteringtonpark.com

North Yorkshire
Pickering, Scarborough

YORKSHIRE 115

BLACK BULL CARAVAN PARK

Family Caravan and Camping Park one mile south of Pickering on the A169, behind a public house. The gateway to the North York Moors! Good base for walking, cycling, visiting the coast and numerous other local attractions.

On-site facilities: playground • games room • sports field refurbished amenities with free hot showers • dishwashing and laundry

Touring pitches in open level field with some shelter. Fully serviced and fully equipped holiday caravans also for hire. Double-glazed and heated.

Terms from £115 to £410.
Four caravans for hire, sleeping six.
Touring pitches available, from £12 per night

Why not view our website for more photographs?
**Malton Road,
Pickering,
North Yorkshire
YO18 8EA**

**www.blackbullpark.co.uk
Tel: 01751 472528**

Harmony Country Lodge

Set in two acres of private land overlooking the National Park and sea. An ideal base for walking or touring in the beautiful North Yorkshire countryside. TWO miles to the north of Scarborough and within easy reach of many nearby attractions and amenities. Spacious five-berth, fully fitted static caravan with two bedrooms. Shower room with hand basin, hot and cold water, and flush toilet. Fully equipped kitchen, gas cooker and microwave, controlled electric heating and colour TV. Pillows, quilts and linen provided. Picnic table and lawned area. Parking. Rates: from £150 to £340 per week, gas/electricity included.

• B&B available from £29.00 to £37.00

**Sue and Tony Hewitt,
Harmony Country Lodge,
Limestone Road, Burniston,
Scarborough YO13 0DG
0800 2985840
Tel & Fax: 01723 870276
e-mail: tony@harmonylodge.net
www.harmonycountrylodge.co.uk**

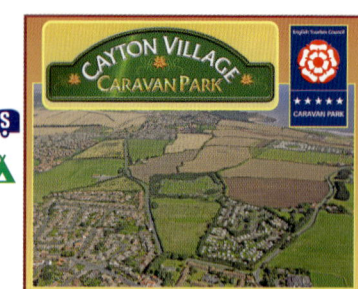

YORKSHIRE — North Yorkshire

Scarborough, Wetherby, Whitby

Cayton Village Caravan Park

The very best of coast and country. Luxurious facilities, adventure playground, site shop, dog walk, bus service at park entrance. Seasonal pitches, supersites, hardstanding and storage. Supersaver and OAP discounts. Open 1st March - 31st October. Location: half-a-mile to beach, three miles to Scarborough, four miles to Filey, adjoining village with pubs, chip shop, PO and bus service.

Prices: Caravans and Motorhomes from £13.50 - £30
Tents from £9 - £20.

Special Offers: Low Season Savers: 7 nights £7 discount, Any 4 nights Sunday to Thursday inclusive £4 discount. Low Season OAP 7 night Special: £10 discount.

Cayton Village Caravan Park Ltd, Mill Lane, Cayton Bay, Scarborough YO11 3NN
Tel: 01723 583171 • e-mail: info@caytontouring.co.uk • www.caytontouring.co.uk

Maustin Caravan Park

ADULTS ONLY

This award-winning Holiday Park is set in the beautiful surroundings of the Lower Wharfe Valley. It is a tranquil and peaceful setting for people without family responsibilities. Whether you hire our latest luxury holiday home or one of our country cottages, bring your own touring caravan or tent, or buy a luxury holiday home, you will be sure of a warm welcome. Visit the Stables Bar and Restaurant serving delicious home-cooked food and fine wines.

Kearby, Near Wetherby,
North Yorkshire LS22 4BZ
Tel: 0113 288 6234
E-Mail: info@maustin.co.uk
www.maustin.co.uk

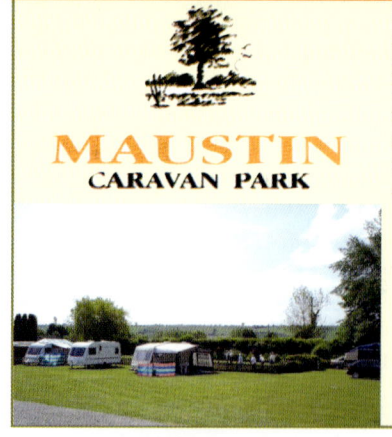

Middlewood Farm Holiday Park

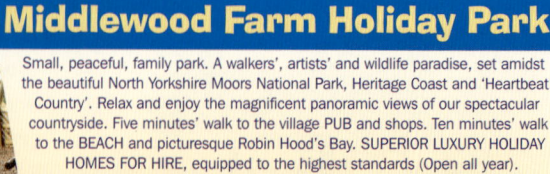

Small, peaceful, family park. A walkers', artists' and wildlife paradise, set amidst the beautiful North Yorkshire Moors National Park, Heritage Coast and 'Heartbeat Country'. Relax and enjoy the magnificent panoramic views of our spectacular countryside. Five minutes' walk to the village PUB and shops. Ten minutes' walk to the BEACH and picturesque Robin Hood's Bay. SUPERIOR LUXURY HOLIDAY HOMES FOR HIRE, equipped to the highest standards (Open all year). TOURERS and TENTS: level, sheltered park with electric hook-ups. Superb heated facilities, free showers and dishwashing. Laundry. Gas. Children's adventure playground. Adjacent dog walk and cycle route. Credit cards accepted. Signposted. A warm welcome awaits you.

Robin Hood's Bay, Near Whitby, Yorkshire YO22 4UF
Tel: 01947 880414
e-mail: info@middlewoodfarm.com • www.middlewoodfarm.com

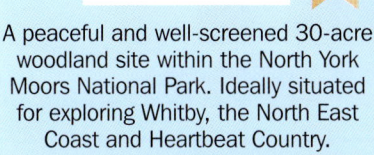

North Yorkshire — YORKSHIRE 117
Whitby, York

Ladycross
TOURING CARAVAN PARK
SITUATED IN SHELTERED WOODLAND
Plantation

A peaceful and well-screened 30-acre woodland site within the North York Moors National Park. Ideally situated for exploring Whitby, the North East Coast and Heartbeat Country. There are lots of activities and visits to suit all tastes within easy reach. Seasonal pitches. No charge for awnings or dogs; two heated amenity blocks, excellent dog walk, launderette, electric hook-ups.
Open March – mid October.

**Ladycross Plantation Touring Caravan Park,
Ladycross Plantation, Egton, Whitby YO21 1UA
Tel: 01947 895502 • enquiries@ladycrossplantation.co.uk
www.ladycrossplantation.co.uk**

The Alders has been sensitively developed in historic parkland on a working farm where visitors may escape from the hustle and bustle of life to peace and tranquillity. The water meadow, wild flowers and woodland walk combine to offer the nature lover an idyllic environment in which to stay. It is a level, dry site with electric hook-ups, fully equipped shower rooms, telephone and gas; nearby village cricket, golf and fishing. Near to A1 and A19 but convenient for York, Harrogate, Dales, Moors, Heritage Coast and National Trust properties. Brochure available.

The Alders
CARAVAN PARK

**Home Farm, Alne, York YO61 1RY
Tel & Fax: 01347 838722
e-mail: enquiries@homefarmalne.co.uk
www.alderscaravanpark.co.uk**

North Yorkshire

York

just 5 miles ...from the centre of York!

OPEN ALL YEAR

This all-new park, which is open all year, has superb facilities including a full length Golf Driving Range and a 9 hole Putting Course.

Tel: 01904 499275
www.yorkcaravansite.co.uk

welcome to our leisure park

Come and see us soon... ...Perfect relaxation

YORK. Goosewood Holiday Park, Sutton-on-the-Forest, York YO61 1ET
Tel: 01347 810829 • Fax: 01347 811498 • www.goosewood.co.uk
A short distance from the centre of York, set in 45 beautiful acres of open countryside. A mixture of woodland and tranquil grassy areas make for the idyllic escape for adults, while there is an adventure playground and play barn for children. Open all year. 52 touring pitches. Caravans and motorhomes welcome.

YORK. Ashfield Holiday Cottages and Caravan Park, Hagg Lane, Dunnington, York YO19 5PE
Tel: 01904 488 631 • www.ashfieldtouringcaravanpark.co.uk
Friendly, family-run site only 10 minutes from the centre of York. Ideal for dog owners and fully equipped with modern, fully functional facilities and separate rally field. Caravans, motorhomes and tents welcome.

YORK. Naburn Lock Caravan Site, Naburn, York YO19 4RU
Tel: 01904 728697 • Fax:01904 728697 • www.naburnlock.co.uk
Well planned site with separate area for adults only. Regular bus service into the centre of historic York. Open from March to November. 96 touring pitches. Caravans, motorhomes and tents welcome.

🚐	Electric hook-ups available	♿	Facilities for disabled visitors
🎠	Children's play area	🐕	Pets welcome
🧺	Laundry facilities	🛒	Shop on site
🍷	Licensed bar on site	W	Wifi access available

FHG Guides

publish a large range of well-known accommodation guides.
We will be happy to send you details or you can use the order form at the back of this book.

North East England

Rothbury Golf Club, Northumberland
Photo courtesy Rothbury Golf Club

Northumberland, County Durham and Tyne and Wear in North East England offer the perfect solution for a break in the open air, whether in the countryside, by the sea or a combination of both. With the Cheviot Hills and the Pennines in the west for walkers, climbers and cyclists, and mile upon mile of beautiful North Sea coast with cliffs, bays and sandy beaches, family resorts and lively city life in the east there is something to suit everyone. Hadrian's Wall is one of the best examples of the Roman occupation, the turmoil of the wars with the Scots has left fortresses and castles to visit, while the advent of Christianity on Holy Island leaves a more peaceful image. Learn more about British history and enjoy the freedom of the open spaces of this lovely region.

Rambling over the heather-clad Cheviot moorlands, exploring the castles and pele towers built to ward off invading Scots, watching the feast of wildlife on the coast and in the countryside, breathing in the wonderful sea air on a golden sandy beach, you'll find it all in **Northumberland**. On the coast, a designated Area of Outstanding Natural Beauty, keen walkers can take the Coast Path from the walled Georgian market town of Berwick-on-Tweed to Cresswell, stopping at little fishing villages on the way. For a shorter route, follow the section along Embleton beach from Craster, best known for its traditionally smoked kippers, to get the best views of the ruins of Dunstanburgh Castle. At the lively market town of Alnwick visit the castle, Hogwarts in the Harry Potter films, with the newly redeveloped gardens, magnificent water features and even a poison garden! Howick Hall gardens are beautiful from the spring snowdrops onwards. Rare and endangered wildlife is found all along the coast and the ultimate destination for enthusiasts is the Farne Islands, with boat trips from the family resort of Seahouses to watch the grey seals and seabirds, including puffins, in the breeding seasons. Wildlife is abundant in the uplands to the west too. In the heather moorlands of the Cheviot Hills there are plenty of opportunities for birdwatching, as well as horse riding, fishing, canoeing and rock climbing. Learn too about the Romans by watching a re-enactment of Roman life at one of the settlements along Hadrian's Wall, or walk along its length from coast to coast. Hexham and Haltwhistle are good bases for a visit, and these and other market towns and villages dotted all over the county make a stay here a very pleasant one.

NORTH EAST ENGLAND

If you're looking for a few days' break somewhere different, why not go to the city of **Durham**? Set between the North Pennines and the Durham Heritage Coast, the old medieval heart with its cobbled streets is dominated by the cathedral and castle, a World Heritage Site, and a must for visitors. On the way back to the modern shopping centre, browse through individual boutiques and galleries in the alleys and vennels, and the stalls of the Victorian market, then enjoy a stroll along the riverside walks. Stay for longer in County Durham, tour all the heritage sites and enjoy invigorating walks and hikes through the dramatic Pennines countryside and along the clifftop path at the coast. There are paths, trails and tracks for all standards of fitness, whether a family ramble or a hike along the Pennine Way. High Force, the highest waterfall in England, on the Raby Castle estate, is easily accessible. Include it in a long distance hike or a gentle wander from the car park. While in the vicinity, pay a visit to this magnificent medieval castle itself near Middleton-in-Teesdale. Keen cyclists can follow the coast to coast route, C2C, which crosses the county. The River Tees presents wonderful opportunities for experienced canoeists, and courses are available at the Teeside White Water Centre at Stockton on Tees in Cleveland, or for a real adrenalin rush, try white water rafting. Enthusiasts will make for Head of Steam, the Darlington Railway Museum to see Locomotion No 1, driven by Stephenson himself on the opening of the very first railway line, and the National Railway Museum, Locomotion, at Shilton. At Killhope go underground at the lead mining museum, and try the hands-on activities.

Accessible with ease from both north and south, the new cosmopolitan city of Newcastle/Gateshead in **Tyne and Wear** is a favourite destination for a short break. Shopping all day followed by a night out at one of the many bars, restaurants and clubs makes for an action-packed, lively weekend. For city centre shopping it takes a lot to beat Eldon Square and Northumberland Street in Newcastle and the elegant streets of nearby Grainger Town are the place to go for designer shopping. At the Metrocentre in Gateshead there are shops for all tastes and price levels, over 50 restaurants, cinema, and a brand new family entertainment area. In addition to the Baltic Centre for Contemporary Art, one of the largest art spaces of its kind in Europe there is a choice of galleries to visit and possibly buy artwork too. Take a closer look at the Angel of the North, the 20 metre high statue that dominates the approach from the south or just wander through one of the parks or alongside the river to see the public artwork on view. Sample the fresh fish and chips in the bracing air of North Shields quay, or take a dip in the water at an award-winning beach at South Shields.

Other specialised holiday guides from FHG
PUBS & INNS OF BRITAIN
• **COUNTRY HOTELS** OF BRITAIN
WEEKEND & SHORT BREAKS
IN BRITAIN & IRELAND
THE GOLF GUIDE
WHERE TO PLAY, WHERE TO STAY
500 GREAT PLACES TO STAY IN BRITAIN
SELF-CATERING HOLIDAYS
BED & BREAKFAST STOPS IN BRITAIN
PETS WELCOME!
FAMILY BREAKS IN BRITAIN

Published annually: available in all good bookshops or direct from the publisher:

e-mail: admin@fhguides.co.uk
www.holidayguides.com

www.holidayguides.com

Durham

Barnard Castle, Bishop Auckland

Durham

NORTH EAST ENGLAND 121

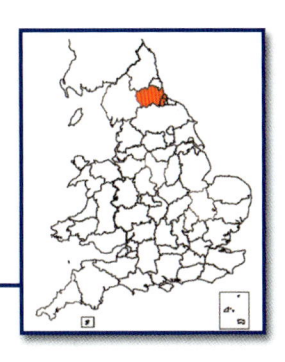

BARNARD CASTLE. East Lendings Caravan Park, Abbey Lane, Barnard Castle DL12 9TJ
Tel: 01833 637171 • Fax: 01833 630578 • www.lakelandleisureestates.co.uk/eastlendings
Popular and sociable park located on the banks of the River Tees, with easy access to the market town of Barnard Castle. On-site pub and club. Open from March to October.

Witton Castle
COUNTRY PARK County Durham

Set within the castle grounds among 338 acres of some of the North's finest and most beautiful countryside, Witton Castle Country Park is fast becoming the number one place to own your own holiday home.

Phase one of the most ambitious project underway in the north east is virtually complete, and with high demand from both first time buyers and people who already have holiday homes and are looking for the best, we now have very limited pitches available on Castle View - so if you're thinking about investing in a holiday home somewhere a bit special, phone for a guided tour now - or just call in. Close to home but a world away.

See you soon!

WANTED
Reasonable site fees ✓
14ft wide, 5 star pitches ✓
Block paved driveways, paths & patios ✓
Piped gas ✓
Bar & restaurant ✓
Over 21s bar ✓
Childrens room ✓
Expansive grounds ✓
Childrens playground ✓
Football & outdoor games ✓
Walking & cycling routes ✓
No tents or rentals ✓
Easy access from home ✓
A country estate not just a caravan park ✓
A castle? ✓

DO YOU OWN YOUR OWN CARAVAN?
DON'T PAY YOUR SITE FEES UNTIL YOU'VE SEEN THE RE-DEVELOPED WITTON CASTLE
2010 SITE FEES FROZEN AGAIN

For a FREE information pack please visit:
www.wittoncastlecountrypark.co.uk
or call us on: **01388 488 230**

For Sat Navs, use:
'Sloshes Lane' and 'DL14 0DE'

Witton Castle Country Park, Sloshes Lane,
Nr Witton-Le-Wear, County Durham, DL14 0DE

The FHG Directory of Website Addresses

on pages 195-210 is a useful quick reference guide for holiday accommodation with e-mail and/or website details

122 NORTH EAST ENGLAND — Northumberland
Bamburgh, Hexham

Northumberland

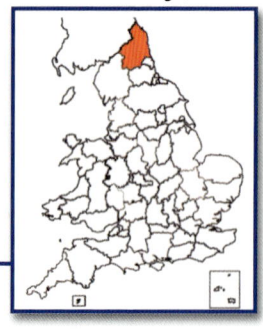

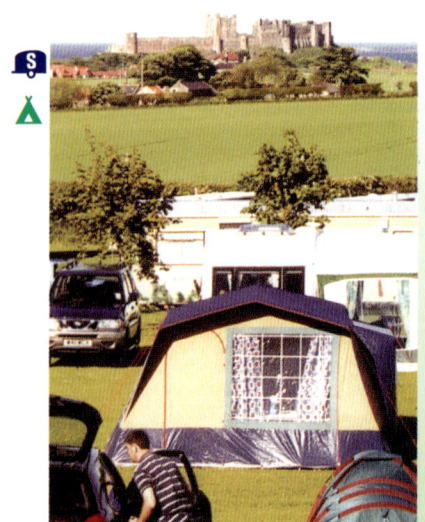

Glororum Caravan Park
Glororum, Bamburgh NE69 7AW

Beautifully situated one mile from Bamburgh on the glorious Northumberland coast. Set in peaceful surroundings within easy reach of Holy Island, the Farne Islands, the Cheviots and many historic castles.

There are ample opportunities locally for swimming, golf, tennis, sailing, water sports, etc.

The park facilities include a shop, toilet blocks with showers, laundry with washing machines and drying facilities and children's play area.

Please send for our colour brochure and tariff leaflet.

e-mail: enquiries@northumbrianleisure.co.uk
www.northumbrianleisure.co.uk

Greencarts is a working farm situated in Roman Wall country, ideally placed for exploring by car, bike or walking. It has magnificent views of the Tyne Valley. Campsite for 30 tents with facilities, and bunk barn with 12 beds, showers and toilet are now open from Easter until the end of October.
Prices for campsite are £5 to £10 per tent, plus £1pp.
Bunk barn beds from £10. Linen available.
Bed and Breakfast also available from £25 to £40.
Mr & Mrs D Maughan, Greencarts Farm,
Humshaugh, Hexham NE46 4BW
Tel/Fax: 01434 681320
e-mail: sandra@greencarts.co.uk

GREENCARTS FARM
www.greencarts.co.uk

Northumberland
Otterburn

NORTH EAST ENGLAND 123

Border Forest Caravan Park
Cottonshopeburnfoot, Otterburn
Northumberland NE19 1TF

We wish you a very warm welcome to the peace and tranquillity of Border Forest Caravan Park Northumberland, a secluded, family-run park situated on the edge of the mighty Kielder Forest.

We are ideally situated to explore the stunning scenery in and around Northumberland and the Border country which is steeped in a sometimes turbulent and violent history.

Only a short drive away is the famous Hadrian's Wall, and in the other direction is the Heritage Coast with beautiful beaches.

- *Touring Site* • *Timber Lodge* • *Self-catering Cottage*
- *Heated Toilet Blocks* • *Free Hot Showers* • *Electric Hook Ups* • *Washing-up Sink*
- *Chemical Disposal Point* • *Spring Water On Tap* • *Calor & Camping Gaz*
- *A paradise for dogs and nature lovers.*
- *Plenty of Dog Walks* • *Tourist Information Area*

There is an abundance of wildlife, numerous walks and nature trails, also direct access to the famous Pennine Way. Or just simply relax on the holiday park and savour the peaceful views without going anywhere.

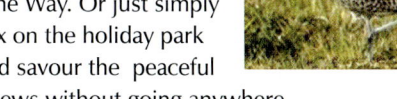

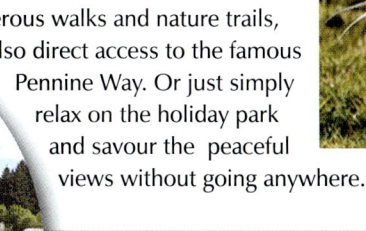

Tel: 01830 520 259
www.borderforest.co.uk
e-mail: borderforest@btinternet.com

Tyne & Wear

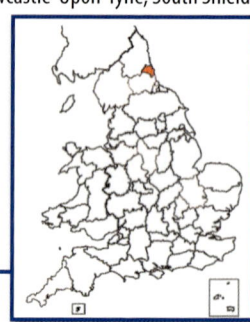

Newcastle-Upon-Tyne, South Shields

Byreside Caravan Site

Hamsterley, Newcastle-upon-Tyne NE17 7RT

The caravan site is on the family-run farm in the beautiful countryside of the Derwent Valley. The site is open all year round and is quiet and secluded. It is very popular with walkers and cyclists as it is adjacent to the Derwent Walk Country Park which is also part of the Coast to Coast route. History looms large in the district with many places to visit in the surrounding area and only a short distance from both Durham and Northumberland.

On site is a small shop and toilet block.

All pitches have electric hook-up points. Camping area. Booking advisable.

Open all year

Contact: Mrs J. Clemitson • 01207 560280

SOUTH SHIELDS. Lizard Lane Caravan And Camping Site, Marsden, South Shields NE34 7AB
Tel: 0191 4544982

Small site catering for tents, tourers and motorhomes. Situated on the edge of town, it has easy access to the beach, and there are delightful walks along the cliff tops. The lively city of Newcastle is just 15 minutes' drive.

SOUTH SHIELDS. Sandhaven Caravan Park, Sea Road, South Shields NE33 2LD
Tel: 0191 454 5194

Miles of sandy beach and traditional seaside fun is on your doorstep at this well equipped park with easy transport links to Newcastle, Gateshead and Sunderland. 25 landscaped pitches include hardstanding. Open March to October.

North West England

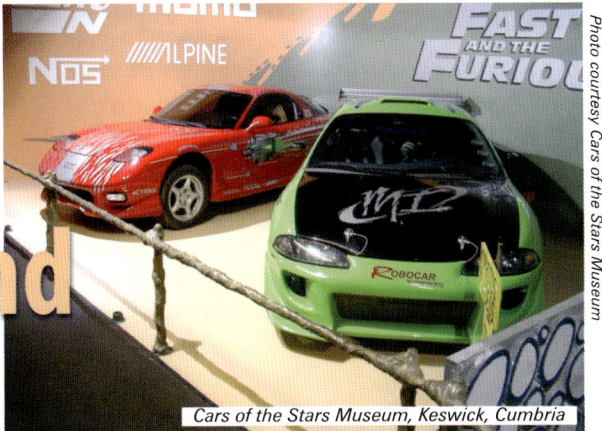

Photo courtesy Cars of the Stars Museum

Cars of the Stars Museum, Keswick, Cumbria

Bright lights and vibrant city nightlife, thrills and entertainment at the seaside, quiet coastal resorts and countryside, and awe-inspiring upland scenery are all to be found in England's North West. From non-stop action in Manchester and Liverpool, the stately homes and glorious gardens of Cheshire, the lively Lancashire seaside and the wonderful walks and climbs of the western Pennines and Cumbria, this region is perfect for a weekend getaway or a longer family holiday.

Manchester and the surrounding area is the place to go for shopping and nightlife, art, music and industrial heritage, and of course, sport. With two famous football teams, international cricket, rugby and all the facilities from the 2002 Commonwealth Games there's plenty to keep sports fans fully occupied. The Arndale Centre in the city, the Trafford Centre just a few miles away and the Lowry Outlet Mall in Salford will ensure that shoppers are happy too. The newly renovated Manchester Art Gallery full of wonderful paintings, MOSI, the Museum of Science and Industry with hands-on exhibitions for all age groups, the Imperial War Museum North and Urbis, a new concept in museums, concentrating on all aspects of contemporary city life are there to browse through and explore.

In **Cheshire**, just south of Manchester, combine a city break in historic Chester with a day or two at one of relaxing spas either in the city itself or in one of the luxury resorts in the rolling countryside. Time your visit to the historic Georgian mansion at Tatton Park to coincide with one of the wide choice of events held there throughout the year, including the annual RHS Flower Show. Chester, with its wonderful array of Roman, medieval and Georgian buildings is a fascinating place to visit. Walk round the most complete example of city walls in the whole country, past the beautiful cathedral, before browsing through the wonderful range of shops, art galleries and museums.

The region now known as **Cumbria**, in England's north west, has been attracting tourists since the end of the 17th century, and the number of visitors has been increasing ever since. The area is a walkers' paradise, and whether on foot, in a wheelchair or a pushchair there's a path and trail for everyone. There are magnificent views from the lakesides as well as from the hill and mountain tops, so whether you're following one of the 'Miles without Stiles' on relatively level, well laid tracks around the towns and villages, climbing in the Langdales or tackling Scafell Pike, the highest mountain in England, you won't miss out on all the Lake District has to offer. The busy market town of Keswick is the ideal centre for exploring the north Lakes, including the historic port of Whitehaven, the former centre for the rum trade. Stay in Penrith, Appleby-in-Westmorland or Kirkby Lonsdale to explore the western Pennines or Silloth-on-Solway to discover the Solway Firth coast. Finally don't miss out Carlisle and its cathedral and castle, the stronghold involved in so many battles with the Scots, the Jacobite rebellions and the Civil War.

Liverpool, an exciting multicultural city built on a history of trade with the Americas, Africa and Asia, is still an important port, but now the emphasis is on art, music and drama and the city's multicultural heritage. Contrasting with this is the tranquil surrounding countryside and coast of the **Merseyside** region, stretching into the counties of Cheshire and Lancashire, where there are ample opportunities for outdoor activities in country parks and nature reserves and on more than 30 miles of coastline and beaches. In Liverpool itself there are theatres, art galleries and museums, cathedrals and endless possibilities for shopping, almost all right in the city centre. Not far from the centre the wonderful interiors and gardens at Speke Hall, a Tudor manor house cared for by the National Trust, are well worth a visit, while back at the Albert Docks the Bugworld Experience, the UK's first insectarium, is just the place to find out all about all kinds of creepy crawlies! Further afield enjoy the views and sea breezes at the Wirral Country Park and beach, and if you're feeling energetic take a walk along the 12 miles of the Wirral Way. City, coast and country, there's plenty to keep the family occupied for an interesting holiday break.

Generations of excited holiday-makers have visited **Lancashire's** coastal resorts, and amongst them Blackpool stands out as the star attraction. For seaside fun, amusements and entertainment it's difficult to beat, but the quieter resorts along the coast with traditional seaside attractions have their own appeal. There's fun for all ages in Blackpool, Britain's most popular resort, from the Big Wheel on Central Pier, the thrilling rides at the Pleasure Beach, and the Winter Gardens with award-winning shows, jazz and rock concerts, to the tropical sharks and reef fish at Sealife, the Sandcastle Waterpark, and a ride in a historic tram along the newly renovated Central Promenade, not forgetting sand, sea and donkey rides. Take a ride to the top of the most famous feature of all, Blackpool Tower, to see the wonderful views and celebrate the arrival of autumn with the annual the spectacle of the Blackpool Illuminations. Further north at Morecambe take part in the Catch the Wind Kite Festival held on the sands in July, just one of a number of events in the town each year. From Clitheroe, with its castle and specialist shops, explore the beautiful Forest of Bowland in the centre of the county, wandering along the lowland riversides or tramping over the moorland hills. Follow the circular Lancashire Cycleway from north to south along sleepy roads through interesting little villages, or test your mountain biking skills in Gisburn Forest where there are trails for everyone from beginners to the highly experienced. Preston, with everything from high street names to farmers' shops and markets, is the destination for shopping, as well as the National Museum of Football.

Photo courtesy Blackpool Tourism

Stanley Park, Blackpool, Lancashire

Cheshire

Knutsford, Macclesfield, Northwich, Wirral

Cheshire

Woodlands Park
Wash Lane, Allostock, Knutsford, Cheshire WA16 9LG
Tel: 01565 723429 or 01332 810818

Woodlands Park is a 16-acre residential and holiday home park set in delightful shrubbery and mature woodland. The park offers homes for sale and has a flat, spacious area for tourers and tents. Facilities include toilet block with showers, laundry room, chemical toilet disposal, electric hook-up points and some hard standings. Brochure and tariff available upon request. Pets welcome by arrangement. Open 1st March to 7th January.

MACCLESFIELD. Stonyfold Caravan Park, Stonyfold Lane, Leek Road, Bosley, Macclesfield SK11 0PR
Tel: 07973 728547 • Fax: 01625 422832.
Adults-only caravan park located south of the market town of Macclesfield. Five touring van pitches available. Lodges, chalets and caravans available for hire. Designated parking.

NORTHWICH. Lamb Cottage Caravan Park, Dalefords Lane, Whitegate, Northwich CW8 2BN
Tel: 01606 882302 • Fax: 01606 888491 • www.lambcottage.co.uk
This caravan park is for adults only. Nearby recreational activities include golf, fishing and horseriding. Open March –end of October (approx.) Caravans and motorhomes are welcome.

WIRRAL. Wirral Country Park Caravan Club Site, Station Rd, Thurstaston, Wirral CH61 0HN
Tel: 0151 648 5228
Set in The Wirral, in an area of great natural beauty, the site offers visitors 2000 acres on which to cycle, explore with the family or simply meander. Open March-November. 93 touring pitches.

FHG Guides

publish a large range of well-known accommodation guides.

We will be happy to send you details or you can use the order form

at the back of this book.

128 NORTH WEST　　　　　　　　　　　　　　　　　　　　　　　　　　Cumbria

Coniston, Grange-Over-Sands

Cumbria

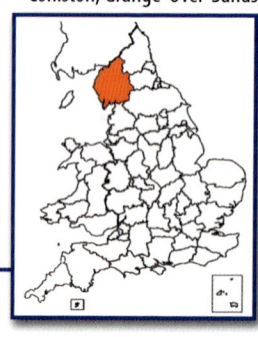

Three six-berth, modern, well-equipped caravans situated on a quiet family-run farm site with beautiful views over Coniston Water.

Showers, toilets, gas cookers, fires and water heaters; electric lighting, fridge, TV, kettle, toaster and microwave.

Pets are welcome, and pony trekking can be arranged from the farm. A good base for walking and touring the area. We have a good pub 200 yards down the road. Weekly terms on request.

Mrs E. Johnson, Spoon Hall, Coniston LA21 8AW
Telephone: 015394 41391

Greaves Farm Caravan Park
Field Broughton, Grange-over-Sands

A small quiet grass site with luxury six-berth caravans.
Family owned and supervised. Beautifully situated in an old orchard. Two miles north of Cartmel, two miles south of foot of Lake Windermere. 30 minutes' from M6. Convenient base for touring Lake District,
Fully serviced. All sites have water, drainage and electricity. Colour TV, fridge. Equipped except for linen. Tourers and tents welcome. Small tented and touring site with electric hook ups if required.
Open March to October.

SAE for details to Mrs E. Rigg, Prospect House, Barber Green, Grange-over-Sands LA11 6HU
Tel: 015395 36329 or 36587

3 Great Sites in Beautiful Lakeland

Tarnside Caravan Park
Braystones, Beckermet, Cumbria CA21 2YL
Tel: 01946 822777 • Fax: 01946 824442
e-mail: reception@seacote.com • www.seacote.com

Situated on seafront on western fringe of Lake District, convenient for Ennerdale, Eskdale, Wasdale and some of England's highest mountains. Good range of tourist attractions in the vicinity. Sea and freshwater fishing.

Licensed club on the park; pubs and shop in Beckermet village (½ mile); Egremont 10 min drive. Modern luxury static holiday caravans; pitches for tourers and motor homes. Dogs welcome.

Seven Acres Caravan Park
www.sevenacres.info
e-mail: reception@seacote.com

Holmrook, Cumbria CA19 1YD
Located alongside the A595 between the villages of Holmrook and Gosforth, Seven Acres is a quiet and peaceful park, with a variety of wildlife. Close to Eskdale, Wasdale and some of England's highest mountains. Modern luxury holiday caravans for hire, fully equipped to sleep up to 8. No additional charge for gas and electricity. Launderette on site. Holiday caravans also for sale. Fully serviced touring pitches and tents also available.
Tel: 01946 822777
Fax: 01946 824442

SEACOTE PARK
The Beach, St Bees, Cumbria CA27 0ET
Tel: 01946 822777
Fax: 01946 824442
reception@seacote.com
www.seacote.com

Adjoining lovely sandy beach on fringe of Lake District, modern luxury holiday caravans for hire, fully equipped to sleep up to 8. Full serviced touring pitches and tent area. St Bees is convenient for touring, with Ennerdale, Eskdale and Wasdale, plus some of England's finest mountain scenery within easy reach. Holiday caravans also for sale.

Greenhowe Caravan Park
Great Langdale, English Lakeland.

Greenhowe is a permanent Caravan Park with Self Contained Holiday Accommodation. Subject to availability Holiday Homes may be rented for short or long periods from 1st March until mid-November. The Park is situated in the heart of the Lake District some half a mile from Dungeon Ghyll at the foot of the Langdale Pikes. It is an ideal centre for Climbing, Fell Walking, Riding, Swimming or just a lazy holiday.

Please ask about Short Breaks.

Greenhowe Caravan Park
Great Langdale,
Ambleside
Cumbria LA22 9JU

For free colour brochure
Telephone: (015394) 37231
Fax: (015394) 37464
www.greenhowe.com

Cumbria
Kendal

NORTH WEST 131

PATTON HALL FARM
kendal, the lake district

luxury static caravan accommodation

Two modern self-catering static caravans located on a 140 acre working sheep farm set in the Mint Valley and offers lovely panoramic views across Kendal and the Lake District fells beyond.
Easily accessible from the M6 motorway; just minutes from Kendal and yet this beautiful, rural location is both peaceful and tranquil.
Fully equipped with modern facilities. Kitchen with full sized cooker and oven, microwave and fridge with freezer box. TV and video.
One twin and one double room and the lounge can also be converted to sleep two people. Bathroom with shower and mirrored vanity unit.
Heated throughout with gas central heating.

Patton Hall Farm
Patton, Kendal,
Cumbria LA8 9DT
Tel: 01539 721590
stay@pattonhallfarm.co.uk
www.pattonhallfarm.co.uk

Modern purpose-built park with top class amenities just three-quarters of a mile from M6 Exit 36. Within easy reach of the Lakes, Yorkshire Dales, West Coast and Morecambe Bay. With licensed lounge bar, off-licence, TV lounge, pool table, facilities for the disabled, shop, Calor gas, barbecues, picnic tables, fully tiled private showers, toilets and wash cubicles, laundry and washing up facilities all with free hot water.
All hardstanding pitches with electric hook-ups.
Many suitable for awnings. Please telephone or write for our free colour brochure. Call for bar opening times.

Waters Edge Caravan Park
Crooklands, Near Kendal LA7 7NN
Tel: 015395 67708

---

symbols

- ☼ Holiday Parks & Centres
- 🚐 Caravans for Hire
- Ⓢ Caravan Sites and Touring Parks
- ⛺ Camping Sites

CASTLERIGG HALL
CARAVAN & CAMPING PARK

In the heart of the English Lake District

"Deep down in the valley, the lakes of Derwentwater and Bassenthwaite gleam blue or silver according to the hues of the weather. This fabulous view is visible from some of the fully serviced pitches which are arranged on hardstanding terraces."

Castlerigg Hall is one of Britain's most spectacularly scenic sites set in the heart of the English Lake District. Its elevated postion provides wonderful panoramic views. The facilities are of a high standard with underfloor heating to one of the toilet buildings, privacy cubicles, laundry and a bathroom to soak those weary legs after a day's walking! The park's shop is well stocked with fresh bread, milk, papers and a wide range of other items. The park's restaurant is popular and open five days a week serving locally sourced food.

Castlerigg Hall's location is ideal for those who wish to leave their motorhome on the pitch as it is only a 25 minute woodland walk to the centre of Keswick. Another popular short walk is to the 400 year old Castlerigg Stone Cicle. Dogs are catered for too, in the form of an area where you can let your dog off the lead - supervised of course. So why not click on the park's website and go the the live webcam and enjoy the view!

Caravans for hire • Camping
Touring Caravans • Motorhomes

Castlerigg Hall
Caravan & Camping Park,
Keswick CA12 4TE
Tel: 017687 74499
info@castlerigg.co.uk
www.castlerigg.co.uk

Two six-berth caravans in own private half-acre site, on quiet farm setting only 5 miles from Kirkby Stephen, 8 miles from Appleby, and 7 miles from Junction 38 of the M6 at Tebay. It is an ideal location for walking, relaxing or touring the Yorkshire Dales, Lake District and many local market towns.

Whygill Head

Both caravans are Quality Cumbria inspected, and fully equipped with TV and DVD player, and all bedding is provided.
All gas, water and electricity included in tariff. Short Breaks available.

Please phone or write for further information, brochure and tariff.

Whygill Head Caravans, Little Asby,
Appleby CA16 6QD
Tel: 07840 656532

Cumbria
Millom, Newby Bridge, Penrith

NORTH WEST 133

Oak Head Caravan Park
English Lake District

A well tended, uncrowded and wooded site set amidst picturesque fells between the Cartmel peninsula and the southern tip of Lake Windermere.

On-site facilities; flush toilets ✧ hot showers ✧ laundry facilities ✧ hair dryers ✧ deep freeze ✧ gas on sale

Tourers (30 pitches) £16 per night (incl. electricity & VAT).
Tents (30 pitches) £14 - £16 per night. Auto homes £16.
All prices for outfit, plus 2 adults and 2 children.
Open March 1st to October 31st.
Oak Head Caravan Park, Ayside, Grange-over-Sands LA11 6JA
www.oakheadcaravanpark.co.uk

Contact: Mr A.S.G Scott
Tel: 015395 31475

Waterside House Campsite
Waterside House, Howtown Road, Pooley Bridge, Penrith, Cumbria CA10 2NA • Tel & Fax: 017684 86332

Farm and campsite situated about one mile from Pooley Bridge. Genuine Lakeside location with beautiful views of Lake Ullswater and Fells. Ideal for windsurfing, canoeing, boating, fell walking and fishing, table tennis, volleyball. Boat, canoe and mountain bike hire on site. Play area, shop and gas exchange also. SAE or telephone for brochure. Open March to October. Directions: M6 Junction 40, A66 follow signs for Ullswater, A592 to Pooley Bridge, one mile along Howtown Road on right - signposted.

e-mail: enquire@watersidefarm-campsite.co.uk
www.watersidefarm-campsite.co.uk

Gillside Caravan & Camping Site,
Gillside Farm, Glenridding, Penrith CA11 0QQ
Tel: 017684 82346

Sited in an idyllic location above Ullswater, five minutes' walk from the village of Glenridding with shops, National Park Information Centre, cafés and restaurants. The path to Helvellyn passes the farm. Well-equipped six-berth holiday homes; bunkhouse, suitable for groups. Facilities include a constant supply of hot and cold water in the shower/toilet block, deep sinks for washing pots and pans and a laundry with washer/drier; electric hook-ups. Fresh milk and eggs available at the farmhouse. Activities include wind surfing, canoeing, sailing on the steamer, pony trekking and rock climbing. Open March to mid-November. Bunkhouse open all year.

e-mail: gillside@btconnect.com
www.gillsidecaravanandcampingsite.co.uk

Looking for holiday accommodation?
for details of hundreds of properties
throughout the UK including
comprehensive coverage of all areas of Scotland try:

www.holidayguides.com

Beckses Holiday Caravan Park

Conveniently situated within six miles of the M6 motorway, this caravan park offers a choice of holiday accommodation on the fringe of the Lake District National Park. Four and six-berth caravans for hire, with mains services, electric light and fridge, gas cooker and fire, toilet, separate double and bunk bedrooms, kitchen area and lounge. Fully equipped except linen. Alternatively those with touring caravans and tents will find excellent facilities on site; toilets, showers, chemical disposal points, stand pipes and laundry facilities. Within easy reach of outdoor heated swimming pool, pony trekking, fishing and fell walking. Some local pubs have restaurant facilities. Full details and terms on request.

Penruddock, Penrith, Cumbria CA11 0RX
Tel: 017684 83224

Park Foot Holiday Park combines an idyllic setting with so much to see and do

A family-run park catering for families and couples only, Park Foot offers touring caravan and camping pitches and self-catering cottages. All touring pitches have electricity and are close to a water point.

- Modern toilets with hot showers
- Laundry room • Shop
- Direct access to Lake Ullswater and Barton Fell
- Two children's playgrounds
- Games and amusements • Pony trekking
- Mountain bike hire • Dog walking areas
- Licensed club with bar, restaurant and takeaways, disco, live entertainment and children's club in the summer season.
- Static caravans and lodges for sale.

Parkfoot Caravan & Camping Park,
Howtown Road, Pooley Bridge, Penrith,
Cumbria CA10 2NA
Tel: 017684 86309 • Fax: 017684 86041
holidays@parkfootullswater.co.uk • www.parkfootullswater.co.uk

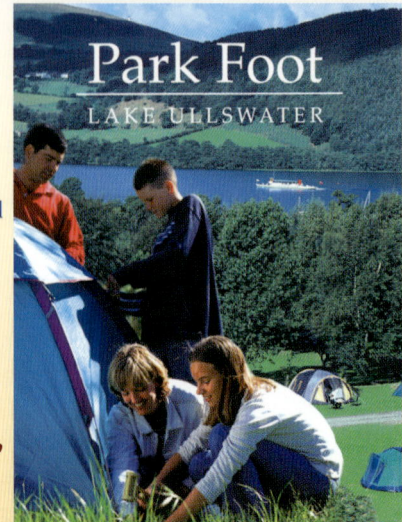

Silloth-on-Solway

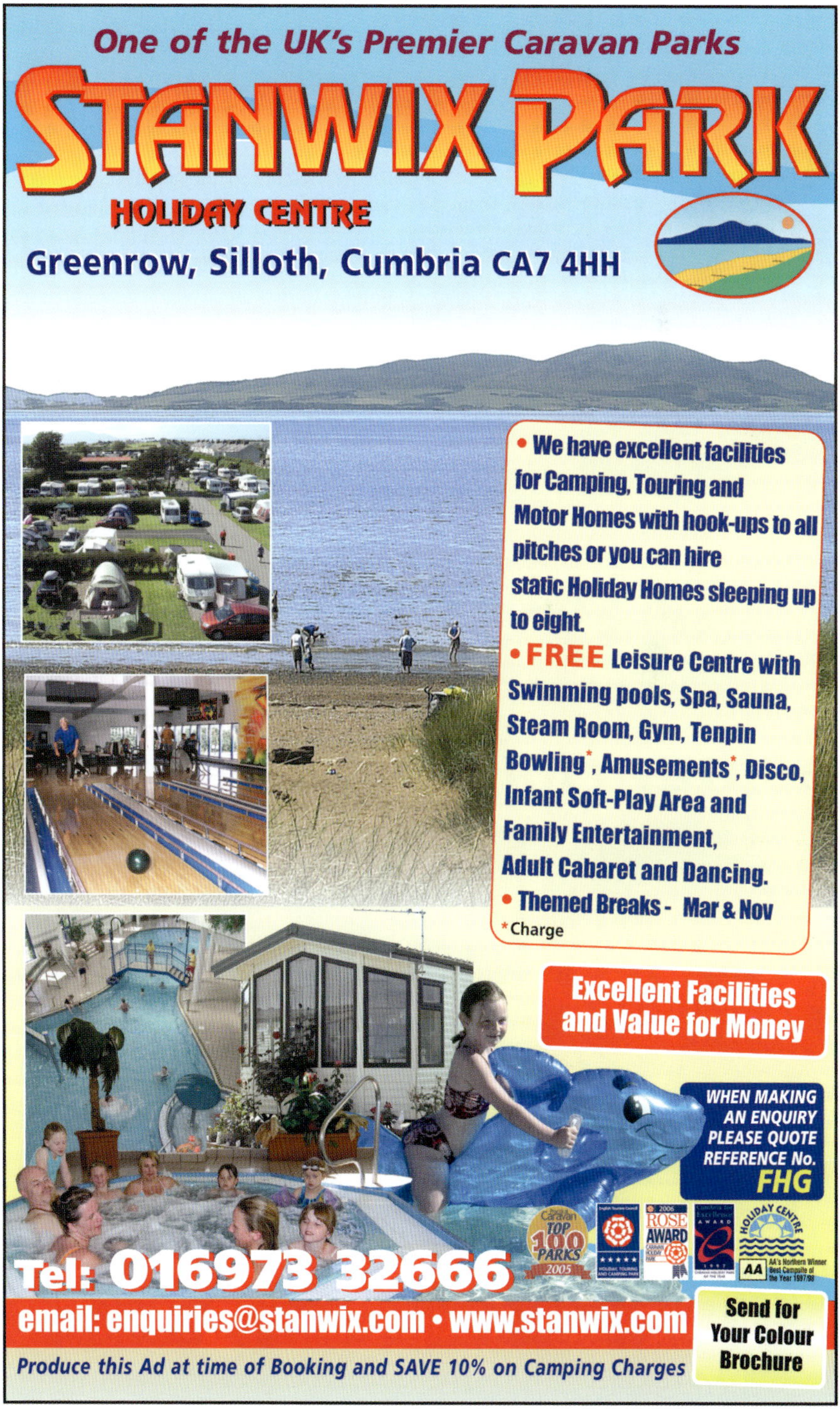

Cumbria
Silloth-on-Solway

Tanglewood Caravan Park
CAUSEWAY HEAD, SILLOTH-ON-SOLWAY, CUMBRIA CA7 4PE

Tanglewood is a family-run park on the fringes of the Lake District National Park. It is tree-sheltered and situated one mile inland from the small port of Silloth on the Solway Firth, with a beautiful view of the Galloway Hills. Large modern holiday homes are available from March to January, with car parking beside each home. Fully equipped except for bed linen, with end bedroom, panel heaters in both bedrooms and the bathroom, electric lighting, hot and cold water, toilet, shower, gas fire, fridge and colour TV, all of which are included in the tariff. Touring pitches also available with electric hook-ups and water/drainage facilities, etc. Play area. Licensed lounge with adjoining children's play room. Pets welcome free but must be kept under control at all times. Full colour brochure available.

★★★ TEL: 016973 31253
e-mail: tanglewoodcaravanpark@hotmail.com
www.tanglewoodcaravanpark.co.uk

Solway Holiday Village
HAGANS LEISURE GROUP

Located in the unspoiled seaside Victorian town of Silloth-on-Solway, this 120-acre family park has something for everyone. A truly idyllic location, the park enjoys breathtaking views out over the Solway Firth to Scotland and offers an ideal touring centre for the Scottish Borders and the English Lake District

- Indoor Leisure Pool
- Fitness Suite
- Tennis Courts
- 9-hole Golf Course
- Licensed Bars
- Live Entertainment
- Kids' Club
- Indoor Play Area
- Outdoor Play Area
- Ten-Pin Bowling
- Pool & Games Room
- Animal Farm
- NEW Italian-themed Courtyard Water Garden

Sale & Hiring from £19pppn
Touring Site from £5.30

Book Now on 016973 31236

solway@hagansleisure.co.uk
www.hagansleisure.co.uk

Cumbria
Ullswater

NORTH WEST 137

Cove Park

The Peaceful Park

Cove Park is a peaceful caravan & camping park overlooking Lake Ullswater, surrounded by Fells with beautiful views. The park is very well-maintained. We are ideally situated for walking, watersports and all of the Lake District tourist attractions in the North Lakes. Facilities include clean heated showers and washrooms with hand and hair dryers, washing and drying machines, iron & board, and a separate washing up area and a freezer for ice packs. We offer electric hook-ups with hardstandings, and plenty of sheltered grass for campers.

The Children's play area offers our younger visitors a safe environment to let off steam. Dogs are most welcome at Cove, (on a lead on the Park please) and we have our own woodland area and fields for exercising.

We do not have a "bar" or "club house" at Cove Park, however, there are many very good local restaurants and pubs in the area, which we will be happy to recommend to you.

Shop nearby (plus Penrith is approx 8 miles away with full range of shops & late opening. Pooley Bridge is also 5 minutes away by car with a range of shops).

Cove Caravan & Camping Park
Watermillock, Penrith, Cumbria CA11 0LS
Tel: 017684 86549 • www.cove-park.co.uk

NORTH WEST

Cumbria

Ullswater, Whicham Valley

Ullswater Caravan Camping & Marine Park

Overlooking Lake Ullswater, this quiet and secluded park provides all amenities and home comforts the discerning holiday maker would expect.

TV lounge • Games room • Private residents' bar area • Washing and ironing facilities

Breathtaking scenery at any time of the year. Some of the best walking country in Britain. Private marina with access to stunning Lake Ullswater (one mile away). Delightful towns and villages dotted throughout the Lake District and Cumbria.

- Electric hook ups available. Camping only areas.
- Static caravans & holiday cottages available to let.
- Cottages are available all year round.
- Static caravans available April-November.

Ullswater Caravan, Camping & Marine Park
Watermillock, Ullswater CA11 0LR

Tel: 017684 86666
www.ullswatercaravanpark.co.uk

Whicham Hall Farm

A truly wonderful location, this single sited modern, static caravan enjoys unspoilt views of the beautiful Whicham Valley. Situated on a working beef/sheep farm at the foot of Backcombe mountain, with plenty of fell and beach walking on our doorstep. The caravan sleeps 4 people in two separate bedrooms, bedding provided. Gas cooking, electric heating and lighting, fridge, microwave and spin dryer. Shower room with basin, w.c. and shaver point. Sorry, no dogs. Ample parking.
Terms from £200 to £350 per week.
Short breaks out of season

Mrs Capstick, Whicham Hall Farm,
Whicham Valley, Silecroft, Cumbria LA18 5LT
Tel: 01229 772637 / 718112
Mobile: 07974 367496

Visit the FHG website
www.holidayguides.com

for details of the wide choice of accommodation featured in the full range of FHG titles

Lancashire
Blackpool, Lune Valley

NORTH WEST 139

Lancashire

Clifton Fields Caravan Park

Situated one mile from the M55, 3.5 miles to Blackpool and 4 miles to Lytham and St Annes. Clifton Fields is a family-owned and run caravan park with a warm welcome to families and couples, offering a touring caravan field with individual hard standing and electric hook-up points, secured by an automatic barrier. Facilities include toilets, showers, elsan disposal point and a launderette.

Directions: exit M55 at Junction 4, turn left, B&Q will be on your right hand side, at the roundabout go straight on then get into the right hand lane, at the traffic lights turn right then immediately left into Peel Road. We are the second caravan park on the right hand side.

CLIFTON FIELDS CARAVAN PARK • Peel Road, Peel, Blackpool FY4 5JU
Tel: 01253 761676

www.clifton-fields.co.uk

Lune Valley

Well equipped, modern static caravan on Yorkshire/ Lancashire border, four miles from Ingleton. In quiet garden on working farm with panoramic views of Ingleborough and surrounding hills, central for dales, coast and the Lakes. Sleeps 4. Double and twin beds, TV, shower, fridge, microwave and garden furniture.

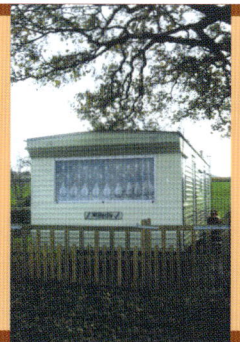

Nearest shop one mile, pub ¾ mile, and two miles from Bentham 18 hole golf course.

From £180 per week including gas, electricity and bed linen.

Mrs B Mason,
Oxenforth Green,
Tatham, Lancaster
LA2 8PL
Tel: 01524 261784

Scotland • Regions

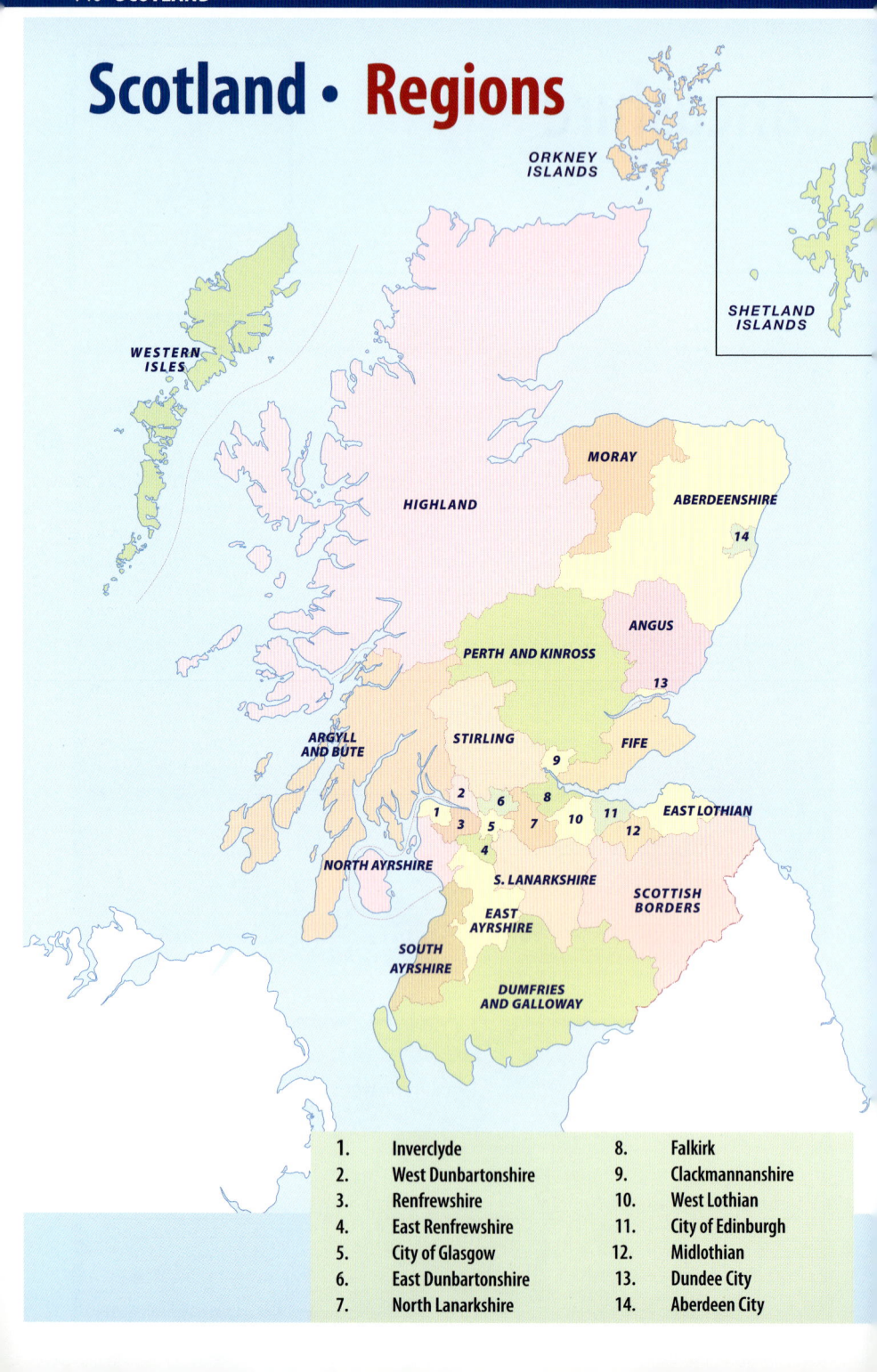

Orkney Islands
Shetland Islands
Western Isles
Moray
Highland
Aberdeenshire
Angus
Perth and Kinross
Argyll and Bute
Stirling
Fife
East Lothian
North Ayrshire
S. Lanarkshire
East Ayrshire
Scottish Borders
South Ayrshire
Dumfries and Galloway

1. Inverclyde
2. West Dunbartonshire
3. Renfrewshire
4. East Renfrewshire
5. City of Glasgow
6. East Dunbartonshire
7. North Lanarkshire
8. Falkirk
9. Clackmannanshire
10. West Lothian
11. City of Edinburgh
12. Midlothian
13. Dundee City
14. Aberdeen City

Scotland

Photo courtesy VisitScotland

Reaching out into the North Sea from the Moray Firth in the north, extending south past Royal Deeside and dominated by the Grampian Highlands to the west, **Aberdeenshire, Banff and Moray** present a wonderful combination of countryside, coast and heritage for the holidaymaker to explore. Easily accessible from Aberdeen, where there are all the attractions of city life, this is an ideal corner of the country for an interesting and relaxing break. Why not follow one of the five tourist trails to see the spectacular scenery and learn more about the area at the same time? On the Victorian Heritage Trail follow in the footsteps of Queen Victoria to Royal Deeside to reach the best-known castle of all, Balmoral, visiting many of her favourite towns and viewpoints on the way. Golfers have 45 inland courses to choose from, some long-established, others more modern developments, like Inchmarlo, as well as the championship links. Aberdeen, a university city of sparkling granite buildings, has museums, art galleries, theatres, films and superb shopping, as well as beaches, golf and fishing.

From the Firth of Tay and westwards from the North Sea coast towards the highlands of the Cairngorm National Park, lies the former Pictish stronghold of **Angus**, its historic burghs and villages and the university city of **Dundee**. The area is renowned for golf, with 50 courses within 30 miles of Dundee, from classic links like Carnoustie to the heathland at Edzell in the north and parkland courses nearer the city. Visit the ancient port of Arbroath during the Sea Fest, celebrating its maritime heritage, and taste a traditional 'smokie'. The more recent past is commemorated in Dundee at Discovery Point, now the home of the RRS Discovery, the ship that took Captain Scott on his ill-fated journey to the Antarctic. The story of the jute industry, on which the wealth of the city was built, is retold at the Verdant Works, and the city formerly associated with jute, jam and journalism now looks to the future at the Sensation Science Centre, with interactive exhibits involving robotics, cybernetics and even keyhole surgery.

Argyll & Bute is a wonderfully unspoilt area, historically the heartland of Scotland and home to a wealth of fascinating wildlife. Here you may be lucky enough to catch a glimpse of an eagle, a wildcat or an osprey, or even a fine antlered stag. At every step the sea fringed landscape is steeped in history, from prehistoric sculpture at Kilmartin, to the elegant ducal home of the once feared Clan Campbell. On the upper reaches of Loch Caolisport can be found St Columba's Cave, and more recent times are illustrated at the Auchindrain Highland Township south of Inveraray, a friendly little town with plenty to see, including the Jail, Wildlife Park and Maritime Museum. Bute is the most accessible of the west coast islands, and Rothesay is its main town. Explore the dungeons and grand hall of Rothesay Castle, or visit the fascinating Bute Museum. The town offers a full range of leisure facilities, including a fine swimming pool and superb golf course, and there are vast areas of parkland where youngsters can safely play.

Ayrshire and The Isle of Arran is situated in the South of Scotland, flanked by the Borders to the south and the Central Belt to the north. Here the warm waters of the Gulf Stream meet with miles of sandy beaches and a dramatic coastline littered with rocky outcrops and caves, once a favourite with smugglers. The Island of Arran, as well as being one of Scotland's most accessible islands, is also arguably one of its most truly representative. From the mountainous north, including Goat Fell, highest peak in the south of Scotland, to the undulating south it is easy to see how the island became known as "Scotland in miniature". The Burns National Heritage Park near Ayr celebrates the life and works of Scotland's national poet, and visitors to the historic town may also enjoy a visit to the racecourse, a shopping spree, or a round on one the area's 44 golf courses.

Covering about 1800 miles, **The Scottish Borders** stretch from the rolling hills and moorland in the west, through gentler valleys to the rich agricultural plains of the east, and the rocky Berwickshire coastline with its secluded coves and picturesque fishing villages. Through the centre, tracing a silvery course from the hills to the sea, runs the River Tweed which provides some of the best fishing in Scotland. As well as fishing there is golf – 18 courses in all, riding or cycling and some of the best modern sports centres and swimming pools in the country. Castles, abbeys, stately homes and museums illustrate the exciting and often bloody history of the area, which is commemorated in the Common Ridings and other local festivals, creating a colourful pageant much enjoyed by visitors and native Borderers alike.

Dumfries & Galloway is a mixture of high moorland and sheltered glens, and presents abundant opportunities for hill walking, rambling, fishing for salmon and sea trout, cycling, bird watching and field sports. There are at least 32 golf courses, ranging from the challenging Stranraer course at Creachmore to the scenic, clifftop course at Portpatrick. The warming influence of the Gulf Stream ensures a mild climate which makes touring a pleasure, and visitors come here to explore the interesting castles, gardens, museums and historic sites. Discover the many hidden secrets of this lovely and unspoilt landscape such as the pretty little villages along the coast or visit some of the interesting towns in the area including Stranraer, the principal town and ferry port with its busy shopping streets, park and leisure centre. Those who love 'the written word' must surely visit the book town of Wigtown, and the gourmet amongst us will love Castle Douglas, the recently designated 'Food Town'.

In the area known as **Edinburgh & The Lothians,** Scotland's capital is home to a wide range of attractions offering something for visitors of all ages. The Royal Mile holds many of the most historic sights, but within a short distance there are fine gardens to visit or the chance to sample the latest in interactive technology. The annual Festival in August is part of the city's tradition and visitors flock to enjoy the performing arts, theatre, ballet, cinema and music, and of course "The Tattoo" itself. At the Festival Fringe there are free shows and impromptu acts, a jazz festival and book festivals. Once thriving fishing villages, North Berwick and Dunbar now cater for visitors who delight in their traditional seaside charm. In Midlothian you can step back in time with a visit to Rosslyn Chapel or Borthwick and Crichton Castles, or seize the chance to brush up on your swing at one of the excellent courses in the area. A network of signposted paths allow walkers of all abilities to enjoy the contrasts of the area, whether for a leisurely stroll or at a more energetic pace.

SCOTLAND

Queen's View, Perthshire

Photo courtesy VisitScotland

Fife - whether as 'County', 'Region' or more traditionally 'Kingdom', this has always been a prosperous and self-contained part of Scotland. The coast, with small ports such as Crail, Anstruther, Pittenweem, St Monance, Elie and the more commercial Methil, Burntisland and Kirkcaldy, has always been interesting and important. St Andrews with its university, castle, cathedral and golf, is the best known and most visited town. Dunfermline has a historic past with many royal associations and was the birthplace of the philanthropist, Andrew Carnegie. Medieval buildings have been restored by the National Trust in nearby Culross. Cupar, Falkland, Kinross (for Loch Leven), Auchtermuchty and Leuchars are amongst the many other historic sites in Fife, and at North Queensferry is one of Fife's newest and most popular attractions, Deep Sea World. The picturesque seaside village of Aberdour with its own castle is nearby.

In one of Europe's most dynamic cultural centres, there's so much to see and do – from the City of **Glasgow** itself, alive with heritage, entertainment and nightlife, to the charm of the bustling towns, scenic villages and countryside of the surrounding districts. Entertainment and sport feature in an exciting year-round calendar that encompasses opera and theatre, Scottish ceilidhs and top sporting events. Glasgow is home to a multitude of shops, from boutiques and specialist stores, to the High Street favourites, and shopping malls. The famous River Clyde links city life to country life as it flows from its source in the Lowther Hills to the Clyde Valley, to the maritime towns and villages of Inverclyde and Renfrewshire, and castles, distilleries, gardens and wildlife await just outside the city.

Apart from the stunning scenery, the major attraction of **The Scottish Highlands** is that there is so much to see and do, whatever the season. Stretching from Fort William in the south, to Wick in the far north, there is a wealth of visitor attractions and facilities. Loch Ness, home of the legendary monster, is perhaps the most famous of these attractions and the Loch Ness Visitor Centre also provides a variety of souvenirs, including kilts and whisky. Make sure that a visit to the bustling Highland capital city of Inverness is on your itinerary, and don't miss Fort William in the Western Highlands, a busy town with a wide range of shops and services, pubs, restaurants and Scottish entertainment. The North West Highlands is home to the nation's first Geopark, underlining the importance of the area's geological past. The famous Inverewe Gardens with its wonderful array of foreign plants, more formal borders and lovely views everywhere is worth a visit at any season. John O'Groats is, of course, the ultimate destination of most travellers as it was for the Norsemen centuries ago, whose heritage is preserved in the Northlands Viking Centre at Auckengill. The main towns in this sparsely populated area are Dornoch, Golspie, Brora and Helmsdale. Popular activities include walking, cycling, pony trekking and golf, and anglers will find good sea fishing, as well as some great value day permits for fresh water fishing.

Perth & Kinross embraces both Highland and Lowland. Close to where the two Scotlands meet, a cluster of little resort towns has grown up: Crieff, Comrie, Dunkeld, Aberfeldy, and Pitlochry, set, some say, right in the very centre of Scotland. No matter where you base yourself, from Kinross by Loch Leven to the south to Blairgowrie by the berryfields on the edge of Strathmore, you can be sure to find a string of interesting places to visit. If your tastes run to nature wild, rather than tamed in gardens, then Perthshire offers not only the delights of Caledonian pinewoods by Rannoch and the alpine flowers of the Lawers range, but also wildlife spectacle such as nesting ospreys at Loch of the Lowes by Dunkeld. There are viewing facilities by way of hides and telescopes by the lochside. Water is an important element in the Perthshire landscape, and it also plays a part in the activities choice. Angling and sailing are two of the 'mainstream' activities on offer, or enjoy a round of golf on any of Perthshire's 40 courses, including those at Gleneagles by Auchterarder. The main town of Perth has plenty of shops and attractions including an excellent repertory theatre and a great choice of eating places, making this is an ideal base to explore the true heartland of Scotland.

At the heart of Scotland, **Stirling & The Trossachs** has played a central role in most aspects of the nation's life. History and geography have converged here in road and rail routes, in decisive sieges and battles, in important industrial developments and heritage. The county enjoys the natural riches of the Forth valley and the economic wealth of Grangemouth and Falkirk. The town of Stirling itself is a natural tourist centre, both for its own attractions, such as the historic castle and the excellent shopping facilities, and as a base for other visitor attractions close at hand. Villages and small towns such as Drymen, Killearn, Fintry and Kippen offer hospitality and interesting outings. Loch Lomond and The Trossachs National Park is less than an hour from Glasgow, yet feels worlds apart from the bustle of city life. Explore wild glens and sparkling lochs, and for the more energetic, low-level walking, cycling, hill walking, and the new sport of canyoning can be enjoyed.

The Falkirk Wheel

Aberdeen, Banff & Moray

Elgin, Huntly

Aberdeen, Banff & Moray

SCOTLAND 145

Station Caravan Park boasts terrific views of the Moray Firth where we often sight the Moray Firth dolphins, and is an ideal place to relax and have a good holiday. As well as the beach, there are caves, rockpools and fossils within walking distance. The village itself has all the shops you will need including a chemist, post office, takeaway food, ice cream, convenience store and pubs. We have luxury caravan holiday homes for hire, many with sea views, plus there are usually a few for sale. For the touring units there are electric hook-ups, water points, modern toilet/shower blocks and a launderette. Open from 28th March till 31st October. For full price information please contact the park direct.

Station Caravan Park • West Beach, Hopeman • Near Elgin IV30 5RU
Tel & Fax: 01343 830880

e-mail: enquiries@stationcaravanpark.co.uk   www.stationcaravanpark.co.uk

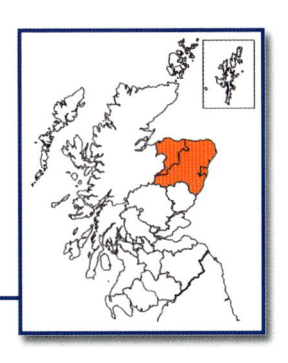

Huntly Castle Caravan Park

Set in the heart of the Grampian countryside, 5 minutes' walk from Huntly town, this 5-Star graded family-run park achieved *AA Best Campsite in Scotland 2008*. It offers the very highest standard of facilities including fully serviced pitches and fully equipped disabled suites.
The park is an ideal base for the Castle Trail, Whisky Trail and North East Coastal Trail. There are 15 golf courses within half an hour's drive.
Why not treat yourself to a break in one of the Thistle Award holiday homes for hire?
Open 26 March to 31 October 2010.

The Meadow, Huntly, Aberdeenshire AB54 4UJ • Tel: 01466 794999
e-mail: enquiries@huntlycastle.co.uk • www.huntlycastle.co.uk

146 SCOTLAND — Aberdeen, Banff & Moray / Angus & Dundee

Laurencekirk

Welcome to Brownmuir Caravan Park

• Laundry Facilities • Washing Facilities • Showers • Shaving Points • Playground •

Ideal for walking and hiking, cycling, fishing, ski-ing, birdwatching, golf and shopping.
Good touring centre for Aberdeen, Royal Deeside, Dundee, Glenshee etc.
Open April to October • Static caravans/hire • Tourers welcome • Tents • Pets welcome

Contact: Mrs Bowers, Brownmuir Caravan Park, Fordoun, Laurencekirk AB30 1SJ
Tel: 01561 320786 • Fax: 01561 320786
email: brownmuircaravanpark@talk21.com
www.brownmuircaravanpark.co.uk

Angus & Dundee

Brechin

Eastmill Caravan Park
Brechin, Angus DD9 7EL

Beautifully situated on flat grassy site along the River South Esk, within easy access of scenic Angus Glens, local walks and 10 miles from sandy east coast beaches; midway between Dundee and Aberdeen. Shop, gas supplies, shower block, laundry and hook-ups on site; licensed premises nearby. Six-berth caravans with mains services available to rent. Facilities for tourers, caravanettes and tents. Dogs welcome. Open April to October.

Telephone: 01356 625206
(out of season 01356 622487)
Fax: 01356 623356)

Argyll & Bute

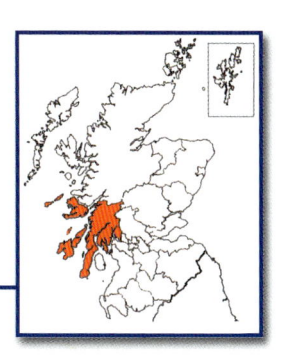

Carradale, Inveraray, Kinlochleven

SCOTLAND 147

CARRADALE. Carradale Bay Caravan Site, Carradale, Kintyre PA28 6QG
Tel: 01583 431665 • www.carradalebay.com
Ideal for a quiet, relaxing holiday, this award-winning park is set on a southerly corner of the Carradale Estate, adjoining a mile of golden sands. Popular activities in the area inlcude walking, cycling, golf, fishing and horse riding. Open April to September.

INVERARAY. Argyll Caravan Park, Inveraray PA32 8XT
Tel: 01499 302285 • www.argyllcaravanpark.com
Just 2½ miles south of the historic town of Inveraray, this park is ideal for relaxing or as a base for exploring this scenic area. 30 serviced pitches are available, 9 with grass for awning. Please note tents are not allowed. Open April to October.

There are 20 static six-berth caravans for holiday hire on this lovely site with breathtaking mountain scenery on the edge of Loch Leven — an ideal touring centre.

Caravans have electric lighting, Calor gas cookers and heaters, toilet, shower, fridge and colour TV. There are two toilet blocks with hot water and showers and laundry facilities. Children are welcome and pets allowed. Open from April to October. Milk, gas, soft drinks available on site; shops three miles. Sea loch fishing, hill walking and boating; boats and rods for hire, fishing tackle for sale.

CAOLASNACON

Caravan & Camping Park, Kinlochleven PH50 4RJ

For details contact Mrs Patsy Cameron

Tel: 01855 831279
e-mail: caolasnacon@hotmail.co.uk
www.kinlochlevencaravans.com

Argyll & Bute
Helensburgh

ROSNEATH CASTLE PARK
SO NEAR... YET SO FAR AWAY

Rosneath Castle Park has everything to offer if you are looking for a relaxing holiday. No more than an hour's drive from Glasgow, the 57 acres that the park occupies along the shore of Gareloch offer the perfect opportunity to relax and discover another world, and another you.

Thistle Awarded Luxury Self-Catering Holiday Homes with superb views. In a beautiful setting with first class facilities including an adventure playground, boat house, fun club, restaurant and bar, there's no end to the reasons why you would 'wish you were here'.

Rosneath Castle Park, Rosneath,
Near Helensburgh, Argyll G84 0QS
Tel: (01436) 831208
Fax: (01436) 831978
enquiries@rosneathcastle.demon.co.uk
www.rosneathcastle.co.uk

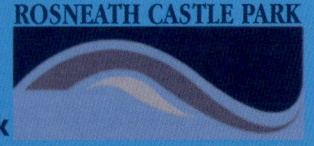

Argyll & Bute
Oban

SCOTLAND 149

Tralee Bay Holidays

Top Graded 5 Star, Tralee Bay Holidays has been a David Bellamy Gold Award Park for the last 5 years.

Located on the West Coast of Scotland near Oban, overlooking Ardmucknish Bay, the wooded surroundings and sandy beach make Tralee the ideal destination for a self-catering lodge or caravan holiday at any time of the year.

The Park offers something for everyone with play area, mini golf, fly fishing, nature walks and boat slipway. Set in breathtaking Highland countryside, the gateway to the Isles.

The choice of self-catering accommodation ranges from 2 and 3 bedroom caravans to brand new, lavishly furnished lodges. Pets welcome.

Tralee Bay Holidays, Benderloch, by Oban, Argyll PA37 1QR
Tel: 01631 720255/217
e-mail: tralee@easynet.co.uk
www.tralee.com

150 **SCOTLAND** Argyll & Bute
Oban, Tarbert

Oban Caravan and Camping Park

Gallanachmore Farm, Oban PA34 4QH • Tel: 01631 562425
e-mail: info@obancaravanpark.com • www.obancaravanpark.com

In an area of outstanding scenic beauty and graded as "Very Good", Gallanachmore Farm is situated on the seafront overlooking the Island of Kerrera. The Park provides excellent toilet and shower facilities, a well-stocked shop, launderette, children's play area and lends itself superbly for boating, fishing, windsurfing and scuba diving holidays. Also our static park has modern caravans for hire, all with sea views. Situated two-and-a-half miles south of Oban; from roundabout in the centre of the town, follow signs to Gallanach. Terms from £10.50 to £13.50 per night (two persons in touring van, tent or motorhome).
Howard and Judy Jones.

AA

Port Ban Holiday Park

Kilberry, Tarbert, Argyll PA29 6YD

Tel: 01880 770224

www.portban.com
e-mail: portban@aol.com

Beautiful, remote, secluded, coastal park enjoying fantastic sunsets over the Paps of Jura. Many sports facilities including Games Hall, Putting Green, Football Pitch, Tennis Court, Crazy Golf, Bowling Green and also Bikes for Hire. Sandy Beaches and rock pools. Organised events during school holidays including children's club, sports competitions and ceilidhs.
Ideal for wildlife enthusiasts – dolphins, seals, birds of prey, wildflowers etc.
Shop selling gifts and basic groceries.
Cafe selling snacks, homemade cakes and freshly ground coffees.
Standard and Luxury caravans for hire from £200 -£455 per week.
Pitches available for tourers and Tents from £8/night.
Reduced rates for Senior Citizens outside school holidays.
Christian Fellowship available and Services held during School Holidays.

Ayrshire & Arran   **SCOTLAND** 151

Ayr

Ayrshire & Arran

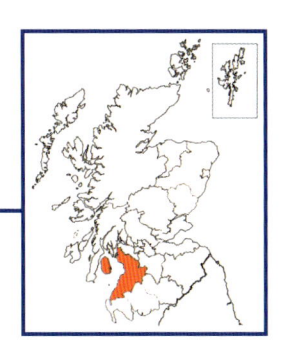

Crofthead
Holiday Park, Ayr

One of Ayrshire's premier 4- Star parks, Crofthead is peacefully situated amidst beautiful Ayrshire countryside, yet just two miles from the fabulous amenities of bustling Ayr. This friendly and relaxing park offers a perfect base for exploring Scotland's glorious south west.

Our family-run ten acre park nestles in a sheltered, tranquil hollow in rolling farmland, with the Annfield burn flowing alongside.

Shop, launderette and snooker facilities available. Pets welcome. Touring sites and tenting pitches, mainly on grass, some hardstanding available. Electric hook-ups.

Local activities include golf, riding, fishing, swimming pool and many sites of historic interest.

Contact: Mr & Mrs McCormack
Crofthead Holiday Park, McNairston, Ayr KA6 6EN
Tel: 01292 263516 • Fax: 01292 263675
e-mail: holidays@croftheadholidaypark.co.uk • www.croftheadholidaypark.co.uk

---

AYR. Craigie Gardens Caravan Club Site, Craigie Road, Ayr KA8 0SS
Tel: 01292 264909
7-acre site set in a beautiful park just a short walk from the centre of Ayr, which has excellent shopping amenities and attractions such as a theatre, racecourse, golf courses and long, sandy beach. Open all year round.

AYR. Heads of Ayr Caravan Park, Dunure Road, Ayr KA7 4LD
Tel: 01292 442269 • Fax: 01292 500298 • www.headsofayr.com
5 miles south of Ayr, this family-owned park (mainly static) has 36 pitches for tourers and also caters for tents. Facilities are excellent, with entertainment in high season, and the beach is just a 15-minute walk away. Open March to October.

Borders

Greenlaw, Jedburgh, Peebles, Selkirk

Greenlaw Caravan Park,
Bank Street, Greenlaw, Duns TD10 6XX
01361 884075 • www.greenlawcaravanpark.co.uk

Picturesque riverside park attached to a friendly country village offering shops, hotels and inns with regular functions; ideal for bowling, fishing, golf, walking or simply relaxing.

New "Blackadder Touring Park". See otters playing and herons fishing at the waterfall, choice of breathtaking riverside pitches. No tents. Well placed for exploring the Borders, the Northumbrian coast, Edinburgh and Newcastle. Short Breaks catered for. Only 37 miles south of Edinburgh on the A697.

Winner/Runner up - Most Improved Park in Scotland 2001.

JEDBURGH. Jedwater Caravan Park, Jedburgh TD8 6PJ
Tel: 01835 840219 • Fax: 01835 869370 • www.jedwater.co.uk
This peaceful country park nestles in a wooded ravine just 4 miles south of Jedburgh, off the A68. A warm welcome is assured from the resident owners and from the friendly animals on the family farm. Open April to October.

PEEBLES. Crossburn Caravan Park, Edinburgh Road, Peebles EH45 8ED
Tel: 01721 720501 • Fax 01721 720501
Secluded and friendly park, well located for a range of activities and within walking distance of the charming market town of Peebles. Tourers, motorhomes and tents welcome. Open April to October.

Selkirk Leisure Centre and Caravan Park
Victoria Park, Buccleuch Road, Selkirk TD7 5DN
Tel: 01750 20897 • e-mail: selkirk@bslt.org.uk

Situated in front of the beautiful River Ettrick, this caravan and camping park sits within the grounds of the town's leisure centre run by Borders Sport and Leisure. Scott's Selkirk, as it is known locally, famous for its association with Sir Walter Scott, is an ideal base for exploring the fabulous scenery and visitor attractions the Borders has to offer. All site users receive access to the leisure facilities.

• Touring caravans • Tents • Pets • Children's play area
• Electric hook-ups available
• Leisure facilities – gym, swimming pool and sauna.

Dumfries & Galloway

Dalbeattie, Dumfries

SCOTLAND 153

Dumfries & Galloway

Glenearly Caravan Park
Dalbeattie, Dumfriesshire DG4 5NE

Touring & Static Park
Luxury Static Caravans for Hire
Holiday Homes for Sale

Scottish Tourist Board ★★★★ HOLIDAY PARK

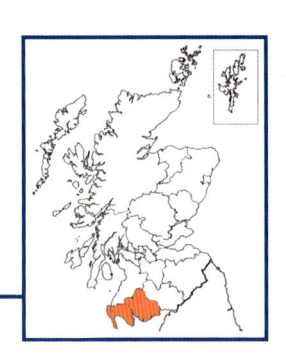

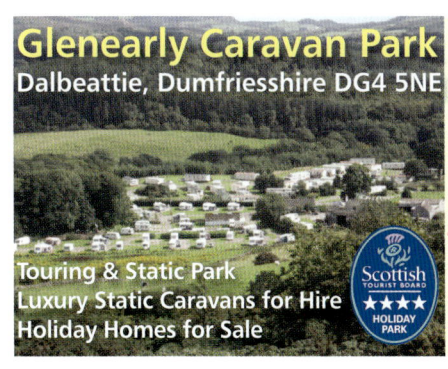

Peaceful, family-run touring and holiday home caravan park in open countryside, 10 minutes' walk into the town of Dalbeattie, with shops, restaurants and takeaway. Level and well-drained touring area with centrally heated toilet block, games room, small play area and a laundry. Perfect for walking, golf, mountain biking and all the attractions in this beautiful area.

If you require further assistance or information please do not hesitate to contact Debbie or Maureen on 01556-611393 or e-mail: glenearlycaravan@btconnect.com
www.glenearlycaravanpark.co.uk

BARNSOUL FARM & WILDLIFE AREA

Open March-October, at other times by arrangement.

Barnsoul, one of Galloway's most scenic working farms, with 300 acres of beautiful wooded parkland abounding in wildlife. Birdwatching, walking, fishing on your doorstep.

- 50 pitches for tents, motor homes or touring caravans on grass, hard standing – level and sloping areas.
- Chalets and static caravans for hire by the week.
- Wigwam bothies for hire by the night, weekend or week.
- Water, electric hook-ups, chemical toilet disposal points.
- Shower block with individual cubicles including shower & vanity unit.
- Kitchen with hot water, cooking facilities and laundry.
- On site barbecues.

Terms: Car/Caravan £12-£18
Car/Tent £12-£18
Cycle/Motorcycle/Tent £12-£14

Our latest accommodation Scandinavian Wigwam Bothies

Irongray, Shawhead, Dumfries DG2 9SQ
Tel: 01387 730249
Tel/Fax: 01387 730453
e-mail: barnsouldg@aol.com
www.barnsoulfarm.co.uk

154 SCOTLAND — Dumfries & Galloway — Newton Stewart, Stranraer

Drumroamin Farm
Camping and Caravan Site

**The natural place...
...to relax and unwind**

A family-run, private site in the heart of Wigtownshire, overlooking Wigtown Bay and the Galloway hills.
Level, well-drained field with electric hook-ups. Modern, well equipped heated shower/toilet block with separate family/disabled shower room. Indoor TV/playroom with sitting area.
Dogs welcome, woodland walks close by.
Two static caravans for holiday letting, screened from main campsite.
Open all year.

1 South Balfern, Kirkinner,
Newton Stewart, Wigtownshire DG8 9DB
Tel: 01988 840613
mobile: 07752 471456
e-mail: enquiry@drumroamin.co.uk
www.drumroamin.co.uk

Aird Donald Caravan Park

London Road, Stranraer, Wigtownshire DG9 8RN
Tel: 01776 702025 • e-mail: enquiries@aird-donald.co.uk
www.aird-donald.co.uk

- Open all year
- Selection of hard standing and grass-sites
- Hook-ups
- Hard roads
- Surrounded by conifers and shrubs
- High standard Caravan & Camping Park
- Super Loos

10 minutes from Stranraer Ferries
Book in up to 12 midnight. Other requests by telephone.
Leisure centre 10 minutes' walk from site.

Edinburgh & Lothians

Dunbar, East Calder, Linlithgow

SCOTLAND 155

Edinburgh
& Lothians

DUNBAR. Thurston Manor Holiday Home Park, Innerwick, Dunbar EH42 1SA
Tel: 01368 840643 • Fax: 01368 840261 • www.thurstonmanor.co.uk
Set in the grounds of a former country estate, Thurston Manor Park provides the highest standards combined with a peaceful, friendly atmosphere. Standard and super pitches are available and there is a clean, fully heated shower block. Tourers, motorhomes and tents welcome. Open March to January.

DUNBAR. Belhaven Bay Caravan Park, Edinburgh Road, Dunbar EH42 1TU
Tel: 01368 865956 • www.meadowhead.co.uk/belhaven
Award-winning park adjoining the John Muir Country Park and close to the beach, Belhaven is just two minutes off the A1 north of Dunbar, with convenient rail links to Edinburgh. on an 18-acre site, pitches range from fully serviced hard standings to traditional grass. Open March to October.

A family-run touring park set in countryside, just west of Edinburgh, with excellent facilities and lovely walks to the Union Canal and Almondell Country Park. Ideal for visiting Edinburgh, with nearby Park and Ride, Royal Highland Showground and the Falkirk Wheel, or touring with excellent access to all routes for travelling further afield. Or try our timbertents, a warm and dry alternative to camping. We are an ideal stop-over on your way north or south, or stay awhile, you will be most welcome.

Linwater Caravan Park, West Clifton, East Calder, West Lothian EH53 0HT
Tel: 0131 333 3326 • www.linwater.co.uk

LINLITHGOW. Beecraigs Caravan and Camping Site, Linlithgow EH49 6PL
Tel: 01506 844516 • www.beecraigs.com
Popular site in a country park just 2 miles from the historic town of Linlithgow, midway between Glasgow and Edinburgh. Spread over 100 acres, the site offers hardstanding pitches and is open to caravans, motorhomes and tents. Open all year.

Readers are requested to mention this FHG guidebook when seeking accommodation

Fife

Crail, Glenrothes, Kinghorn, Leven, St Andrews

CRAIL. Sauchope Links Caravan Park, Near Crail KY10 3XL
Tel: 01333 450460 • Fax: 01333 450246 • www.largoleisure.co.uk
Well laid out and landscaped park with superb sea views to the Isle of May. Close to many fine golf courses and other tourist attractions, and ideal for a relaxing holiday. Facilities include a heated outdoor pool and indoor recreation room. Tourers welcome. Open March to November.

GLENROTHES. Kingdom Caravan Park, Overstenton Farm, Glenrothes KY6 2NG
Tel & Fax: 01592 772226 • www.kingdomcaravanpark.com
A modern site with good amenities for visitors to this popular area. Glenrothes has good shopping and leisure amenities, and all the attractions of St Andrews and the East Neuk are just a short drive away. Open March to October.

KINGHORN. Pettycur Bay Holiday Park, Burntisland Road, Kinghorn KY3 9YE
Tel: 01592 892200 • Fax: 01592 892206 • www.pettycur.co.uk
Overlooking miles of golden sands, this is an ideal base for enjoying the wealth of leisure facilities in the area. Facilities are excellent, with a Leisure Centre with a swimming pool and entertainment. Open from March to October.

LEVEN. Leven Beach Caravan Site, North Promenade, Leven KY8 4HY
Tel: 01333 426008 • www.pettycur.co.uk
Located on the promenade with direct access to the beach, the park's location makes it an ideal base for exploring the Kingdom of Fife; Edinburgh only 35 minutes by road or rail. Hardstanding and grassed pitches are well laid out, and there is a modern utility block.

ST ANDREWS. Clayton Caravan Park, Near St Andrews KY16 9YE
Tel: 01334 870242 • Fax: 01334 870057 • www.clayton-caravan-park.co.uk
All touring pitches at this popular site just outside St Andrews are super pitches and are sheltered by trees, within a short distance of the main facilities. Tents not accepted. Open April to October.

Please note

All the information in this book is given in good faith in the belief that it is correct. However, the publishers cannot guarantee the facts given in these pages, neither are they responsible for changes in policy, ownership or terms that may take place after the date of going to press. Readers should always satisfy themselves that the facilities they require are available and that the terms, if quoted, still apply.

Highlands

Arisaig, Aviemore, Dingwall

Highlands

Camusdarach Campsite

Arisaig, Inverness-shire PH39 4NT

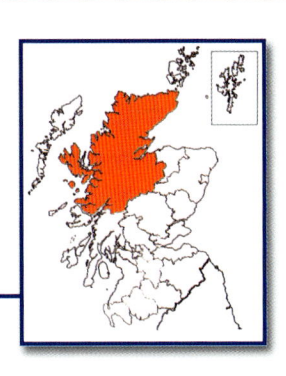

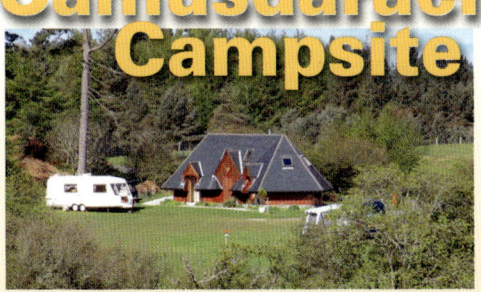

Camusdarach Campsite is the ideal base from which to explore the beautiful scenery of the 'Road to the Isles and the Western Highlands and Islands. The undulating, grassy site has 42 pitches for tents or vans and of these 20 are Serviced Pitches with electric hook-up including 6 pitches on hard-standing. The unique shower/toilet block also has sheltered, washing-up sinks, a laundry and a separate fully fitted room with nappy-changing facilities suitable for families with young children or for the disabled. A short walk down from the site brings you to the fabulous, white-sand beaches featured in the film 'Local Hero'. Local shops, restaurants and ferries are within easy reach at Arisaig (4 miles) and Mallaig (6 miles). Traigh Golf Course, probably 'the most beautifully sited 9-hole course in the world', is 1 mile away.

2010 Fees: Tent and 2 adults £14 per night: Motorhome/caravan and 2 adults £16 per night
Large tent and 2 adults on serviced pitch £19 per night
Motorhome/carvan and 2 adults on serviced pitch £19 per night
Fees include electricity if appropriate and use of showers which are not metered.
Booking essential in July and August.
Tel: 01687 450 221
e-mail: asimpson@camusdarach.com • www.camusdarach.com
Member of the Road to the Isles Marketing Group at www.road-to-the-isles.org.uk/camusdarach.html

---

AVIEMORE. Dalraddy Holiday Park, Aviemore PH22 1QB
Tel: 01479 810330 • www.alvie-estate.co.uk/dalraddy_holiday_park.htm
Quiet family park in 25 acres of woodland, just 3 miles south of Aviemore, with spectacular views of the Cairngorms. Tourers, motorhomes and tents welcome. Open all year.

DINGWALL. Black Rock Caravan and Camping Park, Evanton, Dingwall IV16 9UN
Tel & Fax: 01349 830917 • www.blackrockscotland.co.uk
In the shadow of Ben Wyvis, this is an ideal base for a relaxing break, or to explore the local area which takes in some of the most spectacular and unspoiled scenery in the Highlands. Dingwall is 4 miles away and Inverness 15 miles. Touring caravans and tents welcome. Open April to October.

Highlands
Aviemore

SPEYSIDE LEISURE PARK
Self-Catering Holidays in the Heart of the Highlands

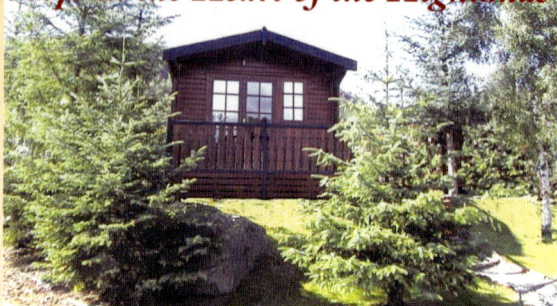

The park is situated in a quiet riverside setting with mountain views, only a short walk from Aviemore centre and shops. We offer a range of warm, well equipped chalets, cabins and caravans, including a caravan for the disabled. Prices include electricity, gas, linen, towels and use of our heated indoor pool and sauna. There are swings, a climbing frame and low level balance beams for the children. Permit fishing is available on the river. Discounts are given on some local attractions.

Families, couples or groups will find this an ideal location for a wide range of activities including:

- Horse riding • Golf • Fishing • Hillwalking
- RSPB Reserves • Mountain and Watersports • Reindeer herd
- Steam railway and the Whisky Trail

Only slightly further afield you will find Culloden Moor, the Moray Firth dolphins and of course, the not to be missed, Loch Ness. Accommodation sleeps from 1-6, and we offer a reduced rate for a couple or one single person. Short Breaks are available.
Sorry, no pets, except guide and hearing dogs. No tents or camper vans.

Speyside Leisure Park
Dalfaber Road, Aviemore,
Inverness-shire PH22 1PX
Tel: 01479 810236
Fax: 01479 811688
e-mail:
fhg@speysideleisure.com
www.speysideleisure.com

Highlands — Beauly, Dornoch **SCOTLAND** 159

Cannich Caravan & Camping Park

At the head of Glen Affric National Nature Reserve. Scenic, family-run site in the heart of Strathglass set amidst stunning glens with sparkling lochs, rivers and waterfalls. Breathtaking scenery, superb walking and biking through Caledonian pine forests and rugged mountains. We welcome touring caravans, motorhomes and tents. Choose from our open grassy pitches or the shelter of the Scots pines, and enjoy free HOT showers, indoor washing up, TV room, laundry and playpark. Comfortable, luxury fully equipped static caravans are available for weekly or nightly hire. Visit our cafe serving drinks and snacks all day. Central heating, double glazing. Ideal for a winter getaway. ON SITE BIKE HIRE.

Cannich, Strathglass
Inverness-shire IV4 7RN
Tel & Fax: 01456 415364
www.highlandcamping.co.uk

Scottish Tourist Board ★★★★ HOLIDAY PARK

Dornoch Caravan and Camp Park
the perfect spot for your camping holiday!

Billy and Sandra Macrae would like to give you "A Highland Family Welcome" to Dornoch Caravan and Camp Park. We hope you'll enjoy your stay with us.

Situated in the Royal Burgh of Dornoch on the east coast of Sutherland, next to Dornoch's award-winning beautiful golden beaches and magnificent golf course.

• ample touring pitches • tent pitches • static vans to let • shop
• TV room • launderette • free showers • electric hook-ups
• children's play area • games room

The Links, Dornoch IV25 3LX • Tel/Fax: 01862 810 423
info@dornochcaravans.com • www.dornochcaravans.com

FREE AND REDUCED RATE HOLIDAY VISITS!

Don't miss our
Readers' Offer Vouchers
on pages 211-234

Linnhe
LOCHSIDE HOLIDAYS

Almost a botanical garden, Linnhe is recognised as one of the best and most beautful Lochside parks in Britain. Magnificent gardens contrast with the wild, dramatic scenery of Loch Eil and the mountains beyond. Superb amenities, launderette shop & bakery, and free fishing on private shoreline with its own jetty all help give Linnhe its Five Star grading. Linnhe Lochside Holidays is ideally situated for day trips with Oban, Skye, Mull, Inverness and the Cairngorms all within easy driving distance.

- ◆ **Holiday Caravans from £240 per week**
- ◆ **Touring pitches from £16 per night**
- ◆ **Tent pitches from £12 per night**
- ◆ **Pets welcome**
- ◆ **Tourer playground, pet exercise area**
- ◆ **Motorhome waste and water facilities**
- ◆ **Recycling on park**
- ◆ **Colour brochure sent with pleasure.**

www.linnhe-lochside-holidays.co.uk/brochure
Tel: 01397 772 376 to check availability

Highlands SCOTLAND 161
Glencoe, Inverness, John O'Groats, Laide

INVERCOE HIGHLAND HOLIDAYS
Invercoe, Glencoe, Argyll PH49 4HP • TEL: 01855 811210 • FAX: 01855 811210
www.invercoe.co.uk • e-mail: holidays@invercoe.co.uk

At Invercoe Highland Holidays we offer you quiet, get-away-from-it-all vacations, in what is one of the most picturesque of the Scottish glens. You can have a relaxing break in a stone cottage, luxury timber lodge, mobile holiday homes or bring your own caravan, tent or tourer for the holiday of your choice.

We have been providing holidays for over thirty years and are confident our high standard of accommodation will provide an excellent base to explore the West Highlands.

Self Catering ★ OPEN ALL YEAR ★

INVERCOE HIGHLAND HOLIDAYS

HOLIDAY PARKS & CENTRES

INVERNESS near. Auchnahillin Caravan & Camping Park, Daviot East, Inverness IV2 5XQ (01463 772286).
Friendly, informal family-run ten-acre park, set in tranquil glen, yet conveniently located just off the A9, only eight miles south of Inverness with several other popular destinations being within an easy drive. Informative reception area, small shop, children's play area, laundry and dishwashing facilities, showers, toilets and hairdryers.
Rates: 11 fully equipped, self-contained static caravan/chalet holiday homes for hire, £35 to £65 per night/£170 to £320 per week. 45 pitches for touring units, £9 to £15 per night. Camping ground for up to 30 tents, £8 to £10 per night.
• Disabled/baby changing facilities. • Dogs welcome. • Open April until October.
STB ★★★★ HOLIDAY PARK
e-mail: info@auchnahillin.co.uk   www.auchnahillin.co.uk

CARAVAN SITES & TOURING PARKS

JOHN O'GROATS. John O'Groats Caravan and Camping Site, John O'Groats KW1 4YR (01955 611329/744). At end of A99 on seafront beside "last house in Scotland", caravan and camping site with showers, launderette, electric hook-ups and disabled toilet. Internet access. Caravans, caravanettes and tents welcome. Booking office for day trips to Orkney Islands on site. Hotel, restaurant, cafe, harbour 150 metres. Magnificent cliff scenery with sea birds galore including puffins, guillemots, skuas within one-and-a-half-miles. Seals are often seen swimming to and fro and there is a seal colony only four miles away. From the site you can see the wide panorama of the Orkney Islands, the nearest of which is only seven miles away. Public telephone 150 metres.
Rates: from £13 per night.
STB ★★★ HOLIDAY PARK
e-mail: info@johnogroatscampsite.co.uk   www.johnogroatscampsite.co.uk

Gruinard Bay Caravan Park

Situated just a stone's throw from the beach, Gruinard Bay Caravan Park offers the perfect setting for a holiday or a stopover on the West Coast of Scotland. Family-owned and personally operated, the park boasts magnificent views across Gruinard Bay.
● Sea front Touring Pitches ● Electric Hook-ups ● Camping Pitches ● Free Toilet and Shower facilities ● Gas available on site ● Laundry facilities
● Static Holiday Homes available ● Pets Welcome (not in Holiday Homes)

**Tony & Ann Davis, Gruinard Bay Caravan Park,
Laide, Wester Ross IV22 2ND
Tel/Fax: 01445 731225
www.gruinard.scotshost.co.uk**

CALOR Gas

Hillhead Caravans
Achmelvich

Excellent self-catering accommodation at the beautiful white, safe, sandy beach of Achmelvich, near Lochinver in North West Scotland, one of the country's beauty spots. Ideal for family holidays.

Clean, modern, 6-berth, fully serviced caravans to let, 150 metres from the beach.

Our accommodation and area are perfect for country lovers and a good centre for hillwalking, photography, cycling, climbing, caving, geology, swimming, bird-watching, touring, fishing, sailing – or just relaxing with a good book! Open late March to late October.

Details from Durrant and Maysie Macleod
Hillhead Caravans, Lochinver IV27 4JA
Tel & Fax: 01571 844454
e-mail:info@lochinverholidays.co.uk

Highlands   SCOTLAND 163
Lairg, Scourie, Shielbridge, Strathnaver

Dunroamin Caravan Park
Main Street, Lairg
Sutherland IV27 4AR

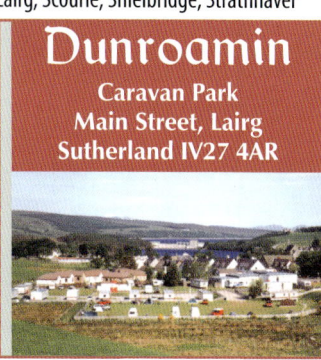

Lew Hudson, his wife Margaret and their family welcome you to Dunroamin Caravan Park. A small family-run park situated in the picturesque village of Lairg by Loch Shin, this is the ideal base for touring the whole of Sutherland and Caithness. Fishing and walking nearby, with golf just 15 miles away. Outstandingly well maintained grounds with Crofters licensed restaurant on site. Electric hook-ups. 200 yards from pub, bank, shops, post office, etc. Holiday caravans for hire, tourers and tents welcome.

Tel: 01549 402447
enquiries@lairgcaravanpark.co.uk
www.lairgcaravanpark.co.uk

Bayview, Badcall, Scourie IV27 4TH

Six-berth caravan with gas cooking, heating, shower and mains electricity. Situated in the beautiful North West Highlands of Scotland, two hours driving time from the city of Inverness. Ideal centre for touring Northern Scotland and the Western Isles (vehicle ferry sails from Ullapool to Stornoway). There are ample opportunities for climbing and hillwalking. Visit the Handa Island bird sanctuary, also local boat trips. Permits available for trout fishing. The scenery around the caravan is breathtaking, and there are many beautiful beaches within a short drive.

Contact: Florence or Bert Macleod
01349 864072

CAMPING SITES

SHIELBRIDGE (Glen Shiel). Shiel Caravan Site, Shielbridge, By Kyle (01599 511221).
Touring site situated at the west end of the spectacular Glen Shiel on the A87 Fort William to Kyle of Lochalsh road (access by shop at Shielbridge). This is an ideal centre from which to explore the beautiful West Coast and is 15 miles from the Isle of Skye bridge at Kyle. There is space for 16 caravans and 50 tents; all usual facilities including showers. Shop adjacent, gas and petrol available. New toilet and shower block opened 2005. Electric hook-ups available.
Rates: from £5 per person per night.
• Pets welcome. • Children welcome. • Open from March 16th to October 16th.

North Sutherland

This is a 30' caravan, sleeping 4/5, situated beside the B871 in the Strathnaver Valley. 6 miles from the coast and Bettyhill village, and 13 miles from Tongue. Ideal for touring the north of Scotland.

The caravan is fully equipped except for linen and towels. Shower, flush toilet, gas cooker, electric light and fridge.

Open May to September.
Terms from £180 to £190 per week

Mrs C.M. MacLeod,
Achnabourin, Strathnaver, Near Bettyhill,
North Sutherland KW11 6UA
Tel: 01641 561210

Lanarkshire

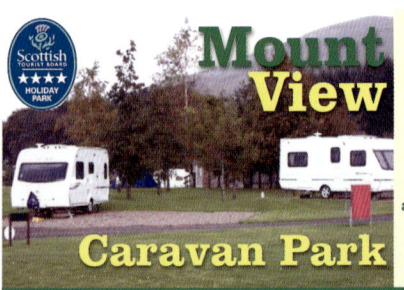

Lanarkshire
Abington, Motherwell, Stepps

Mount View Caravan Park

Luxury holiday homes for hire on caravan park set in peaceful, unspoilt countryside with beautiful views of the Clyde valley. Good for walking, cycling, fishing, golf and touring the area. Near to Moffat, Biggar, Edinburgh, Glasgow and Scottish Borders.
Fully equipped holiday home including microwave, TV/DVD and with double glazing and central heating.
En suite shower room, lounge, dining area, kitchen, twin and double bedrooms. Bedding and towels can be provided at an extra cost. Easy access, just five minutes from J13 of the M74 and a short walk from the village shop.
£170 to £350 per week.

Abington, South Lanarkshire ML12 6RW   Tel: 01864 502808
e-mail: info@mountviewcaravanpark.co.uk • www.mountviewcaravanpark.co.uk

---

MOTHERWELL. Strathclyde Country Park Caravan Site, Hamilton Road, Motherwell ML1 3ED
Tel: 01698 402060 • Fax: 01698 252925
Open from April to October, the site can accommodate up to 100 caravans and 50 tents. Facilities are excellent and it is an excellent base for visiting Glasgow, Edinburgh and the whole of Central Scotland. Strathclyde Country Park has ample opportunities for outdoor activities of every kind, plus a large funfair.

STEPPS. Craigendmuir Park, Stepps, Glasgow G33 6AF
Tel: 0141 779 2973 • Fax: 0141 779 4057 • www.craigendmuir.co.uk
Conveniently situated just off the A80, this friendly park enjoys good public transport links to Glasgow and further afield, making it an ideal base for touring. Hardstanding and grassed pitches are available, and facilities on site are well maintained. Open all year. Tents, caravans and motorhomes welcome.

---

symbols

- ☼ Holiday Parks & Centres
- 🚐 Caravans for Hire
- $ Caravan Sites and Touring Parks
- ⛺ Camping Sites

Perth & Kinross
Blairgowrie

Perth & Kinross

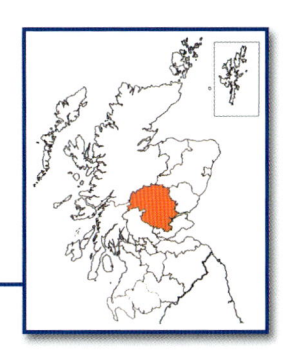

For a peaceful break in the Perthshire countryside, Five Roads is the perfect location. It is situated on the outskirts of Alyth, a small, historic town offering a wide variety of attractions in close proximity. The park is open all year and welcomes tourers and tents. Each pitch has an electric hook-up. There are two Thistle Award holiday homes for hire; each has central heating, double glazing, shower, microwave, TV and is fully furnished. WiFi available. Bed linen is provided. Play area for small children. Pets not permitted in holiday homes. There are three golf courses within a one mile radius.

FIVE ROADS CARAVAN PARK, Alyth, Blairgowrie PH11 8NB
Tel: 01828 632255
steven.ewart@btopenworld.com • www.fiveroads-caravan-park.co.uk

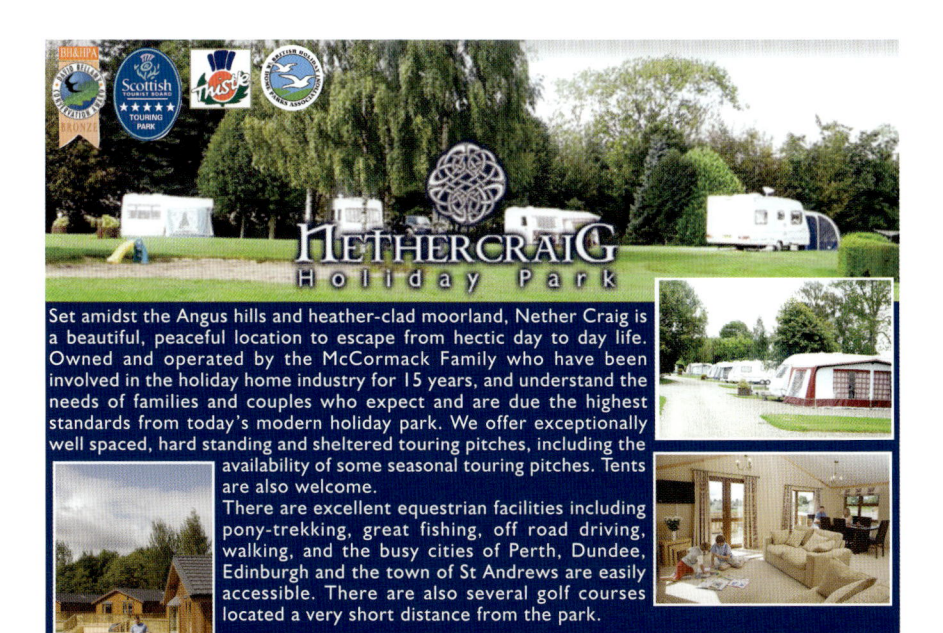

NETHERCRAIG
Holiday Park

Set amidst the Angus hills and heather-clad moorland, Nether Craig is a beautiful, peaceful location to escape from hectic day to day life. Owned and operated by the McCormack Family who have been involved in the holiday home industry for 15 years, and understand the needs of families and couples who expect and are due the highest standards from today's modern holiday park. We offer exceptionally well spaced, hard standing and sheltered touring pitches, including the availability of some seasonal touring pitches. Tents are also welcome.

There are excellent equestrian facilities including pony-trekking, great fishing, off road driving, walking, and the busy cities of Perth, Dundee, Edinburgh and the town of St Andrews are easily accessible. There are also several golf courses located a very short distance from the park.

Nethercraig Caravan Park, By Alyth, Blairgowrie, Perthshire PH11 8HN
Tel: 01575 560204 • e-mail: nethercraigholidaypark@btconnect.com
www.nethercraigholidaypark.co.uk

Largo Leisure Park

For Living Life to the Full

Our holiday parks are ideally suited for those seeking a tran[quil] retreat with beautiful scenery, whilst enjoying the many [and] varied attractions of the Kingdom of Fife and Perthshire areas [of] Scotland.

Holiday homes are perfect for getting away from it all. Our parks offer [an] atmosphere to relax and enjoy the long holiday or short break.

Sauchope Links Park is situated on the shoreline, near the eastern most ti[p of] Fife in a beautiful, unspoilt position close to the historic town of Crail. This aw[ard] winning park with stunning views makes the perfect holiday destination.

Letham Feus Park is situated only 3 miles from Lundin Links with its championship [golf] course and beautiful sandy beach. The park is blessed with breathtaking views over [the] Forth Estuary to the South and beautiful woodland to the north. Letham Feus is [the] perfect place to take that well earned break.

Braidhaugh Park is situated on the banks of the River Earn amid the s[cenic] surroundings of Crieff. The park is an ideal base from which to explore not [only] the beautiful surroundings of Perthshire, but also the magnificent scenic gran[deur] of Central Scotland.

Loch Tay Highland Lodges Holiday Park is beautifully situated on a well established [ ] acre Highland Estate nestling on the shores of Loch Tay in Perthshire. It is the perfect all round holiday destination for those who love pure relaxation or for those energetic types [who] love the great outdoors.

Sauchope Links Holiday Park, Crail, Fife KY1[0]
Tel: 01333 450 460 info@sauchope.[ ]

Letham Feus Holiday Park, Cupar Rd by Lundin Links KY8
Tel: 01333 351 900 info@lethamfeus.[ ]

Braidhaugh Holiday Park, South Bridgend, Crieff PH7
Tel: 01764 652951 info@braidhaugh.[ ]

Loch Tay Highland Lodges, Milton Morenish Estate by K[ ]
Perthshire FK21 8TY Tel: 01567 82[ ]
info@lochtay-vacations.co.uk www.lochtay-vacations.[ ]

Bring this advert with you on the day of [ ]
check in, and receive a FREE bottle of [ ]

Largo Leisure Parks
www.largoleisure.co.uk

Perth & Kinross   SCOTLAND 167
Auchterarder, Blair Atholl, Blairgowrie, Loch Rannoch, Lochearnhead

AUCHTERARDER. Auchterarder Caravan park, Auchterarder PH3 1ET
Tel & Fax: 01764 663119 • www.prestonpark.co.uk/caravan.htm
Family-run park with modern facilities, in a secluded location two miles from Auchterarder and 12 miles from Perth. Pitches are generously spaced, with level hardstandings and a separate area for tents. Open all year.

BLAIR ATHOLL. River Tilt Park, Bridge of Tilt, Blair Atholl, Pitlochry PH18 5TE
Tel: 01796 481467 • Fax: 01796 481511 • www.rivertiltpark.co.uk
Family-owned and run park which has been awarded the highest gradings for the quality of its facilities. The touring park has a separate area for dog owners and for tents, and offers hardstanding or grassed pitches. Tourers, motorhomes and tents welcome. Open March to November.

BLAIRGOWRIE. Five Roads Caravan Park, By Alyth, Blairgowrie PH11 8NB
Tel: 01828 632155 • Fax: 01828 633324 • www.fiveroads-caravan-park.co.uk
With three golf courses within a one mile radius, and pony trekking, fishing and walking in the area, as well as beautiful scenery, this site is very popular with those seeking a base for an active or leisurely holiday. Caravans, motorhomes and tents welcome. Open all year.

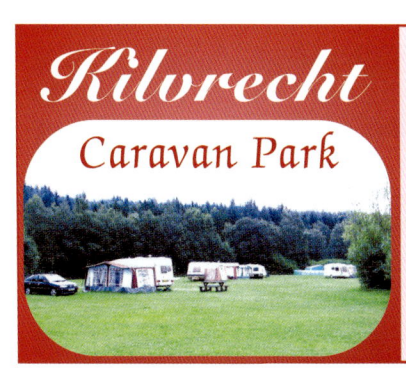

Kilvrecht Caravan Park

Secluded campsite on a level open area in quiet and secluded woodland setting. There is fishing available for brown trout on Loch Rannoch. Several trails begin from the campsite.

Please write, fax or telephone for further information.

Loch Rannoch, Perthshire PH8 0JR
Tel: 01350 727284
Fax: 01350 727811
e-mail: hamish.murray@forestry.gsi.gov.uk

LOCHEARNHEAD. Balquhidder Braes Caravan and Camping Park, Near Lochearnhead FK19 8NX
Tel & Fax: 01567 830293 • www.balquhidderbraes.co.uk
Centrally located for touring and sightseeing, this small, family-run park offers modern self-catering holiday homes, as well as touring caravan and tent pitches. Set within the Trossachs National Park, a great location for outdoor pursuits. Open March to October.

The FHG Directory of Website Addresses

on pages 211-234 is a useful quick reference guide for
holiday accommodation with e-mail and/or website details

168 **SCOTLAND** — Perth & Kinross
Pitlochry, Tyndrum

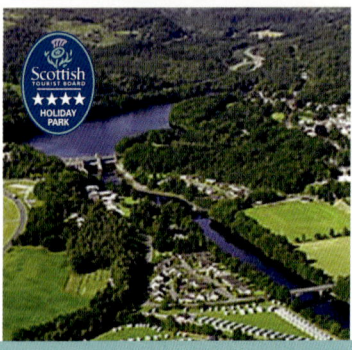

A 16 acre site with 154 touring pitches (last arrival 9pm) with electricity and awnings extra and 36 caravans to let, sleep six (minimum let two nights) with mains water, shower, toilet, TV, etc. Site facilities include showers, electric hook-ups, chemical disposal point, telephone, shop, etc. Shops and eating out places one mile. We also take tents. Fishing available. Children and pets welcome. Caravans from £280 to £530 per week; pitches from £16.00 per night. Open March to October.

Milton of Fonab Caravan Park
Pitlochry PH16 5NA • 01796 472882 • Fax: 01796 474363
e-mail: info@fonab.co.uk • www.fonab.co.uk

Unique holiday accommodation in a heated wooden wigwam!

Wigwams are sturdy insulated wooden camping cabins, large enough to stand in, with removable sleeping platforms, easily accommodating 4-5 people. Comfortably equipped, with foam mattresses and electricity for light, heating and personal electrical equipment. Bring your own sleeping bags etc, though linen can be hired. Each has its own car parking and play area, picnic bench and campfire.

The Facility Blocks have fully equipped large kitchens (pans, crockery and cutlery included); large dining/TV lounge area; showers and toilets, with disabled facilities.

Farm Shop has all the necessities plus local food and supplies, logs or charcoal. There is also a pets' corner for the children.

Super Deluxe Lodges with own kitchenette, bedroom, shower room and toilet; each sleeps up to 6.

Located at SAC's Auchtertyre Highland Estate - open access to all encouraged.
Members of wigwamholidays.com

Mrs Rena Baillie, Strathfillan Wigwams,
Auchtertyre, Tyndrum, Perthshire FK20 8RU
Tel: 01838 400251
e-mail: wigwam@sac.ac.uk
www.wigwamholidays.com/strathfillan

Stirling & The Trossachs

Dollar, Stirling

Stirling & The Trossachs

RIVERSIDE CARAVAN PARK

This is a well established family-run park in a sheltered position on the banks of the River Devon, half a mile south of Dollar. It makes an ideal base for hill walking, bird watching, fishing and Golf.
On our doorstep there is much to offer the visitor:

- **Dollar Glen** ● **Castle Campbell**
- **The Mill Trail** ● **Wallace Monument**
- **Bannockburn** ● **Knockhill Racing Circuit**

Edinburgh, St Andrews, Dundee, Perth, Gleneagles, Glasgow, Loch Lomond and the Trossachs are all within an hour's drive
On-site facilities include electric hookup, well equipped toilets, Calor gas sales and private fishing. Golf, swimming and riding nearby.
Open from March to January (including Christmas and New Year).
We welcome caravans, motorvans and tents.

Riverside Caravan Park
Dollarfield, Dollar, Clackmannanshire FK14 7LX
Tel: 01259 742 896
E-mail: info@riverside-caravanpark.co.uk
www.riverside-caravanpark.co.uk

STIRLING. Witches Craig Caravan & Camping Park, Blairlogie, Stirling FK9 5PX
Tel: 01786 474947 • Fax: 01786 447286 • www.witchescraig.co.uk
Attractive, well maintained site at the foot of the Ochil Hills, ideal for relaxing and centrally located for exploring Central Scotland. Winner of many awards including Gold David Bellamy Award and National Loo of the Year. Tourers, motorhomes and tents welcome. Open April to October.

STIRLING. Auchenbowie Caravan Site, Auchenbowie, Stirling FK7 8HE
Tel: 01324 823999/822141
Touring and tent pitches are available on this well kept site located off the M80/M9, just four miles from historic Stirling. Rates for overnight stays are very reasonable, and visitors will appreciate the peaceful surroundings. Open April to October.

Scottish Islands

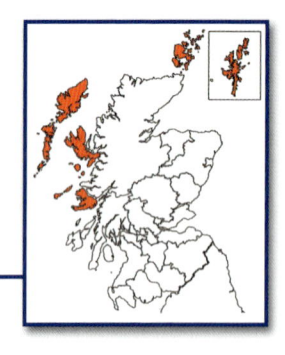

Orkney Islands

Kirkwall

The Pickaquoy Centre Caravan & Camping Park • Kirkwall, Orkney
Tel: 01856 879900 • www.pickaquoy.co.uk • e-mail: enquiries@pickaquoy.com
The St Magnus Cathedral is the central feature of Kirkwall, Orkney's main town, a relaxing and interesting centre from which to explore the surrounding areas. The site is situated within The Pickaquoy Centre complex, an impressive modern leisure facility offering a range of activities for all the family.

Birsay Outdoor Centre/ Caravan & Camping Site
A new site located in the picturesque north west of Orkney

Point of Ness Caravan & Camping Site • Stromness, Orkney.
Stromness is a small, picturesque town with impressive views of the hills of Hoy. The site is one mile from the harbour in a quiet, shoreline location. Many leisure activities are available close by, including fishing, sea angling, golf and a swimming & fitness centre.

For Birsay and Point of Ness contact: Department of Education & Recreation Services, Orkney Islands Council, Kirkwall, Orkney KW15 1NY • Tel: 01856 873535 ext. 2404

Other specialised holiday guides from FHG
PUBS & INNS OF BRITAIN • **SELF-CATERING HOLIDAYS** IN BRITAIN
WEEKEND & SHORT BREAKS IN BRITAIN & IRELAND
THE GOLF GUIDE WHERE TO PLAY, WHERE TO STAY
500 GREAT PLACES TO STAY IN BRITAIN • **FAMILY BREAKS** IN BRITAIN
BED & BREAKFAST STOPS IN BRITAIN • **PETS WELCOME!**
COUNTRY HOTELS OF BRITAIN

Published annually: available in all good bookshops or direct from the publisher:
FHG Guides, Abbey Mill Business Centre, Seedhill, Paisley PA1 1TJ
Tel: 0141 887 0428 • Fax: 0141 889 7204
e-mail: admin@fhguides.co.uk • www.holidayguides.com

Mount Pleasant

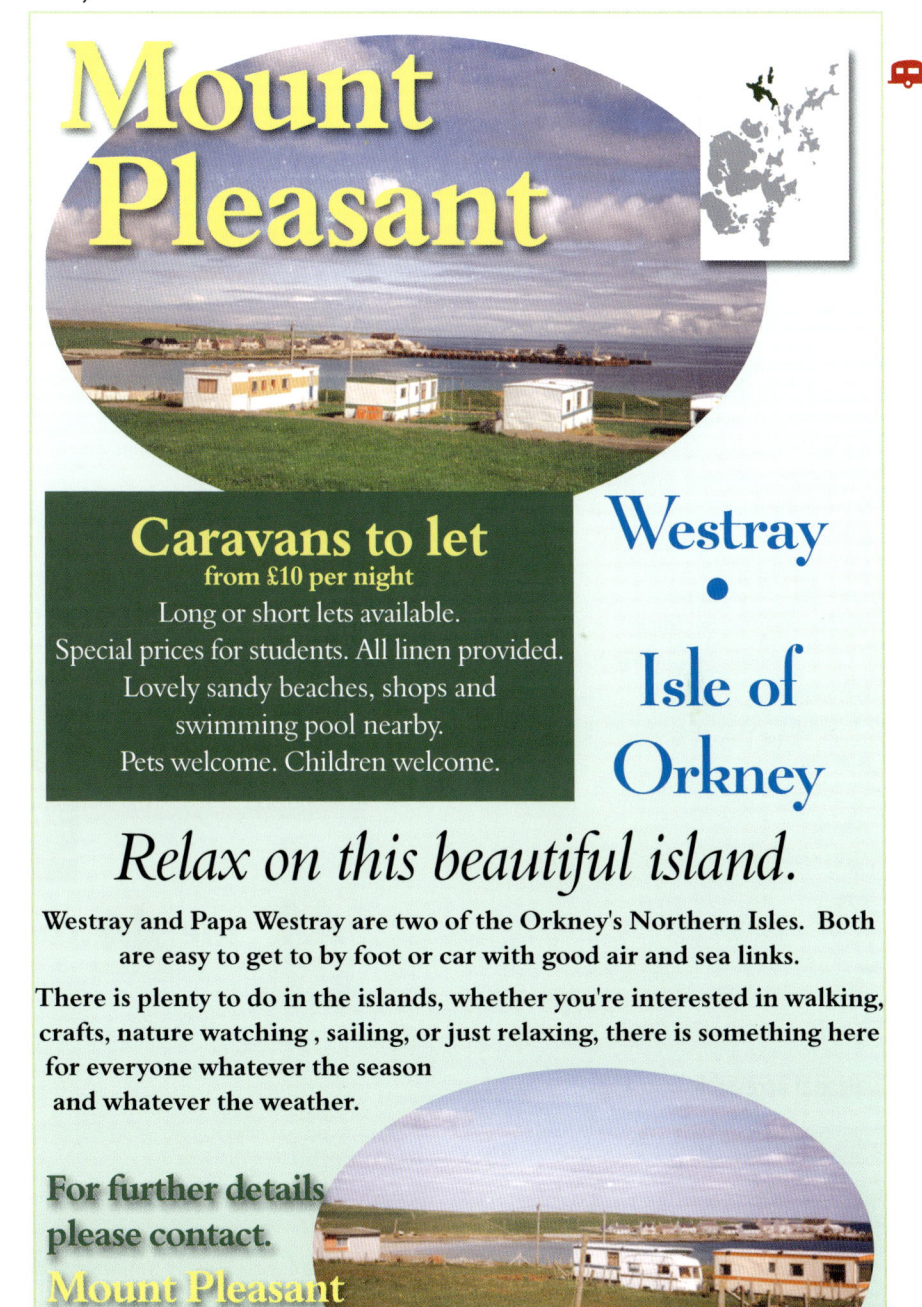

Caravans to let
from £10 per night

Long or short lets available.
Special prices for students. All linen provided.
Lovely sandy beaches, shops and swimming pool nearby.
Pets welcome. Children welcome.

Westray
•
Isle of Orkney

Relax on this beautiful island.

Westray and Papa Westray are two of the Orkney's Northern Isles. Both are easy to get to by foot or car with good air and sea links.

There is plenty to do in the islands, whether you're interested in walking, crafts, nature watching, sailing, or just relaxing, there is something here for everyone whatever the season and whatever the weather.

For further details please contact.

Mount Pleasant
Westray, Orkney Isands KW17 2DH
Tel: 01857 677229

Ratings & Awards

For the first time ever the AA, VisitBritain, VisitScotland, and the Wales Tourist Board will use a single method of assessing and rating serviced accommodation. Irrespective of which organisation inspects an establishment the rating awarded will be the same, using a common set of standards, giving a clear guide of what to expect. The RAC is no longer operating an Hotel inspection and accreditation business.

Accommodation Standards: Star Grading Scheme

Using a scale of 1-5 stars the objective quality ratings give a clear indication of accommodation standard, cleanliness, ambience, hospitality, service and food, This shows the full range of standards suitable for every budget and preference, and allows visitors to distinguish between the quality of accommodation and facilities on offer in different establishments. All types of board and self-catering accommodation are covered, including hotels, B&Bs, holiday parks, campus accommodation, hostels, caravans and camping, and boats.

VisitBritain and the regional tourist boards, enjoyEngland.com, VisitScotland and VisitWales, and the AA have full details of the grading system on their websites

The more stars, the higher level of quality

★★★★★
exceptional quality, with a degree of luxury

★★★★
excellent standard throughout

★★★
very good level of quality and comfort

★★
good quality, well presented and well run

★
acceptable quality; simple, practical, no frills

National Accessible Scheme

If you have particular mobility, visual or hearing needs, look out for the National Accessible Scheme. You can be confident of finding accommodation or attractions that meet your needs by looking for the following symbols.

Typically suitable for a person with sufficient mobility to climb a flight of steps but would benefit from fixtures and fittings to aid balance

Typically suitable for a person with restricted walking ability and for those that may need to use a wheelchair some of the time and can negotiate a maximum of three steps

Typically suitable for a person who depends on the use of a wheelchair and transfers unaided to and from the wheelchair in a seated position. This person may be an independent traveller

Typically suitable for a person who depends on the use of a wheelchair in a seated position. This person also requires personal or mechanical assistance (eg carer, hoist).

Wales

Cardiff Castle, South Wales

Anglesey & Gwynedd is rich in archaeological and historical heritage, and is home to a diversity of wildlife which inhabit the cliffs, estuaries, heaths and rich farmland. Tourists love the unspoilt beaches and extensive sands, and the popular seafront at Benllech offers miles of clean golden sands, safe bathing, boating, fishing and windsurfing activities, as well as the usual ice cream kiosks, seaside shops, and food. Snowdonia to the west attracts climbers and walkers, but the less active will enjoy the 9 mile return journey on Bala Lake Railway which runs alongside Llyn Tegid, or Bala Lake as it also known, and through the beautiful Snowdonia National Park to the market town of Bala. The small, peaceful seaside village of Aberdovey within Snowdonia National Park is a popular resort with a thriving little harbour and very popular with those who enjoy a more active holiday. All kinds of watersports, including sailing, sailboarding, fishing, and boat trips, are available, and there is also an 18-hole championship golf course. The Llyn Peninsula also boasts some of the best sailing and surfing beaches in North Wales and its capital, Pwllheli, has an impressive marina which berths over 400 boats and has space for overnight mooring. No holiday in the area can be complete without a visit to the Royal town of Caernarfon with its wonderful views across the Menai Straits, and the mountains of Snowdonia in the background. The majestic Caernarfon Castle, one of Europe's greatest medieval fortresses famous for the investiture of Prince Charles as Prince of Wales in 1969, houses the Royal Welsh Fusiliers Regimental Museum.

In **North Wales** there are charming towns and villages to explore, soft sandy beaches and rugged coastline, and as many castles, stately homes, gardens, parks, craft centres, museums and steam trains as anyone could desire. Better book a long holiday to start the grand tour, and then come back again to catch up with all that you will surely have missed. Betws-y-Coed, North Wales' most popular inland resort, houses The Snowdonia National Visitor Centre with its craft units and thrilling video presentations – always worth a visit. For fun filled family holidays try Llandudno, where a whole host of summer events and activities can be enjoyed, or Rhyl with its Children's Village on the Promenade, plus amusements, boating ponds and fairground. Walkers and cyclists will revel in the breathtaking scenery of the Prestatyn hillside and the Clwydian Range and will find all the information that they need at Offa's Dyke Visitor Centre. Most people would enjoy a break in Llangollen with its variety of attractions. The town hosts many different international events each year, including the famous Eisteddfod Music Festival which attracts visitors from all over the world. Throughout North Wales there can be found a variety of good restaurants, cafes and traditional country pubs, so eating out is never a problem, and the abundance of shops and open-air markets, as well as the many quality craft shops, ensure that you return home with those special little gifts for your family or friends.

Carmarthenshire is surely the best region for an activity or leisure break, with activities for everyone from cycling to bird watching, and from walking to sailing and fishing. The region also boasts many good golf courses, offering affordable golf to players of all abilities. The Millennium Coastal Park is one of the most popular tourist attractions in Britain, with breathtaking views of the Gower Peninsula, and a unique variety of attractions stretching from Pembrey Country Park with its acres of beautiful parkland, and one of the best beaches in the UK, as well as many excellent family attractions. Visitors will enjoy exploring the many interesting little villages, and there is an endless choice of places to eat and drink, including pubs, restaurants, inns and cafes.

Although it is one of the largest counties within Wales, **Ceredigion** is one of the least populated. There is plenty of variety and spectacular coastal and countryside scenery to be enjoyed. The Cambrian Mountains are only some half an hour's drive from most coastal areas and the coast is similarly accessible to inland areas. Aberaeron's most notable feature is its architecture - one house in every four is listed as being of special architectural or historical interest. Beyond Cardigan, to the south, are the high hills of the Preseli mountains and the Pembrokeshire Coast National Park whilst inland lies the Teifi Valley - offering marvellous angling - and Cenarth's famous falls. Tresaith is one of the locations most favoured by visitors to Ceredigion. It is almost a picture-book seaside village and offers a wonderful sandy beach, ideal for families, with clean sands, clear waters, and rocks to climb. There are many species of bird to be seen along the coastline including Red Kite, and you may be able to spot dolphins and seals in the waters.

Pembrokeshire's entire coastline is a designated National Park, with its sheltered coves and wooded estuaries, fine sandy beaches and some of the most dramatic cliffs in Britain. The islands of Skomer, Stokholm and Grasholm are home to thousands of seabirds, and Ramsey Island, as well as being an RSPB Reserve boasts the second largest grey seal colony in Britain. Pembrokeshire's mild climate and the many

Conwy Castle, North Wales

delightful towns and villages, family attractions and outdoor facilities such as surfing, water skiing, diving, pony trekking and fishing make this a favourite holiday destination.

Powys is situated right on England's doorstep and boasts some of most spectacular scenery in Europe. It is ideal for an action-packed holiday with fishing, golf, pony trekking, sailing and canal cruising readily available, and walkers have a choice of everything from riverside trails to mountain hikes. Offa's Dyke Path runs for 177 miles through Border country, often following the ancient earthworks, while Glyndwr's Way takes in some of the finest landscape features in Wales on its journey from Knighton to Machynlleth and back to the borders at Welshpool. There are border towns with Georgian architecture and half-timbered black and white houses to visit, or wander round the wonderful shops in the book town of Hay, famous for its Literary Festival each May. There are Victorian spa towns too, with even the smallest of places holding festivals and events throughout the year.

As well as being an ideal holiday destination in its own right Swansea Bay is a perfect base for touring the rest of **South Wales**. A great place for all sorts of watersports such as sailing canoeing, fishing and waterskiing, or you may prefer such land based activities as walking, cycling and horse riding. Just a short journey from the City you will find the beautiful Glamorgan Heritage Coast, overlooked by dramatic cliffs. Especially popular with walkers and hikers this area is also ideal for long, leisurely strolls in the secluded coves and inlets along the coast. There are more than 15 golf courses here including the famous Royal Porthcawl. For something different visit the Wye Valley and the Vale of Usk with awesome castles, breathtaking scenery and a rich and colourful history. The area is steeped in industrial heritage, and at Blaenavon World Heritage Site visitors can go underground with a

Brecon Beacons, South Wales

miner and uncover real stories about people from the past. The 13th century castle of Caerphilly is the largest in Wales and home to the ghostly Green Lady who haunts its halls. Many staff at Rhondda Heritage Park claim to have seen a phantom miner, or the ghost of a woman with two young children, and the legendary King Arthur is also reputed to have connections to the valleys. The area is popular for leisurely walks, or serious hikes and there are dedicated paths, challenging bike trails and, of course, plenty of opportunities for a game of golf.

Cardiff is one of the UK's top shopping venues, with malls, quaint arcades and markets, as well as independent chain stores and boutiques. The architecture is a blend of the old and the new, from the 2000 year old Cardiff Castle, one of Wales's leading tourist attractions with its enchanting fairytale towers and splendid interior, to the impressive and ultra-modern Wales Millennium Centre.

176 WALES — Anglesey & Gwynedd

Anglesey, Bala

Anglesey & Gwynedd

Minffordd Caravan Park, Minffordd, Lligwy, Dulas, Isle of Anglesey LL70 9HJ
01248 410678 • Fax: 01248 410378

Modern caravans to let on small 5★ garden park near the safe sandy beach of Lligwy (approx half a mile). Surrounded by flowers and lawns, each caravan is a recent model, complete with shower, W.C., wash basin, colour TV, fridge, microwave, and are fully equipped with the exception of personal linen. **TWO CARAVANS HAVE BEEN SPECIALLY DESIGNED AND EQUIPPED FOR ACCOMPANIED PHYSICALLY DISABLED GUESTS.**

Nearby, in their own separate gardens, are a luxury four-bedroom detached house, a superb two-bedroom cottage, and two new semi-detached cottages - all 5★. Please contact us for availability and brochure. Telephone, fax, e-mail or send SAE. Personally managed by the owners.
WALES IN BLOOM AWARD WINNERS 2002/3/4/5/6/7.

e-mail: enq@minffordd-holidays.com • www.minffordd-holidays.com

❖ Ty Gwyn ❖

Static six-berth luxury caravan with two bedrooms, shower, bathroom, colour TV, microwave, etc. on private grounds.

Situated two miles from Bala in beautiful country area.

Ideal for walking, sailing,

fishing and canoeing.

30 miles from nearest beach.

Pets welcome.

Contact: **MRS A. SKINNER,
TY GWYN, RHYDUCHAF,
BALA, GWYNEDD LL23 7SD**
Tel: **01678 521267**

Anglesey & Gwynedd | **WALES** 177
Anglesey

Tyddyn Isaf
Camping and Caravan Park

Lligwy Bay, Dulas, Anglesey LL70 9PQ
Tel: 01248 410203 • Fax: 01248 410667

Award-winning superior park which has been described as a 'wild life wonderland' by David Bellamy. Touring caravans and tents are catered for by the high standard of facilities – "Loo of the Year" award. The site facilities include sanitation, water, electricity, gas, shop, swings, licensed restaurant, take-away food and laundry facilities. Safe, sandy beach reached directly from the site. Golf, tennis, fishing, riding and bathing all within easy reach. Open from 1st March to 31st October.

Children welcome.
Pets by arrangement.
Tourers from £18.
Six acres for campers
from £15 per tent.
CALOR GAS 'FINALIST'
BEST TOURING PARK
IN WALES

www.tyddynisaf.co.uk

178 WALES — Anglesey & Gwynedd
Barmouth

HENDRE MYNACH
TOURING CARAVAN AND CAMPING PARK

SOUTHERN SNOWDONIA

Award winning caravan park close to the beautiful Mawddach Estuary. 100 metres from safe sandy beach. Excellent base for walking and cycling, close to Cycle Route 8. All modern amenities. Hard standings available. Pets welcome, dog walk on site. Approximately 20 minutes pleasant walk along promenade to Barmouth town centre. Bus service and train station close by.

SPECIAL OFFERS AVAILABLE SPRING & AUTUMN

PHONE FOR COLOUR BROCHURE

Barmouth, Gwynedd, LL42 1YR
Tel: 01341 280 262
E-mail: info@hendremynach.co.uk
www.hendremynach.co.uk

photo: J.A. Morris

FHG Guides

publish a large range of well-known accommodation guides. We will be happy to send you details or you can use the order form at the back of this book.

---

symbols

- ☀ Holiday Parks & Centres
- 🚐 Caravans for Hire
- Ⓢ Caravan Sites and Touring Parks
- ⛺ Camping Sites

Islawrffordd Caravan Park

Situated on the Snowdonia coastline, just north of Barmouth, our park offers a limited number of caravans for hire, most of which come with double glazing and central heating along with laundered bedding.

Our touring caravan field has been modernised to super pitch quality including hard standing with each plot being reservable.

Camping is also available on a first-come, first-served basis.

Park facilities include
- shop • bar • laundry
- indoor heated pool
- jacuzzi • sauna
- amusements • food bars
- state of the art toilet/shower block

Enquiries regarding any of the above to John or Jane.

Tel: 01341 247269
Fax: 01341 242639
e-mail: info@islawrffordd.co.uk
www.islawrffordd.co.uk

Tal-y-Bont, Gwynedd LL43 2BQ

180 WALES — **Anglesey & Gwynedd**

Benllech

Sports and Leisure

We have horse riding facilities on the site together with beach donkeys that work regularly depending on the tide and weather. Immediately adjacent to the site there are tennis courts and a bowling green. There is also a golf course within two miles. A particular feature of the site is that whilst having the benefits of the village on one side, it has an attractive cliff path for walkers between the site and sea that stretches for miles. It is the intention of the local council to extend this walk right around the island.

The Site.....

There are a number of flush toilet blocks together with two shower blocks. Mains water is laid in all fields, and dustbins and skips are regularly serviced. There are electric hook-ups to numerous marked-out touring caravan pitches, and hook-ups are available for tents. We have a designated family field, and one of the most popular features of the camping site is that it is split up into numerous hedged enclosures.

We do not take advanced bookings for tents and touring caravans in the main designated area, as there is usually plenty of room, although electric hook-ups cannot be guaranteed. However we do take advanced bookings for touring caravans, only a small number of which are situated within the main caravan park. During the peak season and Bank Holidays, bookings will only be taken for a minimum of a week. Seasonal tourers are welcome, and reservations can be made for these.

Organised Camps

Organised camps for schools, scouts, guides etc are welcome, and we give quotations on enquiry. Each organised camp can have its own separate field with mains water and full facilities.

GOLDEN SUNSET HOLIDAYS
BENLLECH
ANGLESEY LL74 8SW
TEL: 01248 852345
www.goldensunsetholidays.com

Anglesey & Gwynedd

Caernarfon

Coastal Snowdonia
300 YARDS FROM LONG SANDY BEACH

ENJOY THE BEST OF BOTH WORLDS, BETWEEN SEA AND MOUNTAINS

LUXURY HOLIDAY HOMES FOR SALE AND HIRE

- Licensed Club House
- Pets Welcome
- Heated Swimming Pool
- Games Room
- Electrical Hook-ups available
- Super Pitches available
- Two Shower Blocks
- Two Children's Play Areas
- Touring & Camping on level grassland
- Washing-up and Laundry facilities

To request a brochure please contact:
Dinlle Caravan Park, Dinas Dinlle, Caernarfon LL54 5TS
Tel: 01286 830324
www.thornleyleisure.co.uk

Plas-Y-Bryn Chalet Park

Bontnewydd,
Near Caernarfon LL54 7YE
Tel: 01286 672811

Our small park is situated two miles from the historic town of Caernarfon.

Set into a walled garden it offers safety, seclusion and beautiful views of Snowdonia. It is ideally positioned for touring the area. Shop and village pub nearby.

A selection of chalets and caravans available at prices from £195 (low season) to £445 (high season) per week for the caravans and £140 (low season) to £580 (high season) per week for the chalets. Well behaved pets always welcome.

e-mail: philplasybryn@aol.com
www.plasybryn.co.uk

Llwyn-Yr-Helm Farm

- Caravans, Dormobiles and tents; electric hook-ups.
- Pets welcome.
- Facilities for the disabled.
- Toilet block
- Laundry
- Self-catering accommodation also available.

Mrs Helen Rowlands
Llwyn-Yr-Helm Farm, Brithdir, Dolgellau LL40 2SA
Tel: 01341 450254
e-mail: info@llwynyrhelmcaravanpark.co.uk
www.llwynyrhelmcaravanpark.co.uk

Situated on a minor road half a mile off B4416 which is a loop road between A470 and A494, this is a quiet, small working farm site, four miles from Dolgellau in beautiful countryside, ideal for walking and mountain biking.

Many places of interest in the area including slate mines, narrow gauge railways, lakes and mountains and nine miles from sandy beaches.

Anglesey & Gwynedd
Snowdonia, Tal-y-Llyn, Trearddur Bay

WALES 183

BrynGloch
CAMPING & CARAVANNING PARK

www.bryngloch.co.uk
01286 650216

Nestled in a picturesque valley on the banks of the river Gwyrfai at the foot of Snowdon. Bryn Gloch boasts level all weather Super Pitches, Touring Pitches, Tent Pitches, Motorhome Pitches. Static Caravans and bunkhouse also for hire.

- Electric Hook-ups
- Luxury Toilet-Shower Blocks
- Mother & Baby Room
- Disabled Facilities
- Fishing • Games Room
- Shop/Off Licence
- Pub & Restaurant within 1 mile

Dôl-Einion is perhaps the prettiest campsite in the Snowdonia National Park. It is a flat three-acre meadow bordered by colourful rhododendrons in season and there is an attractive trout stream. The site nestles at the foot of mighty Cader Idris, at the start of the main path to the summit. Easy access on B4405 for caravans, camping vans. Hard standing area useful in bad weather. Hook - ups available. Good centre for walking or touring. Castle, narrow gauge railway and lake fishing nearby. On a bus route. Pub and restaurant at walking distance. Toilets and showers.

M. Rees, Dôl-Einion, Tal-y-Llyn, Tywyn LL36 9AJ • 01654 761312

Managed by resident owner. Terms on application.

TYN RHÔS CAMPING SITE

Ravenspoint Road,
Trearddur Bay, Holyhead,
Isle of Anglesey LL65 2AX
Tel: 01407 860369

Clean facilities, hot showers, toilets, chemical disposal, electric hook-ups etc. Couples and families welcome; separate rally field available. Bookings for electric pitches advisable, some disabled access – access statement/further information on request.

Wales Cymru ★★★

Rocky coves and sandy bays, Blue Flag beaches and public slipway, horse riding, golf. Spectacular coastal views all on the doorstep. Discover this diverse island steeped in history with its many attractions. The Royal town of Caernarfon and Snowdonia all within easy reach. Ferries to Ireland 3 miles.

Access from the A55. Junction 2 for Trearddur Bay on the B4545, turn right onto Ravenspoint Road, (after Spar shop), one mile to shared entrance, bear left.

North Wales

Abergele, Bangor-on-Dee, Betws-y-Coed, Mold

Static Caravan Park in peaceful location in North Wales

This small caravan site is situated in beautiful unspoilt countryside, 10 miles from the coast and 12 miles from Betws-y-coed, ideal for touring North Wales. The six-berth caravans are fully equipped except for linen and towels and have shower, flush toilets, hot and cold water, Calor gas cooker, electric light and fridge. Children especially will enjoy a holiday here, there being ample play space and facilities for fishing and pony riding. Pets are allowed but must be kept under control. Terms on application. SAE please. Open March- Oct.

Pen Isaf Farm Caravan Park
Llangernyw, Abergele LL22 8RN
Tel: 01745 860276
Mr and Mrs T.P. Williams

www.caravan-park-wales.co.uk

ABERGELE. Hunters Hamlet Caravan Park, Sirior Goch Farm, Betws yn Rhos, Abergele LL22 8PL
Tel: 01745 832237 • www.huntershamlet.co.uk
A quiet, peaceful site set among country lanes which can cater for 23 touring units (8 pitches have full services). Just a little further afield are the lively resorts of the North Wales coast. Open March to October.

BANGOR-ON-DEE. Emral Gardens Caravan Park, Holly Bush, Bangor-on-Dee, Wrexham LL13 0BG
Tel: 01948 770401 • www.emralgardens.co.uk
An adults-only site, partly surrounded by woodland, and with views across the fields. Level grass pitches have basic or luxury hook-ups, and there is a washing up area and TV room. Open March to October.

BETWS-Y-COED. Rynys Farm Camping Site, Llanrwst, Betws-y- Coed LL26 0RU
Tel: 01690 710218 • www.rynys-camping.co.uk
The views from this from this small, friendly site are simply breathtaking, and it lies within easy reach of many attractions and superb walking country. It caters mainly for tents and camper vans, plus a few touring caravans.

MOLD. Fron Farm Caravan and Camping Park, Rhes y Cae Road, Hendre, Mold CH7 5QW
Tel: 01352 741482 • www.fronfarmcaravanpark.co.uk
A spacious 5-acre site with stunning views of the Clwydian Mountains, with modern purpose-built facilities. It is very popular with children, who love the friendly farm animals and well equipped play area. Open April to October.

Readers are requested to mention this FHG guidebook when seeking accommodation

Ceredigion
Aberystwyth, Llanarth, Llandysul

WALES 185

ABERYSTWYTH. Aberystwyth Holiday Village, Penparcau Road, Aberystwyth SY23 1TH
Tel: 01970 624211 • Fax: 01970 611536 • www.aberystwythholidays.co.uk
Set in 30 acres, just a few minutes' walk from the town centre and beach, this is an ideal location for a family holiday. The excellent facilities include an indoor pool, fitness centre, bars and entertainment. Open March to October.

LLANARTH. Llanina Caravan Park, Llanarth, New Quay SA47 0NP
Tel & Fax: 01545 580947 • www.llanina-caravan-park.co.uk
Situated close to Cardigan Bay, this sheltered site is within easy walking distance of local amenities. Wildlife lovers will delight in spotting Red Kites, seals and dolphins, and there are many attractions in the area to interest all the family. 30 pitches for tourers/motorhomes and 20 for tents. Open April to October.

Treddafydd Farm Caravan Site

Treddafydd, being a small site, offers a peaceful and restful holiday overlooking the beautiful Hoffnant and Penbryn valley. All caravans have inside toilet and shower, fridge and Calor gas cookers, spacious lounge with gas heater and TV; dining area. Hot and cold water. All are fully equipped with electricity and mains water. Linen not supplied. Launderette on site, also a toilet block with two shower rooms. Safe beach at Penbryn, one mile away, cliff walks, sea and river fishing, pony rides available locally. Children are most welcome, with plenty of room for them to play. Treddafydd is a working dairy farm: cows, young calves. Children are welcome to see life on the farm. Pitches also available for tents and touring vans.

Sarnau, Llandysul SA44 6PZ • Tel: 01239 654551

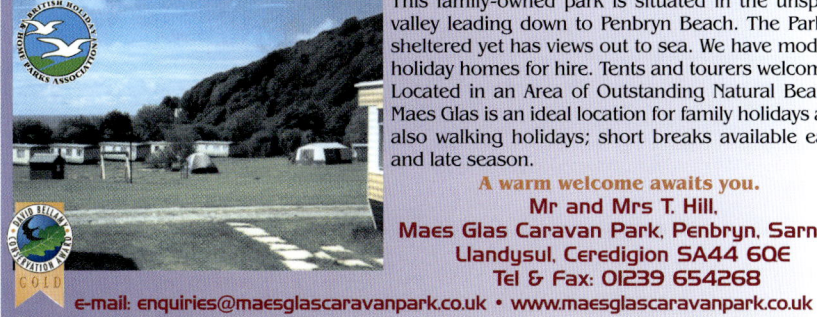

This family-owned park is situated in the unspoilt valley leading down to Penbryn Beach. The Park is sheltered yet has views out to sea. We have modern holiday homes for hire. Tents and tourers welcome. Located in an Area of Outstanding Natural Beauty, Maes Glas is an ideal location for family holidays and also walking holidays; short breaks available early and late season.

A warm welcome awaits you.
Mr and Mrs T. Hill,
Maes Glas Caravan Park, Penbryn, Sarnau,
Llandysul, Ceredigion SA44 6QE
Tel & Fax: 01239 654268
e-mail: enquiries@maesglascaravanpark.co.uk • www.maesglascaravanpark.co.uk

Pembrokeshire

Haverfordwest, St Davids, Saundersfoot, Tenby

❖ Brandy Brook ❖
Caravan and Camping Site

Rhyndaston, Hayscastle, Haverfordwest SA62 5PT

This is a small, secluded site in very attractive surroundings, a quiet valley with a trout stream. The ideal situation for the true country lover. Campers welcome. Hot water/showers on site.
Car essential to get the most from your holiday. Take A487 from Haverfordwest, turn right at Roch Motel, signposted from turning.
Pets accepted at £1.50 per night per pet. Children welcome £1.50 per night.

Rates: £10.40 per night for 2 adults with one tent and a car.

Tel: 01348 840272   ❖   e-mail: f.m.rowe@btopenworld.com

ST DAVIDS. Porthclais Farm Campsite, Porthclais, St Davids SA62 6RR
Tel: 01437 720616 • www.porthclais-farm-campsite.co.uk
This spacious, flat site caters for tents and up to 12 touring vans. Near the Coastal Path, it is ideally located for enjoying the spectacular scenery and tranquil coastal surroundings (small boats can be launched). Open Easter to October.

ST DAVIDS. Tretio Caravan and Camping, Tretio, St Davids SA62 6DE
Tel: 01437 781600
Set against a stunning backdrop of the Pembrokeshire National Park this site is just 3 miles from some of the most beautiful beaches in Britain. Touring caravans, tents and campervans welcome. Open March to October.

SAUNDERSFOOT. Trevayne Farm Caravan & Camping Park, Monkstone, Saundersfoot SA69 9DL
Tel: 01834 813402 • www.camping-pembrokeshire.co.uk
Whether you are looking for a quiet short break away or a great base for a family holiday. Trevayne is the perfect rustic getaway, with access to a clean bathing beach. Open Easter to October.

TENBY. Rowston Holiday Park, New Hedges, Tenby SA70 8TL
Tel: 01834 842178 • Fax: 01834 842177 • www.rowston-holiday-park.co.uk
With easy access to the Pembrokeshire Coast National Park, this beautifully landscaped park is ideal for a peaceful and relaxing holiday. An on-site diner offers a wide range of meals and snacks, and there is a games room (peak season). Open March to October for touring vans, motorhomes and tents.

A useful index of towns/counties appears at the back of this book

Powys
Brecon, Builth Wells, Rhayader

Powys

BRECON. Pencelli Castle Caravan & Camping Park, Pencelli, Brecon LD3 7LX
Tel: 01874 665451 • www.pencelli-castle.com
A multi-award winning family-run park in the heart of the Brecon Beacons National Park, ideal for walking, cycling, pony trekking and canoeing, as well as simply relaxing. The historic town of Brecon is 4 miles away. Closed December.

BUILTH WELLS. Fforest Fields Caravan & Camping Park, Hundred House, Builth Wells LD1 5RT
Tel: 01982 570406 • www.fforestfields.co.uk
A secluded 7-acre rural site a few miles from the market town of Builth Wells. It is landscaped with lots of trees to provide shelter and screening, and there is no traffic noise, so a relaxing stay is guaranteed. Open Easter to November.

The Pines Caravan Park

Small, peaceful, family-run park, with views in glorious mid-Wales. Situated on A470 four miles south of Rhayader – a good central position for exploring the Elan and Wye Valleys. A bird watchers' paradise, with many varieties of birds including the Red Kite.

Luxury modern holiday homes for hire and for sale. Fully equipped with shower, flush toilet, hot and cold water, cooker, fridge, microwave, colour TV. Weekly hire terms from £220 per week.

Mid-week bookings accepted. Shop and cafe close by. Pets welcome. Wheelchair accessible caravan available for hire. Please send for brochure. Philip and Sally Tolson.

**Doldowlod,
Llandrindod Wells LD1 6NN
Tel/Fax: 01597 810068**
www.pinescaravanpark.co.uk
email: info@pinescaravanpark.co.uk

South Wales

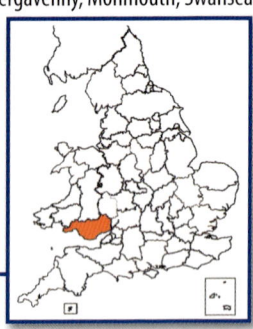

Abergavenny, Monmouth, Swansea

ABERGAVENNY. Pont Kemys Caravan Park, Chainbridge, Abergavenny NP7 9DS
Tel: 01873 880688 • Fax: 01873 880270 • www.pontkemys.co.uk
Lying adjacent to the River Usk, this family-run park has been popular for many years with caravanners and campers. There is an adults-only area with 20 fully serviced pitches. Open March to October.

MONMOUTH. Glen Trothy Caravan & Camping, Mitchel Troy, Monmouth NP25 4BD
Tel: 01600 712295 • www.glentrothy.co.uk
A 6½ acre site offering 74 touring pitches (all with electric hook-ups) and two fields for tents. Amenities are good, and there is a well equipped children's play area. Open March to October.

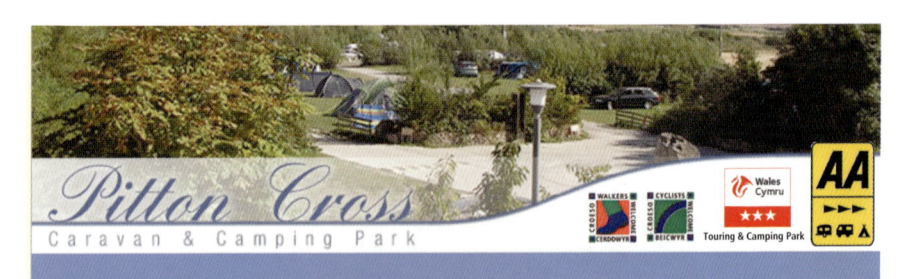

Close to the village of Rhossili, comprising six level paddocks each with 15-20 pitches, some with sea views, others offering peace and privacy. Convenient water and hook-up points. 'Dog free' and 'families only' areas. Clean modern shower and utility block, dish washing area, laundry room, parent and toddler room with baby bath and changing facilities. On-site shop for food and other essentials. Breathtaking coastal scenery, unrivalled countryside and fabulous sunsets. Walking, water sports, rock climbing, cycling.

See our kite centre for an extensive range of kites. Also fishing tackle and a selection of gifts and crafts.

Pitton Cross Caravan & Camping Park Rhossili, Swansea SA3 1PH
Tel: 01792 390 593 • Fax: 01792 391 010 • www.pittoncross.co.uk

South Wales
Merthyr Tydfil

GRAWEN
Caravan and Camping Park,
Grawen Farm, Cwm-Taff, Cefn Coed, Merthyr Tydfil CF48 2HS
Tel: 01685 723740

- Picturesque surroundings with forest, mountain, reservoir walks from site
  - Reservoir trout fishing
- Ideally located for touring, visiting places of historic interest and enjoying scenic views
  - Clean, modern Facilities
    - Free Hot Showers
    - Electric hook-ups
- Washing Machines, Dryers
  - Washing-up facilities
- Two Children's Play Areas
    - Dogs on Leads

Open April to the end of October.

Pre-booking is not always necessary but may be advisable at peak times particularly Bank Holidays

- Easy access A470 Brecon Beacons road, 1½ miles Cefn Coed, 3½ miles Merthyr Tydfil, 2 miles from A456 (known as the Heads of the Valleys)

Car, tent, two persons from £10-£12.   Caravan, car, two persons from £12-£15.

e-mail: grawen.touring@virgin.net
www.walescaravanandcamping.com

Ireland

Kylemore Abbey, Connemara
Photo courtesy PDPhoto.org

A LAND OF HISTORY AND HERITAGE, myths and magic, Ireland is easily accessible by plane or ferry, and ideal for a Short Break holiday at any time of year.

Northern Ireland's beauty is intertwined with tragic history, rich culture and the renowned friendliness of its people. The wild craggy mountains, splendid lakes and sweeping coastline make it an ideal playground for watersports enthusiasts, walkers, cyclists, hikers, rock climbers and sailors. But there are lots of things to keep those after a dose of culture enthralled, too. From oyster festivals to authentic horse fairs, and from ancient castles to elegant country houses, this spectacular part of Ireland is packed with things to do.

From the endless attractions of Dublin with its lively nightlife, museums and art galleries and, of course, its literary connection with Swift, Shaw, Yeats, Joyce and Beckett, to the charming west of Ireland where genuine hospitality is part of the culture, there are plenty of things to do and places to visit. The south-east area is steeped in history and boasts a heritage trail unrivalled by any other region in Ireland. Cork and Kerry to the south are perhaps the most attractive holiday areas, with a long coastline, mountains, many rivers and lakes. Some of Ireland's finest heritage attractions are to be found in the eastern coastal and midlands region, including prehistoric monuments, Celtic monasteries, castles, and grand houses and gardens. But it's not all about action. There's plenty of opportunity to relax; perhaps to enjoy a peaceful cruise on the waterways, or a chat with the locals in one of the friendly pubs and, best of all, to experience the warmest of warm welcomes wherever you go.

Tourism Ireland
0808 234 2009
www.discoverireland.com

Co Antrim   **IRELAND** 191

Antrim, Ballycastle, Bushmills

Co. Antrim

Six Mile Water Caravan Park

Lough Road, Antrim BT41 4DG

The Six Mile Water Caravan and Camping Park is situated on the beautiful shores of Lough Neagh, an area steeped in history and natural beauty, with many attractions and activities to enjoy. On-site facilities include a modern toilet and shower block, fully equipped laundry room, hard stands with 20 electric hook-up caravan pitches, 24 tent pitches and visitor information services. There is also a TV lounge, games room and reception.

The park's central location, coupled with its close proximity to the ports of Larne and Belfast, make it an ideal base for touring not only the Borough of Antrim, but all of Northern Ireland. The park accommodates touring caravans, motor caravans and tents.

NITB ★★★★★

Tel: 028 9446 4963
e-mail: sixmilewater@antrim.gov.uk
www.antrim.gov.uk/caravanpark

BALLYCASTLE. Watertop Farm, 188 Cushendall Road, Ballycastle BT54 6RN
Tel: 028 2076 2576 • Fax: 028 2076 2175 • www.watertopfarm.co.uk
Children will love a holiday at this friendly farm, where the fun is guaranteed. Open all year round. 14 touring pitches. 4 tent pitches. Caravans, motorhomes and tents welcome.

BUSHMILLS. Ballyness Caravan Park, 40 Castlecatt Road, Bushmills BT57 8TN
Tel: 028 2073 2393 • Fax: 028 2073 2713 • www.ballynesscaravanpark.com
Multi-award winning park set in Northern Ireland's breathtaking Ballyness countryside. Dogs welcome. Open from March to November. 46 touring pitches. 6 tent pitches. Caravans, motorhomes and tents welcome.

Co. Down

Ballywalter, Hillsborough, Kilkeel, Killyleagh, Newcastle

BALLYWALTER. Sandycove Holiday Park, 191 Whitechurch Road, Ballywalter BT22 2JZ
Tel: 07801 228814 • Fax: 028 4275 8079

Excellent facilities including a tennis court and direct access to beach. Ideal for day trips to Newtownards and Bangor. Open from March to November. No tents. 40 touring pitches. Caravans and motorhomes welcome.

HILLSBOROUGH. Lakeside View, 71 Magheraconluce Road, Annahilt, Hillsborough BT26 6PR
Tel: 028 92 682098

Idyllic getaway situated near Lough Aghery Lake where visitors can enjoy watching summer water sports and the surrounding natural wildlife. Open from March to October. 25 touring pitches. 15 tent pitches. Caravans, motorhomes and tents welcome.

KILKEEL. Cranfield Caravan Park, 123 Cranfield Road, Kilkeel BT34 4LJ
Tel: 028 417 62572 • Fax: 028 417 69642 • www.cranfieldcaravanpark.co.uk

Enjoy the glorious sea views at this family-run park situated on the most southerly point of Northern Ireland. High standard facilties and direct access to the beach. Open from March to October. 45 touring pitches. Caravans, motorhomes and tents welcome.

KILLYLEAGH. Delamont Country Park, Downpatrick Road, Killyleagh BT30 9TZ
Tel: 028 4482 1833 • www.delamontcountrypark.com

Located close to the beautiful Strangford Lough, an ideal location to get away from it all. Children will love the miniature railway. Open all year round. 60 touring pitches. Caravans, motorhomes and tents welcome.

NEWCASTLE. Murlough Cottage Caravan Park, 180- 182 Dundrum Road, Newcastle BT33 0LN
Tel: 028 437 23184 • Fax: 028 437 26436 • www.murloughcottage.com

With an outstanding selection of activities and facilities, this site makes a fun yet relaxing base from which to explore the area. Ideal for all the family. Open all year round. 25 touring pitches. Caravans and motorhomes welcome.

NEWCASTLE. Sunnyholme Caravan Park, 33 Caslewellan Road, Newcastle BT33 0JY
Tel: 028 437 22739

Charming park situated just on the border of the town. Touring guests can expect top of the range facilities for a relaxing and peaceful holiday. Open from March-November. 20 touring pitches. Caravans, motorhomes and tents welcome.

🚐	Electric hook-ups available	♿	Facilities for disabled visitors
🛝	Children's play area	🐕	Pets welcome
🧺	Laundry facilities	🛒	Shop on site
🍷	Licensed bar on site	W	Wifi access available

Fermanagh / Londonderry IRELAND 193

Enniskillen, Kesh

Fermanagh

ENNISKILLEN. Blaney Caravan Park, Blaney, Enniskillen BT93 7ER
Tel: 028 6864 1634 • www.blaneycaravanpark.com/
Beautiful fishing location, central for a number of rural activities in and around this delightful area. Open all year round. 20 touring pitches. 10 tent pitches. Caravans, motorhomes and tents welcome.

KESH. Loaneden Caravan Park, Muckross Bay, Kesh BT93 1TZ
Tel: 028 68 631603
Relax with the family on Lower Lough Erne. With modern facilities and numerous attractions including superb countryside. Waterskiing/wakeboarding, jet skiing and banana boating nearby. Open from March to November.

Londonderry

Coleraine, Portstewart

COLERAINE. Tullans Park Caravan Park, 46 Newmills Road, Coleraine BT52 2JB
Tel: 028 7034 2309
A working farm where visitors can watch activities such as sheep shearing and see delightful new lambs in Spring. Portrush and Portstewart are just a short distance from the site. Open from March to September. 35 touring pitches. 5 tent pitches. Caravans, motorhomes and tents welcome

COLERAINE. Castlerock Holiday Park, 24 Sea Road Castlerock, Coleraine BT51 4TN
Tel: 028 7084 8381 • Fax: 028 70848381
Set on Northern Ireland's celebrated Causeway Coast, with a delightful beach nearby and great facilities including golf and a children's play park. Open from March to October. Touring pitches. Caravans and motorhomes welcome.

PORTSTEWART. Millfield Holiday Village, 80 Mill Road, Portstewart BT55 7SW
Tel: 028 70 833308 • Fax: 028 70 833308
Modern park offering unparalleled cliff-top views. Promenade, beach and local shops/restaurants nearby. Open from March to October. 16 touring pitches. Caravans and motorhomes welcome.

Please note

All the information in this book is given in good faith in the belief that it is correct. However, the publishers cannot guarantee the facts given in these pages, neither are they responsible for changes in policy, ownership or terms that may take place after the date of going to press. Readers should always satisfy themselves that the facilities they require are available and that the terms, if quoted, still apply.

194 IRELAND — Kerry

Kerry

Killorglin, Lauragh

"Where relaxing comes as naturally as the surrounding beauty"

West's Caravan Park
Killarney Road, Killorglin, Ring of Kerry, SW Ireland
Tel: 00 353 66 9761240

Mobile Homes for hire on family-run park situated on banks of River Laune overlooking Ireland's highest mountain. Ideal touring centre for Ring of Kerry, Dingle Peninsula, Cork, Blarney Stone, Killarney National Park and Tralee.

Park: Pool table, tennis, table-tennis, laundry. Town one mile.

Open Easter to end October

Sited mobile homes on park from 6000 Euros

e-mail: enquiries@westcaravans.com

Creveen Lodge

Immaculately run small hill farm overlooking Kenmare Bay in a striking area of County Kerry. Reception is found at the Lodge, which also offers guests a comfortable sitting room, while a separate block has well-equipped and immaculately maintained toilets and showers, plus a communal room with a large fridge, freezer and ironing facilities. The park is carefully tended, with bins and picnic tables informally placed, plus a children's play area with slides and swings.

There are 20 pitches in total, 16 for tents and 4 for caravans, with an area of hardstanding for motor caravans. Electrical connections are available. Fishing, bicycle hire, water sports and horse riding available nearby. SAE please, for replies.

Mrs M. Moriarty, Creveen Lodge, Healy Pass Road, Lauragh
00 353 64 66 83131
e-mail: info@creveenlodge.com • www.creveenlodge.com

DIRECTORY OF WEBSITE AND E-MAIL ADDRESSES

A quick-reference guide to holiday accommodation with an e-mail address and/or website, conveniently arranged by country and county, with full contact details.

Self-Catering
Hoseasons Holidays Ltd, Lowestoft, Suffolk NR32 2LW
Tel: 01502 502628
• website: www.hoseasons.co.uk

•LONDON

Hotel
Athena Hotel, 110-114 Sussex Gardens, Hyde Park, LONDON W2 1UA
Tel: 020 7706 3866
• e-mail: athena@stavrouhotels.co.uk
• website: www.stavrouhotels.co.uk

Hotel
Gower Hotel, 129 Sussex Gardens, Hyde Park, LONDON W2 2RX
Tel: 020 7262 2262
• e-mail: gower@stavrouhotels.co.uk
• website: www.stavrouhotels.co.uk

B & B
Hanwell B & B, 110a Grove Avenue, Hanwell, LONDON W7 3ES
Tel: 020 8567 5015
• e-mail: tassanimation@aol.com
• website: www.ealing-hanwell-bed-and-breakfast.co.uk/new/index

Hotel
Queens Hotel, 33 Anson Road, Tufnell Park, LONDON N7 0RB
Tel: 020 7607 4725
• e-mail: queens@stavrouhotels.co.uk
• website: www.stavrouhotels.co.uk

B & B
S. Armanios, 67 Rannoch Road, Hammersmith, LONDON W6 9SS
Tel: 020 7385 4904
• website: www.thewaytostay.co.uk

www.holidayguides.com

•BERKSHIRE

Guest House
Clarence Hotel, 9 Clarence Road, WINDSOR Berkshire SL4 5AE
Tel: 01753 864436
• e-mail: clarence.hotel@btconnect.com
• website: www.clarence-hotel.co.uk

•CAMBRIDGESHIRE

B & B
Mrs Hatley, Manor Farm, Landbeach, CAMBRIDGE, Cambridgeshire CB25 9FD
Tel: 01223 860165
• e-mail: vhatley@btinternet.com
• website: www.manorfarmcambridge.co.uk

•CORNWALL

Self-Catering
Cornish Traditional Cottages, Blisland, BODMIN, Cornwall PL30 4HS
Tel: 01208 821666
• e-mail: info@corncott.com
• website: www.corncott.com

Self-Catering
Mineshop Holiday Cottages, CRACKINGTON HAVEN, Bude, Cornwall EX23 0NR
Tel: 01840 230338
• e-mail: info@mineshop.co.uk
• website: www.mineshop.co.uk

Self-Catering
Mr P. Watson, Creekside Holiday Houses, Restronguet, FALMOUTH, Cornwall
Tel: 01326 372722
• website: www.creeksideholidayhouses.co.uk

Self-Catering
Mrs Terry, "Shasta", Carwinion Road, Mawnan Smith, FALMOUTH, Cornwall TR11 5JD
Tel: 01326 250775
• e-mail: katerry@btopenworld.com

196 WEBSITE DIRECTORY

Self-Catering / Caravan
Mrs A. E. Moore, Hollyvagg Farm,
Lewannick, LAUNCESTON,
Cornwall PL15 7QH
Tel: 01566 782309
• website: www.hollyvaggfarm.co.uk

Self-Catering
Celia Hutchinson,
Caradon Country Cottages, East Taphouse,
LISKEARD, Cornwall PL14 4NH
Tel: 01579 320355
• e-mail: celia@caradoncottages.co.uk
• website: www.caradoncottages.co.uk

Self- Catering
Mr Lowman, Cutkive Wood Holiday Lodges,
St Ive, LISKEARD, Cornwall PL14 3ND
Tel: 01579 362216
• e-mail: holidays@cutkivewood.co.uk
• website: www.cutkivewood.co.uk

Self-Catering
Valleybrook Holidays, Peakswater, Lansallos,
LOOE, Cornwall PL13 2QE
Tel: 01503 220493
• website: www.valleybrookholidays.com

B & B
Heidi Swire, Penrose B & B, 1 The Terrace,
LOSTWITHIEL, Cornwall PL22 0DT
Tel: 01208 871417
• e-mail: enquiries@penrosebb.co.uk
• website: www.penrosebb.co.uk

Self-catering Lodges
Blue Bay Lodge, Trenance, MAWGAN
PORTH, Cornwall TR8 4DA
Tel: 01637 860324
• e-mail: hotel@bluebaycornwall.co.uk
• website: www.bluebaycornwall.co.uk

Self-Catering
Ged & Lora Millward, Churchtown &
Churchgate Cottages, 6 Halwyn Road,
Crantock, NEWQUAY, Cornwall TR8 5RT
Tel: 01637 830046
• e-mail: info@crantockcottages.co.uk
• website: www.crantockcottages.co.uk

Guest House
Mrs Dewolfreys, Dewolf Guest House, 100
Henver Road, NEWQUAY, Cornwall TR7 3BL
Tel: 01637 874746
• e-mail: holidays@dewolfguesthouse.com
• website: www.dewolfguesthouse.com

Caravan / Camping
Quarryfield Caravan & Camping Park,
Crantock, NEWQUAY, Cornwall
Contact: Mrs A Winn, Tretherras, Newquay,
Cornwall TR7 2RE
Tel: 01637 872792
• e-mail: quarryfield@crantockcaravans.orangehome.co.uk
• website: www.quarryfield.co.uk

Self-Catering
Classy Cottages, POLPERRO, Cornwall
Contact: Fiona and Martin Nicolle
Tel: 01720 423000
• e-mail: nicolle@classycottages.co.uk
• website: www.classycottages.co.uk

Caravan / Camping
Globe Vale Holiday Park, Radnor, REDRUTH,
Cornwall TR16 4BH
Tel: 01209 891183
• e-mail: info@globevale.co.uk
• website: www.globevale.co.uk

Guest House
Mr S Hope, Dalswinton House,
ST MAWGAN-IN-PYDAR, Cornwall TR8 4EZ
Tel: 01637 860385
• e-mail: dalswintonhouse@tiscali.co.uk
• website: www.dalswinton.com

Self-Catering
Mrs R. Reeves, Polstraul, Trewalder,
Delabole, ST TUDY, Cornwall PL33 9ET
Tel: 01840 213120
• e-mail: ruth.reeves@hotmail.co.uk
• website: www.maymear.co.uk

Self-Catering
Whitsand Bay Self Catering, Portwrinkle,
TORPOINT, Cornwall, PL11 3BU
Tel: 01579 345688
• e-mail: ehwbsc@hotmail.com
• website: www.whitsandbayselfcatering.co.uk

Self-Catering
The Garden House, Port Isaac, Near
WADEBRIDGE, Cornwall
Contact: Mr D Oldham, Travella, Treveighan,
St Teath, Cornwall PL30 3JN
Tel: 01208 850529
• e-mail: david.trevella@btconnect.com
• website: www.trevellacornwall.co.uk

Self-Catering
Great Bodieve Farm Barns, Molesworth
House, WADEBRIDGE, Cornwall PL27 7JE
Tel: 01208 814916
• e-mail: enquiries@great-bodieve.co.uk
• website: www.great-bodieve.co.uk

FHG Guides

•CUMBRIA

Self-Catering
Kirkstone Foot Apartments Ltd, Kirkstone Pass Road, AMBLESIDE, Cumbria LA22 9EH
Tel: 015394 32232
- e-mail: enquiries@kirkstonefoot.co.uk
- website: www.kirkstonefoot.co.uk

Guest House / Self-Catering
Cuckoo's Nest & Smallwood House, Compston Road, AMBLESIDE, Cumbria LA22 9DJ
Tel: 015394 32330
- e-mail: enq@cottagesambleside.co.uk
  enq@smallwoodhotel.co.uk
- website: www.cottagesambleside.co.uk
  www.smallwoodhotel.co.uk

Caravan Park
Greenhowe Caravan Park, Great Langdale, AMBLESIDE, Cumbria LA22 9JU
Tel: 015394 37231
- e-mail: enquiries@greenhowe.com
- website: www.greenhowe.com

Hotel / Guest House
Mrs Liana Moore, The Old Vicarage, Vicarage Road, AMBLESIDE, Cumbria LA22 9DH
Tel: 015394 33364
- e-mail: info@oldvicarageambleside.co.uk
- website: www.oldvicarageambleside.co.uk

Self-Catering
43A Quarry Rigg, BOWNESS-ON-WINDERMERE, Cumbria.
Contact: Mrs E. Jones, 45 West Oakhill Park, Liverpool L13 4BN. Tel: 0151 228 5799
- e-mail: eajay@btinternet.com

Self-Catering
Mrs Almond, Irton House Farm, Isel, Near Keswick, COCKERMOUTH, Cumbria CA13 9ST
Tel: 017687 76380
- e-mail: joan@irtonhousefarm.co.uk
- website: www.irtonhousefarm.com

Self-Catering
Fisherground Farm Holidays, ESKDALE
Contact: Ian & Jennifer Hall, Orchard House, Applethwaite, Keswick, Cumbria CA12 4PN
Tel: 017687 73175
- e-mail: holidays@fisherground.co.uk
- website: www.fisherground.co.uk

Self-Catering
2 Moot Hall, Ireby, Near KESWICK, Cumbria CA7 1DU
Contact: Ruth Boyes, Anglers Lodge, Main Street, Helperby, North Yorkshire YO61 2NT
Tel: 01840 213 120
- e-mail: ruthboyes@virgin.net
- website: irebymoothall.co.uk

Self-Catering
Mr D Burton, Lakeland Cottage Holidays, Bassenthwaite, KESWICK CA12 4QX
Tel: 017687 76065
- e-mail: info@lakelandcottages.co.uk
- website: www.lakelandcottages.co.uk

Self-Catering
Mr D Williamson, Derwent Water Marina, Portinscale, KESWICK, Cumbria CA12 5RF
Tel: 017687 72912
- e-mail: info@derwentwatermarina.co.uk
- website: www.derwentwatermarina.co.uk

Inn
Mr I Court, Horse and Farrier Inn, Threlkeld, KESWICK, Cumbria CA12 4SQ
Tel: 017687 79688
- e-mail: info@horseandfarrier.com
- website: www.horseandfarrier.com

Self-Catering
Mrs J Fallon, South Lakes Cottages, Sunset Cottage, 1 Friars Ground, KIRKBY-IN-FURNESS, Cumbria LA17 7YB
Tel: 01229 889601
- e-mail: enquiries@southlakes-cottages.com
- website: www.southlakes-cottages.com

Self-Catering
Mrs S.J. Bottom, Crossfield Cottages, KIRKOSWALD, Penrith, Cumbria CA10 1EU
Tel: 01768 898711
- e-mail: info@crossfieldcottages.co.uk
- website: www.crossfieldcottages.co.uk

Self-Catering
Mr & Mrs Iredale, Carrock Cottages, Carrock House, Hutton Roof, PENRITH, Cumbria CA11 0XY
Tel: 01768 484111
- e-mail: info@carrockcottages.co.uk
- website: www.carrockcottages.co.uk

Guest House / Inn
The Troutbeck Inn, Troutbeck, PENRITH, Cumbria CA11 0SJ. Tel: 01768 483635
- e-mail: info@troutbeckinn.co.uk
- website: www.thetroutbeckinn.co.uk

Caravan & Camping
Cove Caravan & Camping Park, Watermillock, ULLSWATER, Penrith, Cumbria CA11 0LS
Tel: 017684 86549
- e-mail: info@cove-park.co.uk
- website: www.cove-park.co.uk

B & B / Self-Catering
Barbara Murphy, Land Ends Country Lodge, Watermillock, Near ULLSWATER, Cumbria CA11 0NB
Tel: 01768 486438
- e-mail: infolandends@btinternet.com
- website: www.landends.co.uk

198 WEBSITE DIRECTORY

Guest House
Mr Shaw, Meadfoot Guest House, New Road, WINDERMERE, Cumbria LA23 2LA
Tel: 01539 442610
• e-mail: enquiries@meadfoot-guesthouse.co.uk
• website: www.meadfoot-guesthouse.co.uk

Hotel
The Famous Wild Boar, Crook, Near WINDERMERE, Cumbria LA23 3NF
Tel: Reservations 08458 504604
• website: www.elh.co.uk

• DERBYSHIRE

Self-Catering Holiday Cottages
Mark Redfern, Paddock House Farm Holiday Cottages, Peak District National Park, Alstonefield, ASHBOURNE, Derbyshire DE6 2FT
Tel: 01335 310282 / 07977 569618
• e-mail: info@paddockhousefarm.co.uk
• website: www.paddockhousefarm.co.uk

Self-Catering
Keith & Joan Lennard, Windlehill Farm, Sutton-on-the-Hill, ASHBOURNE, Derbyshire DE6 5JH
Tel: 01283 732377
• e-mail: windlehill@btinternet.com
• website: www.windlehill.btinternet.co.uk

Self-Catering
Burton Manor Farm Cottages, BAKEWELL, Derbyshire DE45 1JX
Contact: Mrs R Shirt, Holmelacy Farm, Tideswell, Buxton SK17 8LW
Tel: 01298 871429
• e-mail: cshirt@burtonmanor.freeserve.co.uk
• website: www.burtonmanor.freeserve.co.uk

Hotel
Biggin Hall, Biggin-by-Hartington, BUXTON, Derbyshire SK17 0DH
Tel: 01298 84451
• e-mail: enquiries@bigginhall.co.uk
• website: www.bigginhall.co.uk

Caravan
Golden Valley Caravan Park, Coach Road, RIPLEY, Derbyshire DE55 4ES
Tel: 01773 513881
• e-mail: enquiries@goldenvalleycaravanpark.co.uk
• website: www.goldenvalleycaravanpark.co.uk

• DEVON

Self-Catering
Helpful Holidays, Mill Street, Chagford, DEVON TQ13 8AW
Tel: 01647 433593
• e-mail: help@helpfulholidays.com
• website: www.helpfulholidays.com

Self-Catering
Farm & Cottage Holidays, DEVON
Tel: 01237 459897
• website: www.holidaycottages.co.uk

Self-Catering
Wooder Manor, Widecombe-in-the-Moor, ASHBURTON, Devon TQ13 7TR
Tel: 01364 621391
• e-mail: angela@woodermanor.com
• website: www.woodermanor.com

Farm B & B
Mrs J Ley, West Barton, Alverdiscott, Near BARNSTABLE, Devon EX31 3PT
Tel: 01271 858230
• e-mail: ela@andrews78.freeserve.co.uk

Self-Catering / Organic Farm
Little Comfort Farm Cottages, Little Comfort Farm, BRAUNTON, North Devon EX33 2NJ
Tel: 01271 812414
• e-mail: info@littlecomfortfarm.co.uk
• website: www.littlecomfortfarm.co.uk

Guest House
Woodlands Guest House, Parkham Road, BRIXHAM, South Devon TQ5 9BU
Tel: 01803 852040
• e-mail: woodlandsbrixham@btinternet.com
• website: www.woodlandsbrixham.co.uk

Farm / Self-Catering / B&B
Mrs Lee, Church Approach Cottages, Church Green, Farway, COLYTON, Devon EX24 6EQ
Tel: 01404 871383/871202
• e-mail: lizlee@eclipse.co.uk
• website: www.churchapproach.co.uk

Holiday Park
Manleigh Holiday Park, Rectory Road, COMBE MARTIN, North Devon EX34 0NS
Tel: 01271 883353
• e-mail: info@manleighpark.co.uk
• website: www.manleighpark.co.uk

Self-Catering / Holiday Park
Mrs Helen Scott, Cofton Country Holidays, Starcross, Near DAWLISH, Devon EX6 8RP
Tel: 01626 890111
• e-mail: info@coftonholidays.co.uk
• website: www.coftonholidays.co.uk

www.holidayguides.com

WEBSITE DIRECTORY 199

Inn
The Blue Ball Inn, Countisbury, LYNMOUTH, Near Lynton, Devon EX35 6NE
Tel: 01598 741263
• website: www.BlueBallinn.com
   www.exmoorsandpiper.com

Self-Catering
G Davidson Richmond, Clooneavin, Clooneavin Path, LYNMOUTH, Devon EX35 6EE • Tel: 01598 753334
• e-mail: relax@clooneavinholidays.co.uk
• website: www.clooneavinholidays.co.uk

Self-Catering
C & M Hartnoll, Little Bray House, Brayford, Barnstable, LYNTON, Devon EX32 7QG
Tel: 01598 710295
• e-mail: holidays@littlebray.co.uk
• website: www.littlebray.co.uk

B & B / Guest House / Farm
Mrs E A Forth, Fluxton Farm, OTTERY ST MARY, Devon EX11 1RJ
Tel: 01404 812818
• website: www.fluxtonfarm.co.uk

Hotel
Christine Clark, Amber House Hotel, 6 Roundham Road, PAIGNTON, Devon TQ4 6EZ
Tel: 01803 558372
• e-mail: enquiries@amberhousehotel.co.uk
• website: www.amberhousehotel.co.uk

Guest House
The Commodore, 14 Esplanade Road, PAIGNTON, Devon TQ4 6EB
Tel: 01803 553107
• e-mail: info@commodorepaignton.com
• website: www.commodorepaignton.com

Hotel / Inn / Self Catering
Port Light Hotel & Bolberry Farm Cottages, Bolberry Down, Near SALCOMBE, Devon TQ7 3DY • Tel: 01548 561384
• e-mail: info@portlight.co.uk
• website: www.portlight.co.uk
   www.bolberryfarmcottages.co.uk

Guest House
A J Hill, Beaumont, Castle Hill, SEATON Devon EX12 2QW
Tel: 01297 20832
• e-mail: jane@lymebay.demon.co.uk
• website: www.smoothhound.co.uk/hotels/beaumon1.html

Self-Catering
M Courtney, West Millbrook, Twitchen, SOUTH MOLTON, Devon EX36 3LP
Tel: 01598 740382
• e-mail: wmbselfcatering@aol.com
• website: www.westmillbrook.co.uk

Self-Catering / Camping
Dartmoor Country Holidays, Magpie Leisure Park, Bedford Bridge, Horrabridge, Yelverton, TAVISTOCK, Devon PL20 7RY
Tel: 01822 852651
• website: www.dartmoorcountryholidays.co.uk

Guest House
John O'Flaherty, Overcombe House, Old Station Road, Horrabridge, Yelverton, TAVISTOCK, Devon, PL20 7RA
Tel: 01822 853501
• e-mail: enquiries@overcombehotel.co.uk
• website: www.overcombehotel.co.uk

Hotel
Riviera Lodge Hotel, 26 Croft Road. TORQUAY, Devon TQ2 5UE
Tel: 01803 209309
• e-mail: stay@rivieralodgehotel.co.uk
• website: www.rivieralodgehotel.co.uk

Self-Catering
Marsdens Cottage Holidays, 2 The Square, Braunton, WOOLACOMBE, Devon EX33 2JB
Tel: 01271 813777
• e-mail: holidays@marsdens.co.uk
• website: www.marsdens.co.uk

Holiday Park
Woolacombe Bay Holiday Parks, WOOLACOMBE, North Devon EX34 7HW
Tel: 0844 770 0379
• e-mail: goodtimes@woolacombe.com
• website: www.woolacombe.com

Caravan & Camping
North Morte Farm Caravan & Camping Park, Mortehoe, WOOLACOMBE, Devon EX34 7EG
Tel: 01271 870381
• e-mail: info@northmortefarm.co.uk
• website: www.northmortefarm.co.uk

•DORSET

Self-Catering
Luccombe Farm Cottages, Luccombe Farm, Milton Abbas, BLANDFORD FORUM, Dorset DT11 0BE
Tel: 01258 880558
• e-mail: mkayll@aol.com
• website: www.luccombeholidays.co.uk

FHG Guides

200 WEBSITE DIRECTORY

Hotel
Southbourne Grove Hotel, 96 Southbourne Road, BOURNEMOUTH, Dorset BH6 3QQ
Tel: 01202 420503
• e-mail: neil@pack1462.freeserve.co.uk
• website: www.bournemouth.co.uk/southbournegrovehotel

Self-Catering
C. Hammond, Stourcliffe Court, 56 Stourcliffe Avenue, Southbourne, BOURNEMOUTH, Dorset BH6 3PX
Tel: 01202 420698
• e-mail: rjhammond1@hotmail.co.uk
• website: www.stourcliffecourt.co.uk

Self-Catering Cottage / Farmhouse B & B
Mrs S. E. Norman, Frogmore Farm, Chideock, BRIDPORT, Dorset DT6 6HT
Tel: 01308 456159
• e-mail: bookings@frogmorefarm.com
• website: www.frogmorefarm.com

Golf Club
Came Down Golf Club, Higher Came, DORCHESTER, Dorset DT2 8NR
Tel: 01305 813494
• e-mail: manager@camedowngolfclub.co.uk
• website: www.camedowngolfclub.co.uk

Self-Catering
Josephine Pearse, Tamarisk Farm Cottages, Beach Road, West Bexington, DORCHESTER DT2 2DF
Tel: 01308 897784
• e-mail: holidays@tamariskfarm.com
• website: www.tamariskfarm.com/holidays

Hotel / Self Catering
Cromwell House Hotel, LULWORTH COVE, Dorset BH20 5RJ
Tel: 01929 400253
• e-mail: catriona@lulworthcove.co.uk
• website: www.lulworthcove.co.uk

Hotel
Fairwater Head Hotel, Hawkchurch, Near Axminster, LYME REGIS, Dorset EX13 5TX
Tel: 01297 678349
• e-mail: info@fairwaterheadhotel.co.uk
• website: www.fairwaterheadhotel.co.uk

Self-Catering
Westover Farm Cottages, Wootton Fitzpaine, Near LYME REGIS, Dorset DT6 6NE
Tel: 01297 560451/561295
• e-mail: wfcottages@aol.com
• website: www.westoverfarmcottages.co.uk

Self-Catering
Mrs E Melville, Wood Dairy, Wood Lane, NORTH PERROTT, Somerset/Dorset TA18 7TA
Tel: 01935 891532
• e-mail: liz@acountryretreat.co.uk
• website: www.acountryretreat.co.uk

Farm / Self-Catering
White Horse Farm, Middlemarsh, SHERBORNE, Dorset DT9 5QN
Tel: 01963 210222
• e-mail: enquiries@whitehorsefarm.co.uk
• website: www.whitehorsefarm.co.uk

Hotel
The Knoll House, STUDLAND BAY, Dorset BH19 3AW
Tel: 01929 450450
• e-mail: info@knollhouse.co.uk
• website: www.knollhouse.co.uk

Self-Catering
Dorset Coastal Cottages, 3 Station Road, Wood, WAREHAM, Dorset BH20 6BL
Tel: 0800 980 4070
• e-mail: hols@dorsetcoastalcottages.com
• website: www.dorsetcoastalcottages.com

Guest House
Kemps Country House, East Stoke, WAREHAM, Dorset BH20 6AL
Tel: 0845 862 0315
• e-mail: info@kempscountryhouse.co.uk
• website: www.kempshotel.com

Inn / Self-Catering
The Lugger Inn, 30 West Street, Chickerell, WEYMOUTH, Dorset DT3 4DY
Tel: 01305 766611
• e-mail: info@theluggerinn.co.uk
• website: www.theluggerinn.co.uk

Guest House / Self-Catering
Olivia Nurrish, Glenthorne, 15 Old Castle Road, WEYMOUTH, Dorset DT4 8QB
Tel: 01305 777281
• e-mail: info@glenthorne-holidays.co.uk
• website: www.glenthorne-holidays.co.uk

•ESSEX

Farm House B&B / Self-Catering
Mrs Brenda Lord, Pond House B & B and Self-Catering, Earls Hall Farm, St Osyth, CLACTON ON SEA, Essex CO16 8BP Tel: 01255 820458
• e-mail: brenda_lord@farming.co.uk
• website: www.earlshallfarm.info

FHG Guides

•GLOUCESTERSHIRE

Hotel
Tudor Farmhouse Hotel, CLEARWELL, Forest of Dean, Gloucs GL16 8JS
Tel: 01594 833046
• e-mail: info@tudorfarmhousehotel.co.uk
• website: www.tudorfarmhousehotel.co.uk

Guest House
Mr John Sparrey, Parkview Guest House, 4 Pittville Crescent, CHELTENHAM, Gloucs GL52 2QZ
Tel: 01242 575567
• e-mail: stay@parkviewguesthouse.me.uk
• website: www.parkviewguesthouse.me.uk

Hotel
Tudor Farmhouse Hotel, CLEARWELL Near Coleford, Gloucs GL16 8JS
Tel: 01929 450450
• e-mail: info@tudeorfarmhousehotel.co.uk
• website: www.tudorfarmhousehotel.co.uk

Self-Catering
Two Springbank, 37 Hopton Road, Cam, DURSLEY, Gloucs GL11 5PD
Contact: Mrs F A Jones, 32 Everlands, Cam, Dursley, Gloucs G11 5NL
Tel: 01453 543047
• e-mail: info@twospringbank.co.uk
• website: www.twospringbank.co.uk

Caravan & Camping
Tudor Caravan Park, Shepherds Patch, SLIMBRIDGE, Gloucestershire GL2 7BP
Tel: 01453 890483
• e-mail: fhg@tudorcaravanpark.co.uk
• website: www.tudorcaravanpark.com

Guest House
Elizabeth Warland, Hambutts Mynd, Edge Road, PAINSWICK, Gloucs GL6 6UP
Tel: 01452 812352
• e-mail: ewarland@supanet.com.
• website: www.accommodation.uk.net/painswick.htm

Self-Catering
Nicky Cross, Wharton Lodge Cottages, Weston-Under-Penyard, ROSS-ON-WYE, Gloucs HR9 7JX
Tel: 01989 750140
• e-mail: ncross@whartonlodge.co.uk
• website: www.whartonlodge.co.uk

B & B
Mrs A Rhoton, Hyde Crest, Cirencester Road, Minchinhampton, STROUD, Gloucs GL6 8PE
Tel: 01453 731631
• e-mail: stay@hydecrest.co.uk
• website: www.hydecrest.co.uk

•HAMPSHIRE

Holiday Park
Downton Holiday Park, Shorefield Road, MILFORD-ON-SEA, New Forest, Hampshire SO41 0LH
Tel: 01425 476131 / 01590 642515
• e-mail: info@downtonholidaypark.co.uk
• website: www.downtonholidaypark.co.uk

•ISLE OF WIGHT

Farmhouse B & B / Self-Catering Cottages
Mrs F.J. Corry, Little Span Farm, Rew Lane, Wroxall, VENTNOR, Isle of Wight PO38 3AU
Tel: 01983 852419
• e-mail: info@spanfarm.co.uk
• website: www.spanfarm.co.uk

•KENT

Hotel
The Hanson, 41 Belvedere Road, BROADSTAIRS, Kent CT10 1PF
Tel: 01843 868936
• e-mail: hotel.hanson@yahoo.co.uk
• website: www.hansonhotel.co.uk

Hotel
Mr M Collins, The Bell Hotel, The Quay, SANDWICH, Kent CT13 9EF
Tel: 01304 613388
• e-mail: reservations@bellhotelsandwich.co.uk
• website: www.bellhotelsandwich.co.uk

Self-Catering
Mr A Vincent, Golding Hop Farm, Bewley Lane, Plaxtol, SEVENOAKS, Kent TN15 0PS
Tel: 01732 885432
• e-mail: info@goldinghopfarm.com
• website: www.goldinghopfarm.com

•LINCOLNSHIRE

Lodges / Touring Caravan Park
Mr & Mrs A Potts, Walnut Lake Lodges & Camping Park, Main Road, Algarkirk, BOSTON, Lincs PE20 2LQ
Tel: 01205 460482
• e-mail: mariawalnutlakes@yahoo.co.uk
• website: www.walnutlakes.co.uk

www.holidayguides.com

202 WEBSITE DIRECTORY

Lodges / Touring Caravan Park
Mrs D Corradine, Woodland Waters, Willoughby Road, Ancaster, GRANTHAM, Lincs NG2 3RT
Tel: 01400 230888
• e-mail: info@woodlandwaters.co.uk
• website: www.woodlandwaters.co.uk

Farm B & B / Self-catering cottage
Mrs C.E. Harrison, Baumber Park, Baumber, HORNCASTLE, Lincolnshire LN9 5NE
Tel: 01507 578235/07977 722376
• e-mail: mail@baumberpark.com
  mail@gathmanscottage.co.uk
• website: www.baumberpark.com
  www.gathmanscottage.co.uk

Self Catering / B & B
Mr A Tuxworth, Poachers Hideaway Holiday Cottages, Flintwood Farm, Belchford, HORNCASTLE, Lincolnshire LN9 5QN
Tel: 01507 533555
• e-mail: info@poachershideaway.com
• website: www.poachershideaway.com

Farmhouse B & B
S Evans, Willow Farm, Thorpe Fendykes, SKEGNESS, Lincolnshire PE24 4QH
Tel: 01754 830316
• e-mail: willowfarmhols@aol.com
• website: www.willowfarmholidays.co.uk

B & B
Mrs Hodgkinson, Kirkstead Oldmill Cottage, Tattershall Road, WOODHALL SPA, Lincolnshire LN10 6UQ
Tel: 01526 353637
• e-mail: barbara@woodhallspa.com
• website: www.woodhallspa.com

Hotel
Petwood Hotel, Stixwould Road, WOODHALL SPA, Lincolnshire LN10 6QG
Tel: 01526 352411
• e-mail: reception@petwood.co.uk
• website: www.petwood.co.uk

•MERSEYSIDE

Guest House
Holme Leigh Guest House, 93 Woodcroft Road, Wavertree, LIVERPOOL, Merseyside L15 2HG
Tel: 0151 734 2216
• e-mail: info@holmeleigh.com
• website: www.holmeleigh.com

•NORFOLK

Hotel
The Hoste Arms, The Green, BURNHAM MARKET, Norfolk PE31 8HD
Tel: 01328 738777
• e-mail: reception@hostearms.co.uk
• website: www.hostearms.co.uk

Self-Catering
Blue Riband Holidays, HEMSBY, Great Yarmouth, Norfolk NR29 4HA
Tel: 01493 730445
• website: www.BlueRibandHolidays.co.uk

Board /Farm
Mrs L Mack, Hempstead Hall, HOLT, Norfolk NR25 6TN
Tel: 01263 712224
• website: www.hempsteadhall.co.uk

Hotel
The Stuart House Hotel, 35 Goodwins Road, KING'S LYNN, Norfolk PE30 5QX
Tel: 01553 772169
• e-mail: reception@stuarthousehotel.co.uk
• website: www.stuarthousehotel.co.uk

Self-catering
Scarning Dale, Dale Road, SCARNING, Dereham, Norfolk NR19 2QN
Tel: 01362 687269
• e-mail: jean@scarningdale.co.uk
• website: www.scarningdale.co.uk

Self-Catering
Winterton Valley Holidays, Edward Road, WINTERTON-ON-SEA, Norfolk NR29 4BX
Contact: 15 Kingston Avenue, Caister-on-Sea, Norfolk NR30 5ET
Tel: 01493 377175
• e-mail: info@wintertonvalleyholidays.com
• website: www.wintertonvalleyholidays.co.uk

•NORTHUMBERLAND

Inn
The Bay Horse Inn, West Woodburn, HEXHAM, Northumberland NE48 2RX
Tel: 01434 2710218
• e-mail: enquiry@bayhorseinn.org
• website: www.bayhorseinn.org

Self Catering
Mr A. P. Coatsworth, Gallowhill Farm, Whalton, MORPETH, Northumberland NE61 3TX
Tel: 01661 881241
• website: www.gallowhillfarm.co.uk

FHG Guides

Self Catering
Mrs J Younger, Burradon Farm Houses & Cottages, Burradon Farm, Cramlington, NEWCASTLE-ON-TYNE, Northumberland NE23 7ND
Tel: 0191 2683203
• e-mail: judy@burradonfarm.co.uk
• website: www.burradonfarm.co.uk

• NOTTINGHAMSHIRE

Caravan & Camping Park
Orchard Park, Marnham Road, Tuxford, NEWARK, Nottinghamshire NG22 0PY
Tel: 01777 870228
• e-mail: info@orchardcaravanpark.co.uk
• website: www.orchardcaravanpark.co.uk

B & B
Willow House, Burton Joyce, NOTTINGHAM, NG14 5FD Nottinghamshire
Tel: 01159 312070 / 07816 347706
• website: www.willowhousebedandbreakfast.co.uk

• OXFORDSHIRE

Leisure Park
Cotswold Wildlife Park, BURFORD, Oxfordshire OX18 4JN
Tel: 01993 825728
• website: www.cotswoldwildlifepark.co.uk

B & B / Guest House
June Collier, Colliers, 55 Nethercote Road, Tackley, KIDLINGTON, Oxfordshire, OX5 3AT
Tel: 01869 331255 / 07790 338325
• e-mail: colliers.bnb@virgin.net
• website: www.colliersbnb.com

B & B / Self Catering
Julia Tanner, Little Acre, 4 High Street, Tetsworth, THAME, Oxfordshire OX9 7AT
Tel: 01844 281423
• e-mail: julia@little-acre.co.uk
          info@theholliesthame.co.uk
• website: www.little-acre.co.uk
           www.theholliesthame.co.uk

• SHROPSHIRE

Hotel
Longmynd Hotel, Cunnery Rd, CHURCH STRETTON, Shropshire SY6 6AG
Tel: 01694 722244
• e-mail: info@longmynd.co.uk
• website: www.longmynd.co.uk

Self Catering
Mrs N Adams, The Anchorage, Anchor, Newcastle-on-Clun, CRAVEN ARMS, Shropshire S77 8PR
Tel: 01686 670737
• e-mail: nancynewcwm@btinternet.com
• website: www.adamsanchor.co.uk

Self-Catering
Clive & Cynthia Prior, Mocktree Barns Holiday Cottages, Leintwardine, LUDLOW, Shropshire SY7 0LY
Tel: 01547 540441
• e-mail: mocktreebarns@care4free.net
• website: www.mocktreeholidays.co.uk

Self-Catering
Jane Cronin, Sutton Court Farm Cottages, Sutton Court Farm, Little Sutton, LUDLOW, Shropshire SY8 2AJ
Tel: 01584 861305
• e-mail: enquiries@suttoncourtfarm.co.uk
• website: www.suttoncourtfarm.co.uk

• SOMERSET

Farm / Guest House / Self-Catering
Jackie Bishop, Toghill House Farm, Freezing Hill, Wick, Near BATH, Somerset BS30 5RT
Tel: 01225 891261
• e-mail: accommodation@toghillhousefarm.co.uk
• website: www.toghillhousefarm.co.uk

Guest House
Mrs C Bryson, Walton Villa, 3 Newbridge Hill, BATH, Somerset BA1 3PW
Tel: 01225 482792
• e-mail: walton.villa@virgin.net
• website: www.walton.izest.com

Self-Catering
Westward Rise Holiday Park, South Road, BREAN, Burnham-on-Sea, Somerset TA8 2RD
Tel: 01278 751310
• e-mail: info@westwardrise.com
• website: www.westwardrise.com

Self-Catering
Leone & Brian Martin, Riscombe Farm Holiday Cottages, Riscombe Farm, EXFORD, Minehead, Somerset TA24 7NH
Tel: 01643 831480
• e-mail: brian@riscombe.co.uk
• website: www.riscombe.co.uk

Self-Catering / Holiday Park / Touring Pitches
Mary Randle, St Audries Bay Holiday Club, MINEHEAD, Somerset TA4 4DA
Tel: 01984 632515
• e-mail: info@staudriesbay.co.uk
• website: www.staudriesbay.co.uk

204 WEBSITE DIRECTORY

Farm / B & B
North Down Farm, Pyncombe Lane, Wiveliscombe, TAUNTON, Somerset TA4 2BL
Tel: 01984 623730
• e-mail: jennycope@btinternet.com
• website: www.north-down-farm.co.uk

B & B
The Old Mill, Netherclay, Bishop's Hull, TAUNTON, Somerset TA1 5AB
Tel: 01823 289732
• website: www.theoldmillbandb.co.uk / www.bandbtaunton.co.uk

Farm / Guest House
G. Clark, Yew Tree Farm, THEALE, Near Wedmore, Somerset BS28 4SN
Tel: 01934 712475
• e-mail: enquiries@yewtreefarmbandb.co.uk
• website: www.yewtreefarmbandb.co.uk

B & B
Mrs S Crane, Birdwood, Bath Road, WELLS, Somerset BA5 3EW
Tel: 01749 679250
• e-mail: susancrane@mbzonline.net
• website: www.birdwood-bandb.co.uk

Caravan
C G Thomas, Ardnave Holiday Park, Kewstoke, WESTON-SUPER-MARE, Somerset BS22 9XJ
Tel: 01934 622319
• e-mail: enquiries@ardnaveholidaypark.co.uk
• website: www.ardnaveholidaypark.co.uk

• STAFFORDSHIRE

Caravan & Camping
Star Caravan & Camping Park, Woodside Lodge, Ramshorn, Near ALTON TOWERS, Staffordshire ST10 3DW
Tel: 01538 702219
• website: www.starcaravanpark.co.uk

Farm B & B / Self-Catering
Mrs M. Hiscoe-James, Offley Grove Farm, Adbaston, ECCLESHALL, Staffs ST20 0QB
Tel: 01785 280205
• e-mail: enquiries@offleygrovefarm.co.uk
• website: www.offleygrovefarm.co.uk

Self-Catering
T.A. Mycock, Rosewood Cottage, Lower Berkhamsytch, Bottom House, Near LEEK, Staffordshire ST13 7QP
Tel: 01538 308213
• website: www.rosewoodcottage.co.uk

• SUFFOLK

Self-Catering
Annie's Cottage, BUNGAY, Suffolk
Contact: Mrs L Morton, Hill Farm, Beccles, Suffolk NR34 8JE
Tel: 01956 781240
• website: www.hillfarmholidays.com

B & B / Guest House
Dunstin Guest House, 8 Springfield Road, BURY ST EDMUNDS, Suffolk IP33 3AN
Tel: 01284 767981
• e-mail: anndakin@btconnect.com
• website: www.dunstonguesthouse.co.uk

B & B
Mrs Sarah Kindred, High House Farm, Cransford, Woodbridge, FRAMLINGHAM, Suffolk IP13 9PD
Tel: 01728 663461
• e-mail: b&b@highhousefarm.co.uk
• website: www.highhousefarm.co.uk

Self-Catering
Kessingland Cottages, Rider Haggard Lane, KESSINGLAND, Suffolk.
Contact: S. Mahmood, 156 Bromley Road, Beckenham, Kent BR3 6PG
Tel: 020 8650 0539
• e-mail: jeeptrek@kjti.co.uk
• website: www.k-cottage.co.uk

Self-Catering / Caravan
Mr D. Westgate, Beach Farm Holiday Park, Arbor Lane, Pakefield, LOWESTOFT, Suffolk NR33 7BD
Tel: 01502 572794
• e-mail: beachfarmpark@aol.com
• website: www.beachfarmpark.co.uk

• SURREY

Self-Catering / B & B
Mrs J Howell, Little Orchard B & B, 152 London Road North, Merstham, REDHILL, Surrey RH1 3AA
Tel: 01737 558707
• e-mail: jackie@littleorchardbandb.co.uk
• website: www.littleorchardbandb.co.uk

• EAST SUSSEX

Self-Catering
Best of Brighton & Sussex Cottages, Laureens Walk, Nevill Road, Rottingdean, BRIGHTON, East Sussex BN2 7HG
Tel: 01273 308779
• e-mail: enquiries@bestofbrighton.co.uk
• website: www.bestofbrighton.co.uk

FHG Guides

B & B
Maon Hotel, 26 Upper Rock Gardens, BRIGHTON, East Sussex BN2 1QE
Tel: 01273 694400
• e-mail: maonhotel@aol.com
• website: www.maonhotel.co.uk

Self-Catering
"Pekes", CHIDDINGLY, East Sussex
Contact: Eva Morris, 124 Elm Park Mansions, Park Walk, London SW10 0AR
Tel: 020 7352 8088
• e-mail: pekes.afa@virgin.net
• website: www.pekesmanor.com

Guest House / Self-Catering
Longleys Farm Cottage, Harebeating Lane, HAILSHAM, East Sussex BN27 1ER
Tel: 01323 841227
• website: www.longleysfarmcottage.co.uk

Hotel
Grand Hotel, Grand Parade, St Leonards, HASTINGS, East Sussex TN38 0DD
Tel: 01424 428510
• e-mail: info@grandhotelhastings.co.uk
• website: www.grandhotelhastings.co.uk

• WEST SUSSEX

Self-Catering
Mrs M. W. Carreck, New Hall Holiday Flat and Cottage, New Hall Lane, Small Dole, HENFIELD, West Sussex BN5 9YJ
Tel: 01273 492546
• e-mail: norman.carreck@btinternet.com
• website: www.newhallcottage.co.uk

•WARWICKSHIRE

Caravan Touring Park
Dodwell Park, Evesham Road, STRATFORD-UPON-AVON, Warwickshire CV37 9SR
Tel: 01784 204957
• e-mail: enquiries@dodwellpark.co.uk
• website: www.dodwellpark.co.uk

•EAST YORKSHIRE

Hotel
The Old Mill Hotel, Mill Lane, Longtoft, DRIFFIELD, East Yorkshire YO25 3BQ
Tel: 01377 267284
• e-mail: enquiries@old-mill-hotel.co.uk
• website: www.old-mill-hotel.co.uk

•NORTH YORKSHIRE

Farmhouse B & B
Mrs Julie Clarke, Middle Farm, Woodale, COVERDALE, Leyburn, North Yorkshire DL8 4TY • Tel: 01969 640271
• e-mail: j-a-clarke@hotmail.co.uk
• www.yorkshirenet.co.uk/stayat/middlefarm/index.htm

Farm
Mrs Linda Tindall, Rowantree Farm, Fryup Road, Ainthorpe, DANBY, Whitby, North Yorkshire YO21 2LE • Tel: 01287 660396
• e-mail: krbsatindall@aol.com
• website: www.rowantreefarm.co.uk

Farmhouse B&B
Mr & Mrs Richardson, Egton Banks Farmhouse, GLAISDALE, Whitby, North Yorkshire YO21 2QP
Tel: 01947 897289
e-mail: egtonbanksfarm@btconnect.com
•website: www.egtonbanksfarm.agriplus.net

Self-Catering / Lodges & Caravans
Reynard Crag Holiday Park, Reynard Crag Lane, High Birstwith, Near HARROGATE, North Yorkshire HG3 2JQ
Tel: 01423 772828 / 07793 049567
• e-mail: reynardcrag@btconnect.com
• website: www.reynardcragpark.co.uk

Guest House
The New Inn Motel, Main Street, HUBY, York, North Yorkshire YO61 1HQ
Tel: 01347 810219
• enquiries@newinnmotel.freeserve.co.uk
• website: www.newinnmotel.co.uk

Self-Catering
Allaker in Coverdale, West Scrafton, LEYBURN, North Yorkshire DL8 4RM
Contact: Mr Adrian Cave, 21 Kenilworth Road, London W5 5PA Tel: 020 856 74862
• e-mail: ac@adriancave.com
• www.adriancave.com/allaker

Self-Catering
Abbey Holiday Cottages, MIDDLESMOOR. 12 Panorama Close, Pateley Bridge, Harrogate, North Yorkshire HG3 5NY
Tel: 01423 712062
• e-mail: info@abbeyhallcottages.com
• website: www.abbeyholidaycottages.co.uk

Self-Catering
Waterfront House, RIPON
Contact: Mrs C. Braddon, Chantry Bells, Chantry Court, Ripley, Harrogate HG3 3AD
Tel: 01423 770704
• e-mail: chris1.braddon@virgin.net
• website: www.dalesholidayripon.co.uk

www.holidayguides.com

Guest House / Self-Catering
Sue & Tony Hewitt, Harmony Country Lodge, 80 Limestone Road, Burniston, SCARBOROUGH, North Yorkshire YO13 0DG
Tel: 0800 2985840
• e-mail: mail@harmonylodge.net
• website: www.harmonycountrylodge.co.uk

Self-Catering
Mrs Jones, New Close Farm, Kirkby Malham, SKIPTON, North Yorkshire BD23 4DP
Tel: 01729 830240
• e-mail: brendajones@newclosefarmyorkshire.co.uk
• website: www.newclosefarmyorkshire.co.uk

Self-Catering
Greenhouses Farm Cottages, Near WHITBY.
Contact: Mr J.N. Eddleston, Greenhouses Farm, Lealholm, Near Whitby, North Yorkshire YO21 2AD. Tel: 01947 897486
• e-mail: n_eddleston@yahoo.com
• www.greenhouses-farm-cottages.co.uk

Guest House
Mr & Mrs R Brew, The Arches, 8 Havelock Place, WHITBY, North Yorkshire YO21 3ER
Tel: 0800 915 4256 / 01947 601880
• e-mail: archeswhitby@freeola.com
• website: www.whitbyguesthouses.co.uk

B & B
Mr & Mrs Leedham, York House, 62 Heworth Green, YORK, North Yorkshire YO31 7TQ
Tel: 01904 427070
• e-mail: yorkhouse.bandb@tiscali.co.uk
• website: www.yorkhouseyork.co.uk

Self-Catering
York Lakeside Lodges Ltd, Moor Lane, YORK, North Yorkshire YO24 2QU
Tel: 01904 702346
• e-mail: neil@yorklakesidelodges.co.uk
• website: www.yorklakesidelodges.co.uk

Looking for holiday accommodation?
for details of hundreds of properties throughout the UK visit:
www.holidayguides.com

SCOTLAND

ABERDEEN, BANFF & MORAY

Hotel
Glen Lui Hotel, 14 Invercauld Road, BALLATER, Aberdeenshire AB35 5PP
Tel: 01339 755402
• e-mail: info@glen-lui-hotel.co.uk
• website: www.glen-lui-hotel.co.uk

ANGUS & DUNDEE

Golf Club
Edzell Golf Club, High Street, EDZELL, Brechin, Angus DD9 7TF
Tel: 01356 648462
• e-mail: secretary@edzellgolfclub.net
• website: www.edzellgolfclub.net

ARGYLL & BUTE

Self-Catering
Ardtur Cottages, APPIN, Argyll PA38 4DD
Tel: 01631 730223
• e-mail: pery@btinternet.com
• website: www.ardturcottages.com

Self-Catering
Blarghour Farm Cottages, Blarghour Farm, By Dalmally, INVERARAY, Argyll PA33 1BW
Tel: 01866 833246
• e-mail: blarghour@btconnect.com
• website: www.self-catering-argyll.co.uk

Self-Catering
Inchmurrin Island Self-Catering Holidays, Inchmurrin Island, LOCH LOMOND G63 0JY
Tel: 01389 850245
• e-mail: scotts@inchmurrin-lochlomond.com
• website: www.inchmurrin-lochlomond.com

Self-Catering
Colin Mossman, Lagnakeil Lodges, Lerags, OBAN, Argyll PA34 4SE
Tel: 01631 562746
• e-mail: info@lagnakeil.co.uk
• website: www.lagnakeil.co.uk

Hotel
Falls of Lora Hotel, Connel Ferry, By OBAN, Argyll PA37 1PB
Tel: 01631 710483
• e-mail: enquiries@fallsoflora.com
• website: www.fallsoflora.com

Self-Catering
Airdeny Chalets, Glen Lonan, TAYNUILT, Oban, Argyll PA35 1HY Tel: 01866 822648
• e-mail: jenifer@airdenychalets.co.uk
• website: www.airdenychalets.co.uk

•AYRSHIRE & ARRAN

Farmhouse / B & B
Mrs Nancy Cuthbertson, West Tannacrieff, Fenwick, KILMARNOCK, Ayrshire KA3 6AZ
Tel: 01560 600258
• e-mail: westtannacrieff@btopenworld.com
• website: www.smoothhound.co.uk/hotels/westtannacrieff.html

•BORDERS

Guest House
Mr A & Mrs C Swanston, Ferniehirst Mill Lodge, JEDBURGH, Roxburghshire TD8 6PQ
Tel: 01835 863279
• e-mail: ferniehirstmill@aol.com
• website: www.ferniehirstmill.co.uk

Self-Catering
Mrs C. M. Kilpatrick, Slipperfield House, WEST LINTON, Peeblesshire EH46 7AA
Tel: 01968 660401
• e-mail: cottages@slipperfield.com
• website: www.slipperfield.com

•DUMFRIES & GALLOWAY

Self-Catering
Barend Holiday Village, Barend Farmhouse, SANDYHILLS, Dalbeattie, Dumfries & Galloway DG5 4NU
Tel: 01387 780663
• e-mail: info@barendholidayvillage.co.uk
• website: www.barendholidayvillage.co.uk

Self-Catering
Ae Farm Cottages, Gubhill Farm, Ae, DUMFRIES, Dumfriesshire DG1 1RL
Tel: 01387 860648
• e-mail: gill@gubhill.co.uk
• website: www.aefarmcottages.co.uk

Farm / Camping & Caravans / Self-Catering
Barnsoul Farm Holidays, Barnsoul Farm, Shawhead, DUMFRIES, Dumfriesshire DG2 9SQ. Tel: 01387 730249
• e-mail: barnsouldg@aol.com
• website: www.barnsoulfarm.co.uk

WEBSITE DIRECTORY 207

Self-Catering
Rusko, GATEHOUSE OF FLEET, Castle Douglas, Dumfriesshire DG7 2BS
Tel: 01557 814215
• e-mail: info@ruskoholidays.co.uk
• website: www.ruskoholidays.co.uk

Self-Catering
Hope Cottage, THORNHILL, Dumfriesshire G3 5BJ
Contact: Mrs S. Stannett Tel: 01848 331510
• e-mail: a.stann@btinternet.com
• website: www.hopecottage.co.uk

•EDINBURGH & LOTHIANS

Guest House
International Guest House, 37 Mayfield Gardens, EDINBURGH EH9 2BX
Tel: 0131 667 2511
• e-mail: intergh1@yahoo.co.uk
• website: www.accommodation-edinburgh.com

•FIFE

Self-Catering
Pitcairlie House, AUCHTERMUCHTY, Fife KY14 6EU
Tel: 01337 827418
• e-mail: reservations@pitcairlie-leisure.co.uk
• website: www.pitcairlie-leisure.co.uk

•HIGHLANDS

Self-Catering
Cairngorm Highland Bungalows, AVIEMORE. Contact: Linda Murray, 29 Grampian View, Aviemore, Inverness-shire PH22 1TF
Tel: 01479 810653
• e-mail: linda.murray@virgin.net
• website: www.cairngorm-bungalows.co.uk

Self-Catering
Frank & Juliet Spencer-Nairn, Culligran Cottages, Struy, Near BEAULY, Inverness-shire IV4 7JX . Tel: 01463 761285
• e-mail: info@culligrancottages.co.uk
• website: www.culligrancottages.co.uk

Self-Catering
Tyndrum, BOAT OF GARTEN, Inverness-shire Contact: Mrs Naomi C. Clark, Dochlaggie, Boat of Garten PH24 3BU
Tel: 01479 831242
• e-mail: dochlaggie99@aol.com

Please mention this publication when enquiring about accommodation.

WEBSITE DIRECTORY

Self-Catering
Carol Hughes, Glenurquhart Lodges, Balnain, DRUMNADROCHIT, Inverness-shire IV63 6TJ
Tel: 01456 476234
• e-mail: carol@glenurquhartlodges.co.uk
• website: www.glenurquhart-lodges.co.uk

Hotel
The Clan MacDuff Hotel, Achintore Road, FORT WILLIAM, Inverness-shire PH33 6RW
Tel: 01397 702341
• e-mail: reception@clanmacduff.co.uk
• website: www.clanmacduff.co.uk

Caravan & Camping
Auchnahillin Caravan & Camping Park, Daviot East, INVERNESS, Inverness-shire IV2 5XQ • Tel: 01463 772286
• e-mail: info@auchnahillin.co.uk
• website: www.auchnahillin.co.uk

Hotel
Dunain Park Hotel, Loch Ness Road, INVERNESS, Inverness-shire IV3 8JN
Tel: 01463 230512
• e-mail: info@dunainparkhotel.co.uk
• website: www.dunainparkhotel.co.uk

Hotel
Kintail Lodge Hotel, Glenshiel, SHIEL BRIDGE, Ross-shire IV40 8HL
Tel: 01599 511275
• e-mail: kintaillodgehotel@btinternet.com
• website: www.kintaillodgehotel.co.uk

Hotel
Whitebridge Hotel, Whitebridge, LOCH NESS, Inverness-shire IV2 6UN
Tel: 01456 486226
• e-mail: info@whitebridgehotel.co.uk
• website: www.whitebridgehotel.co.uk

Self-Catering
Innes Maree Bungalows, POOLEWE, Ross-shire IV22 2JU • Tel: 01445 781454
• e-mail: info@poolewebungalows.com
• website: www.poolewebungalows.com

Self-Catering
Mr & Mrs S Dennis, Riverside House, Invergloy, SPEAN BRIDGE, Inverness-shire PH34 4DY • Tel: 01397 712684
• e-mail: enquiries@riversidelodge.org.uk
• website: www.riversidelodge.org.uk

•LANARKSHIRE

Caravan & Holiday Home Park
Mount View Caravan Park, Station Road, ABINGTON, South Lanarkshire ML12 6RW
Tel: 01864 502808
• e-mail: info@mountviewcaravanpark.co.uk
• website: www.mountviewcaravanpark.co.uk

•PERTH & KINROSS

Self-Catering
Loch Tay Lodges, Remony, Acharn, ABERFELDY, Perthshire PH15 2HR
Tel: 01887 830209
• e-mail: remony@btinternet.com
• website: www.lochtaylodges.co.uk

Self-Catering
Laighwood Holidays, Laighwood, DUNKELD, Perthshire PH8 0HB
Tel: 01350 724241
• e-mail: holidays@laighwood.co.uk
• website: www.laighwood.co.uk

Self- Catering
Atholl Cottage, Killiecrankie, PITLOCHRY, Perthshire
Contact: Mrs Joan Troup, Dalnasgadh, Killiecrankie, Pitlochry, Perthshire PH16 5LN
Tel: 01796 470017
• e-mail: info@athollcottage.co.uk
• website: www.athollcottage.co.uk

Self-Catering Cottages
Dalmunzie Highland Cottages, SPITTAL OF GLENSHEE, Blairgowrie, Perthshire PH10 7QE Tel: 01250 885226
• e-mail: enquiries@dalmunziecottages.com
• website: www.dalmunziecottages.com

•STIRLING & TROSSACHS

Hotel
Culcreuch Castle Hotel & Estate, Kippen Road, FINTRY, Stirlingshire G63 0LW
Tel: 01360 860555
• e-mail: info@culcreuch.com
• website: www.culcreuch.com

•ORKNEY ISLANDS

Caravan & Camping
Point of Ness, STROMNESS, Orkney
Tel: 01856 850262
• e-mail: recreation@orkney.gov.uk
• website: www.orkney.gov.uk

Caravan & Camping
Pickaquoy Centre, KIRKWALL, Orkney
Tel: 01856 879900
• e-mail: enquiries@pickaquoy.com
• website: www.pickaquoy.co.uk

www.holidayguides.com

•WALES

Self-Catering
Quality Cottages, Cerbid, Solva,
HAVERFORDWEST, Pembrokeshire SA62 6YE
Tel: 01348 837871
- e-mail: reserve@qualitycottages.co.uk
- website: www.qualitycottages.co.uk

•ANGLESEY & GWYNEDD

Self-Catering / Caravan Site
Bryn Gloch Caravan and Camping Park,
Betws Garmon, CAERNARFON, Gwynedd
LL54 7YY Tel: 01286 650216
- e-mail: eurig@bryngloch.co.uk
- website: www.bryngloch.co.uk

Self-Catering Chalet
Chalet at Glan Gwna Holiday Park, Caethro,
CAERNARFON, Gwynedd
Contact: Mr H A Jones, Menai Bridge,
Caernarfon, Gwynedd LL59 5LN
Tel: 01248 712045
- e-mail: hajones@northwales-chalet.co.uk
- website: www.northwales-chalet.co.uk

Self-Catering
Parc Wernol, Chwilog Fawr, Chwilog,
Pwllheli, CRICCIETH, Gwynedd LL53 6SW
Tel: 01766 810506
- website: www.wernol.co.uk

Self-Catering
Mrs E A Williams, Tyddyn Heilyn, Chwilog,
PWLLHELI, Gwynedd LL53 6SW
Tel: 01766 810441
- e-mail: tyddyn.heilyn@tiscali.co.uk

Caravan & Camping Site
Marian Rees, Dôl Einion, Tal-y-Llyn, TYWYN,
Gwynedd LL36 9AJ
Tel: 01654 761312
- e-mail: marianrees@tiscali.co.uk

•NORTH WALES

Guest House
Park Hill/Gwesty Bryn Parc, Llanrwst Road,
BETWS-Y-COED, Conwy LL24 0HD
Tel: 01690 710510
- e-mail: welcome@park-hill.co.uk
- website: www.park-hill.co.uk

Guest House
Mr D E Morgan, The Northwood, Rhos
Road, Rhos-on-Sea, COLWYN BAY, Conwy
LL28 4RS
Tel: 01492 549931
- e-mail: welcome@thenorthwood.co.uk
- website: www.thenorthwood.co.uk

• PEMBROKESHIRE

Self-Catering
Timberhill Farm, BROAD HAVEN,
Pembrokeshire SA62 3LZ
Contact: Mrs L Ashton, 10 St Leonards
Road, Thames Ditton, Surrey KT7 0RJ
Tel: 02083 986349
- e-mail: lejash@aol.com
- website: www.33timberhill.com

Hotel
Michael & Suzy Beales, Castell Malgwyn
Hote, LLechryd, CARDIGAN, Pembrokeshire
SA43 2QA
Tel: 01239 682382
- e-mail: reception@malgwyn.co.uk
- website: www.castellmalgwyn.co.uk

Country House
Angelica Rees, Heathfield Mansion, Letterston,
Near FISHGUARD, Pembrokeshire SA62 5EG
Tel: 01348 840263
- e-mail: angelica.rees@virgin.net
- website: www.heathfieldaccommodation.co.uk

Guest House
Ivybridge, Drim Mill, Dyffryn, Goodwick,
FISHGUARD, Pembrokeshire SA64 0JT
Tel: 01348 875366
- website: www.ivybridgeleisure.co.uk

Caravan & Camping
Nolton Cross Caravan Park, NOLTON
HAVEN, Haverfordwest, Pembrokeshire
SA62 3NP
Tel:01437 710701
- e-mail: info@noltoncross-holidays.co.uk
- website: www.noltoncross-holidays.co.uk

Self-Catering
Capri Cottage, The Ridgeway,
SAUNDERSFOOT, Pembrokeshire
SA69 9LD.
Contact: R Reed, Trevayne Farm,
Saundersfoot, Pembrokeshire SA69 9LD
Tel: 01834 813402
- e-mail: info@camping-pembrokeshire.co.uk
- www.saundersfoot-holidaycottage.co.uk

210 WEBSITE DIRECTORY

Self-catering
Ffynnon Ddofn, Llanon, Llanrhian, Near ST DAVIDS, Pembrokeshire. Contact: Mrs B. Rees White, Brick House Farm, Burnham Road, Woodham Mortimer, Maldon, Essex CM9 6SR. Tel: 01245 224611
- e-mail: daisypops@madasafish.com
- website: www.ffynnonddofn.co.uk

Guest House
Mrs M. Jones, Lochmeyler Farm, Pen-Y-Cwm, Near Solva, ST DAVIDS, Pembrokeshire SA62 6LL
Tel: 01348 837724
- e-mail: stay@lochmeyler.co.uk
- website: www.lochmeyler.co.uk

Self-Catering
Mrs M. Pike, Porthidaly Farm Holiday Cottages, Abereiddy, ST DAVIDS, Pembrokeshire SA62 6DR
Tel: 01348 831004
- e-mail: m.pike@porthiddy.com
- website: www.porthiddy.com

•POWYS

Self-Catering
Old Stables Cottage & Old Dairy, Lane Farm, Paincastle, Builth Wells, HAY-ON-WYE, Powys LD2 3JS
Tel: 01497 851 605
- e-mail: lanefarm@onetel.com
- website: www.lane-farm.co.uk

Self-Catering / Guest House
Park House Motel, LLLANDRINDOD WELLS, Powys LO1 6RF
Tel: 01597 851201 / 07918 660647
- website: www.parkhousemotel.net

•SOUTH WALES

Caravan Park
Mr G. Watkins, Wernddu Caravan Park, Old Ross Road, ABERGAVENNY, Monmouthshire NP7 8NG
Tel:01873 856223
- e-mail: info@wernddu-golf-club.co.uk
- website: www.wernddu-golf-club.co.uk

Self-Catering Cottages
Mrs Norma James, Wyrloed Lodge Holiday Cottages, 3 Wyrloed Lodge Cottage, Manmoel, BLACKWOOD, Caerphilly, South Wales NP12 0RN
Tel: 01495 371198
- e-mail: norma.james@btinternet.com
- website: www.wyrloedlodge.com

Country House Hotel
Egerton Grey Country House Hotel, Porthkerry, Rhoose, CARDIFF, Vale of Glamorgan, South Wales CF62 3BZ
Tel: 01446 711666
- e-mail: info@egertongrey.co.uk
- website: www.egertongrey.co.uk

Self-Catering
Cwrt-y-Gaer, Wolvesnewton, CHEPSTOW, Monmouthshire, South Wales NP16 6PR
Tel: 01291 650700
- e-mail: john.llewellyn11@btinternet.com
- website: www.cwrt-y-gaer.co.uk

FHG Guides

Other specialised holiday guides from FHG
PUBS & INNS OF BRITAIN • **COUNTRY HOTELS** OF BRITAIN
SELF-CATERING HOLIDAYS IN BRITAIN
THE GOLF GUIDE WHERE TO PLAY, WHERE TO STAY
500 GREAT PLACES TO STAY IN BRITAIN • **FAMILY BREAKS** IN BRITAIN
BED & BREAKFAST STOPS IN BRITAIN • **PETS WELCOME!**
WEEKEND & SHORT BREAKS IN BRITAIN •

Published annually: available in all good bookshops or direct from the publisher:
FHG Guides, Abbey Mill Business Centre, Seedhill, Paisley PA1 1TJ
Tel: 0141 887 0428 • Fax: 0141 889 7204
e-mail: admin@fhguides.co.uk • www.holidayguides.com

211

FHG ·K·U·P·E·R·A·R·D·
READERS' OFFER 2010

LEIGHTON BUZZARD RAILWAY
Page's Park Station, Billington Road,
Leighton Buzzard, Bedfordshire LU7 4TN
Tel: 01525 373888
e-mail: station@lbngrs.org.uk
www.buzzrail.co.uk

One FREE adult/child with full-fare adult ticket
Valid 14/3/2010 - 31/10/2010

NOT TO BE USED IN CONJUNCTION WITH ANY OTHER OFFER

FHG ·K·U·P·E·R·A·R·D·
READERS' OFFER 2010

BEKONSCOT MODEL VILLAGE & RAILWAY
Warwick Road, Beaconsfield,
Buckinghamshire HP9 2PL
Tel: 01494 672919
e-mail: info@bekonscot.co.uk
www.bekonscot.co.uk

One child FREE when accompanied by full-paying adult
Valid February to October 2010

NOT TO BE USED IN CONJUNCTION WITH ANY OTHER OFFER

FHG ·K·U·P·E·R·A·R·D·
READERS' OFFER 2010

BUCKINGHAMSHIRE RAILWAY CENTRE
Quainton Road Station, Quainton,
Aylesbury HP22 4BY
Tel: 01296 655720
e-mail: office@bucksrailcentre.org
www.bucksrailcentre.org

One child FREE with each full-paying adult
Not valid for Special Events or Day Out with Thomas

NOT TO BE USED IN CONJUNCTION WITH ANY OTHER OFFER

FHG ·K·U·P·E·R·A·R·D·
READERS' OFFER 2010

THE RAPTOR FOUNDATION
The Heath, St Ives Road,
Woodhurst, Huntingdon, Cambs PE28 3BT
Tel: 01487 741140 • Fax: 01487 841140
e-mail: heleowl@aol.com
www.raptorfoundation.org.uk

TWO for the price of ONE
Valid until end 2010 (not Bank Holidays)

NOT TO BE USED IN CONJUNCTION WITH ANY OTHER OFFER

A 70-minute journey into the lost world of the English narrow gauge light railway. Features historic steam locomotives from many countries. **PETS MUST BE KEPT UNDER CONTROL AND NOT ALLOWED ON TRACKS**	**Open:** Sundays and Bank Holiday weekends 14 March to 31 October. Additional days in summer, and school holidays. **Directions:** on south side of Leighton Buzzard. Follow brown signs from town centre or A505/A4146 bypass.

FHG GUIDES, ABBEY MILL BUSINESS CENTRE, PAISLEY PA1 1TJ • www.holidayguides.com

Be a giant in a magical miniature world of make-believe depicting rural England in the 1930s. "A little piece of history that is forever England."	**Open:** 10am-5pm daily mid February to end October. **Directions:** Junction 16 M25, Junction 2 M40.

FHG GUIDES, ABBEY MILL BUSINESS CENTRE, PAISLEY PA1 1TJ • www.holidayguides.com

A working steam railway centre. Steam train rides, miniature railway rides, large collection of historic preserved steam locomotives, carriages and wagons.	**Open:** daily April to October 10.30am to 4.30pm. Variable programme - check website or call. **Directions:** off A41 Aylesbury to Bicester Road, 6 miles north west of Aylesbury.

FHG GUIDES, ABBEY MILL BUSINESS CENTRE, PAISLEY PA1 1TJ • www.holidayguides.com

Birds of Prey Centre offering audience participation in flying displays which are held 3 times daily. Tours, picnic area, gift shop, tearoom, craft shop.	**Open:** 10am-5pm all year except Christmas and New Year. **Directions:** follow brown tourist signs from B1040.

FHG GUIDES, ABBEY MILL BUSINESS CENTRE, PAISLEY PA1 1TJ • www.holidayguides.com

NENE VALLEY RAILWAY
Wansford Station, Stibbington,
Peterborough, Cambs PE8 6LR
Tel: 01780 784444
e-mail: nvrorg@nvr.org.uk
www.nvr.org.uk

FHG READERS' OFFER 2010

One child FREE with each full paying adult.
Valid Jan. to end Oct. 2010 (excludes galas and pre-ticketed events)

NOT TO BE USED IN CONJUNCTION WITH ANY OTHER OFFER

ANSON ENGINE MUSEUM
Anson Road, Poynton,
Cheshire SK12 1TD
Tel: 01625 874426
e-mail: enquiry@enginemuseum.org
www.enginemuseum.org

FHG READERS' OFFER 2010

Saturdays - 2 for 1 entry (when one of equal or greater value is purchased). Valid 12 April-30 Sept 2010

NOT TO BE USED IN CONJUNCTION WITH ANY OTHER OFFER

NATIONAL SEAL SANCTUARY
Gweek, Helston,
Cornwall TR12 6UG
Tel: 01326 221361
e-mail: seals@sealsanctuary.co.uk
www.sealsanctuary.co.uk

FHG READERS' OFFER 2010

TWO for ONE - on purchase of another ticket of equal or greater value. Valid until December 2010.

NOT TO BE USED IN CONJUNCTION WITH ANY OTHER OFFER

LAPPA VALLEY RAILWAY
Benny Halt, St Newlyn East,
Newquay, Cornwall TR8 5LX
Tel: 01872 510317
e-mail: info@lappavalley.co.uk
www.lappavalley.co.uk

FHG READERS' OFFER 2010

75p per person OFF up to a maximum of £3
Valid Easter to end October 2010.

NOT TO BE USED IN CONJUNCTION WITH ANY OTHER OFFER

Take a trip back in time on the delightful Nene Valley Railway with its heritage steam and diesel locomotives, There is a 7½ mile ride from Wansford to Peterborough via Yarwell, with shop, museum and excellent cafe at Wansford Station (free parking).	**Open:** please phone or see website for details. **Directions:** situated 4 miles north of Peterborough on the A1

FHG GUIDES, ABBEY MILL BUSINESS CENTRE, PAISLEY PA1 1TJ • www.holidayguides.com

As seen on TV, this multi award-winning attraction has a great deal to offer visitors. It houses the largest collection of engines in Europe, local history area, craft centre (bodging and smithy work), with changing exhibitions throughout the season.	**Open:** Easter Sunday until end October, Friday to Sunday and Bank Holidays, 10am to 5pm. **Directions:** approx 7 miles from J1 M60 and 9 miles J3 M60. Follow brown tourist signs from Poynton traffic lights.

FHG GUIDES, ABBEY MILL BUSINESS CENTRE, PAISLEY PA1 1TJ • www.holidayguides.com

Set on the beautiful Helford Estuary, the National Seal Sanctuary is Europe's busiest seal rescue centre. Every year the Sanctuary rescues and releases over 30 injured or abandoned seal pups and provides a refuge for those seals/sea lions unable to be returned to the wild.	**Open:** daily (except Christmas Day) from 10am. **Directions:** from A30 follow signs to Helston, then brown tourist signs to Seal Sanctuary.

FHG GUIDES, ABBEY MILL BUSINESS CENTRE, PAISLEY PA1 1TJ • www.holidayguides.com

Three miniature railways, plus leisure park with canoes, crazy golf, large children's play area with fort, brickpath maze, wooded walks (all inclusive). Dogs welcome (50p).	**Open:** Easter to end October **Directions:** follow brown tourist signs from A30 and A3075

FHG GUIDES, ABBEY MILL BUSINESS CENTRE, PAISLEY PA1 1TJ • www.holidayguides.com

215

FHG
K·U·P·E·R·A·R·D
READERS' OFFER 2010

PORFELL WILDLIFE PARK & SANCTUARY
Trecangate, Near Llanreath,
Liskeard,
Cornwall PL14 4RE
Tel: 01503 220211
www.porfellanimalland.co.uk

One child FREE with one paying adult per voucher
Valid 1st April-31st October 2010.

NOT TO BE USED IN CONJUNCTION WITH ANY OTHER OFFER

FHG
K·U·P·E·R·A·R·D
READERS' OFFER 2010

BRITISH CYCLING MUSEUM
The Old Station,
Camelford,
Cornwall PL32 9TZ
Tel: 01840 212811
www.camelford.org

Child FREE with one paying adult
Valid during 2010

NOT TO BE USED IN CONJUNCTION WITH ANY OTHER OFFER

FHG
K·U·P·E·R·A·R·D
READERS' OFFER 2010

TAMAR VALLEY DONKEY PARK
St Ann's Chapel, Gunnislake,
Cornwall PL18 9HW
Tel: 01822 834072
e-mail: info@donkeypark.com
www.donkeypark.com

50p OFF per person, up to 6 persons
Valid from Easter until end October 2010

NOT TO BE USED IN CONJUNCTION WITH ANY OTHER OFFER

FHG
K·U·P·E·R·A·R·D
READERS' OFFER 2010

CARS OF THE STARS MOTOR MUSEUM
Standish Street, Keswick
Cumbria CA12 5LS
Tel: 017687 73757
e-mail: cotsmm@aol.com
www.carsofthestars.com

One FREE child with two paying adults
Valid during normal opening times.

NOT TO BE USED IN CONJUNCTION WITH ANY OTHER OFFER

Porfell is home to wild and exotic animals from around the world. Idyllically situated amongst the rolling hills of south east Cornwall. It has a beautiful woodland with raised boardwalks over marsh areas, and a children's farm.	**Open:** 10am-6pm daily from April 1st to October 31st. **Directions:** A38 Liskeard, A390 for St Austell. Turn off at East Taphouse on to B3359, follow brown tourist signs.

FHG GUIDES, ABBEY MILL BUSINESS CENTRE, PAISLEY PA1 1TJ • www.holidayguides.com

The nation's foremost and largest museum of historic cycling, with over 400 examples of cycles, and 1000s of items of cycling memorabilia.	**Open:** all year, Sunday to Thursday, 10am to 5pm. **Directions:** one mile north of Camelford, B3266/B3314 crossroads.

FHG GUIDES, ABBEY MILL BUSINESS CENTRE, PAISLEY PA1 1TJ • www.holidayguides.com

Cornwall's only Donkey Sanctuary set in 14 acres overlooking the beautiful Tamar Valley. Donkey rides, goat hill, children's playgrounds, cafe and picnic area. New all-weather play barn.	**Open:** Easter to end Oct: daily 10am to 5pm. Nov to March: weekends and all school holidays 10.30am to 4.30pm **Directions:** just off A390 between Callington and Gunnislake at St Ann's Chapel.

FHG GUIDES, ABBEY MILL BUSINESS CENTRE, PAISLEY PA1 1TJ • www.holidayguides.com

This world famous motor museum features vehicles from TV and film - Chitty Chitty Bang Bang, Batmobiles, A-Team van, KITT and more. Also souvenir and autograph shop.	**Open:** 10am to 5pm February half term, and Easter to end November. Weekends only in December. **Directions:** M6 to Penrith, A66 to Keswick. Located in centre of town, by Bell Close car park.

FHG GUIDES, ABBEY MILL BUSINESS CENTRE, PAISLEY PA1 1TJ • www.holidayguides.com

FHG · K·U·P·E·R·A·R·D · READERS' OFFER 2010

THE BOND MUSEUM
Southey Hill, Keswick,
Cumbria CA12 5NR
Tel: 017687 74044
e-mail: thebondmuseum@aol.com
www.thebondmuseum.com

One FREE child with two paying adults.
Valid February to October 2010.

NOT TO BE USED IN CONJUNCTION WITH ANY OTHER OFFER

FHG · K·U·P·E·R·A·R·D · READERS' OFFER 2010

THE BEACON
West Strand, Whitehaven,
Cumbria CA28 7LY
Tel: 01946 592302 • Fax: 01946 598150
e-mail: thebeacon@copelandbc.gov.uk
www.thebeacon-whitehaven.co.uk

One FREE adult/concesssion when accompanied by one full paying
adult/concession. Under 16s free. Valid from Oct 2009 to end 2010.
Not valid for special events. Day tickets only.

NOT TO BE USED IN CONJUNCTION WITH ANY OTHER OFFER

FHG · K·U·P·E·R·A·R·D · READERS' OFFER 2010

CRICH TRAMWAY VILLAGE
Crich, Matlock
Derbyshire DE4 5DP
Tel: 01773 854321 • Fax: 01773 854320
e-mail: enquiry@tramway.co.uk
www.tramway.co.uk

One child FREE with every full-paying adult
Valid during 2010

NOT TO BE USED IN CONJUNCTION WITH ANY OTHER OFFER

FHG · K·U·P·E·R·A·R·D · READERS' OFFER 2010

THE MILKY WAY ADVENTURE PARK
The Milky Way, Clovelly,
Bideford, Devon EX39 5RY
Tel: 01237 431255
e-mail: info@themilkyway.co.uk
www.themilkyway.co.uk

10% discount on entrance charge.
Valid Easter to end October (not August).

NOT TO BE USED IN CONJUNCTION WITH ANY OTHER OFFER

For all "Bond" or car fans this is a must! Aston Martins, Lotus, even a T55 Russsian tank from the film "Goldeneye". Also cinema and shop.

Open: 10am to 5pm February to end October; weekends November and December.

Directions: from Penrith (M6) take A66 to Keswick. Free parking.

The Beacon is the Copeland area's interactive museum, tracing the area's rich history, from as far back as prehistoric times to the modern day. Enjoy panoramic views of the Georgian town and harbour from the 4th floor viewing gallery. Art gallery, gift shop, restaurant. Fully accessible.

Open: open all year (excl. 24-26 Dec) Tuesday to Sunday, plus Monday Bank Holidays.

Directions: enter Whitehaven from north or south on A595. Follow the town centre and brown museum signs; located on harbourside.

A superb family day out in the atmosphere of a bygone era. Explore the recreated period street and fascinating exhibitions. Unlimited tram rides are free with entry. Play areas, woodland walk and sculpture trail, shops, tea rooms, pub, restaurant and lots more.

Open: daily April to end October 10am to 5.30pm.

Directions: eight miles from M1 Junction 28, follow brown and white signs for "Tramway Museum".

The day in the country that's out of this world! With 5 major rides and loads of great live shows. See Merlin from 'Britain's Got Talent' 5 days a week. All rides and shows included in entrance fee.

Open: 10.30am - 6pm. Check for winter opening hours.

Directions: on the main A39 one mile from Clovelly.

FHG
·K·U·P·E·R·A·R·D·
READERS' OFFER 2010

THE BIG SHEEP
Abbotsham, Bideford,
North Devon EX39 5AP
Tel: 01237 472366 • Fax: 01237 477916
e-mail: info@thebigsheep.co.uk
www.thebigsheep.co.uk

2 for 1 admission. Valid all year

NOT TO BE USED IN CONJUNCTION WITH ANY OTHER OFFER

FHG
·K·U·P·E·R·A·R·D·
READERS' OFFER 2010

DEVONSHIRE COLLECTION OF PERIOD COSTUME
Totnes Costume Museum,
Bogan House, 43 High Street,
Totnes,
Devon TQ9 5NP

FREE child with a paying adult with voucher
Valid from Spring Bank Holiday to end of Sept 2010

NOT TO BE USED IN CONJUNCTION WITH ANY OTHER OFFER

FHG
·K·U·P·E·R·A·R·D·
READERS' OFFER 2010

WOODLANDS FAMILY THEME PARK
Blackawton, Dartmouth,
Devon TQ9 7DQ
Tel: 01803 712598 • Fax: 01803 712680
e-mail: fun@woodlandspark.com
www.woodlandspark.com

12% discount off individual admission price.
No photocopies. Valid 26 March to 7 November 2010.

NOT TO BE USED IN CONJUNCTION WITH ANY OTHER OFFER

FHG
·K·U·P·E·R·A·R·D·
READERS' OFFER 2010

COMBE MARTIN WILDLIFE & DINOSAUR PARK
Higher Leigh, Combe Martin,
North Devon EX34 0NG
Tel: 01271 882486
e-mail: info@dinosaur-park.com
www.dinosaur-park.com

One child FREE with two paying adults.
Valid February to November 2010

NOT TO BE USED IN CONJUNCTION WITH ANY OTHER OFFER

The best day of your holiday baa none! Sheep racing, dog and duck trialling, huge indoor playground, animal barn with pets' corner and lamb bottle feeding, train and tractor rides, and much more.

Open: 10am-6pm daily April to October. From Nov-March weekends and school holidays only. Please check opening times before visiting.

Directions: two miles west of Bideford, on the A39 Atlantic Highway. Look for the big flag.

FHG GUIDES, ABBEY MILL BUSINESS CENTRE, PAISLEY PA1 1TJ • www.holidayguides.com

---

Themed exhibition, changed annually, based in a Tudor house. Collection contains items of dress for women, men and children from 17th century to 1990s, from high fashion to everyday wear.

Open: Open from Spring Bank Holiday to end September. 11am to 5pm Tuesday to Friday.

Directions: centre of town, opposite Market Square. Mini bus up High Street stops outside.

FHG GUIDES, ABBEY MILL BUSINESS CENTRE, PAISLEY PA1 1TJ • www.holidayguides.com

---

A wide variety of rides, plus zoo and farm, makes a fantastic day out for all ages. Awesome indoor adventure centres, ball blasting arenas, mirror maze and soft play ensures wet days are fun. 16 family rides including white knuckle Swing Ship, electrifying Watercoasters, terrifying Toboggan Run, Superb Falconry Centre, Big Fun Farm, animals, tractor ride, weird and wonderful zoo creatures. An all-weather attraction.

Open: 26 March to 7 November 2010 open daily 9.30am. In winter open weekends and local school holidays.

Directions: 5 miles from Dartmouth on A3122. Follow brown tourist signs from A38.

FHG GUIDES, ABBEY MILL BUSINESS CENTRE, PAISLEY PA1 1TJ • www.holidayguides.com

---

*The home of the only full size animatronic T-Rex. Explore 26 acres of stunning gardens with cascading waterfalls, exotic birds and animals. Daily sea lion shows, falconry displays, lemur encounters, 3 magnificent lions, brass rubbing centre.
A great day out for all the family.*

Open: 10am to 5pm (last entry 3pm). February half term to 8th Nov.

Directions: take M5 to Junction 27. Go west along the A361 towards Barnstaple, turn right on to the A399, and then follow signs for Combe Martin and Ilfracombe.

FHG GUIDES, ABBEY MILL BUSINESS CENTRE, PAISLEY PA1 1TJ • www.holidayguides.com

FHG READERS' OFFER 2010

DINOSAUR ISLE
Culver Parade, Sandown,
Isle of Wight PO36 8QA
Tel: 01983 404344 • Fax: 01983 407502
e-mail: dinosaur@iow.gov.uk
www.dinosaurisle.com

*One child FREE when accompanied by full paying adult.
Valid from February to December 24th 2010.*

NOT TO BE USED IN CONJUNCTION WITH ANY OTHER OFFER

FHG READERS' OFFER 2010

ROMNEY, HYTHE & DYMCHURCH RAILWAY
New Romney Station,
New Romney,
Kent TN28 8PL
Tel: 01797 362353
www.rhdr.org.uk

*One child FREE with every two full paying adults.
Valid until end 2010 except on special event days.*

NOT TO BE USED IN CONJUNCTION WITH ANY OTHER OFFER

FHG READERS' OFFER 2010

CHISLEHURST CAVES
Old Hill, Chislehurst,
Kent BR7 5NL
Tel: 020 8467 3264 • Fax: 020 8295 0407
e-mail: info@chislehurstcaves.co.uk
www.chislehurstcaves.co.uk

*FREE child entry with full paying adult.
Valid until end 2010 (not Bank Holiday weekends)*

NOT TO BE USED IN CONJUNCTION WITH ANY OTHER OFFER

FHG READERS' OFFER 2010

NATURELAND SEAL SANCTUARY
North Parade, Skegness
Lincolnshire PE25 1DB
Tel: 01754 764345
e-mail: info@skegnessnatureland.co.uk
www.skegnessnatureland.co.uk

*One child admitted FREE when accompanied by full
paying adult on production of voucher. Valid to end 2010.*

NOT TO BE USED IN CONJUNCTION WITH ANY OTHER OFFER

In a spectacular pterosaur-shaped building, watching over Sandown's Blue Flag beach, is Britain's first purpose-built dinosaur museum. Walk back through fossilised time and meet life-size model dinosaurs including an animated Neovenator.	**Open:** open all year except 24-26th December and 1st January (call for opening hours Jan/Feb). Daily 10am-5pm (March-Oct), 10am-4pm (Nov-Feb). **Directions:** on B3395 coastal road.

FHG GUIDES, ABBEY MILL BUSINESS CENTRE, PAISLEY PA1 1TJ • www.holidayguides.com

Heritage steam miniature railway and model exhibition. 27 miles round trip following the Kent coastline. The railway runs from Hythe, Dymchurch, New Romney, Romney Sands and Dungeness.	**Open:** 9.45am to 6pm. Check website for details.

FHG GUIDES, ABBEY MILL BUSINESS CENTRE, PAISLEY PA1 1TJ • www.holidayguides.com

Miles of mystery and history beneath your feet! Grab a lantern and get ready for an amazing underground adventure. Your whole family can travel back in time as you explore this labyrinth of dark mysterious passageways. See the caves, church, Druid altar and more.	**Open:** Wed to Sun from 10am; last tour 4pm. Open daily during local school and Bank holidays (except Christmas). Entrance by guided tour only. **Directions:** A222 between A20 and A21; at Chislehurst Station turn into Station Approach; turn right at end, then right again into Caveside Close.

FHG GUIDES, ABBEY MILL BUSINESS CENTRE, PAISLEY PA1 1TJ • www.holidayguides.com

A specialised collection of animals including seals, penguins, tropical birds and butterflies (April to October), reptiles, aquarium, pets' corner etc. Known worldwide for rescuing orphaned and injured seal pups and returning almost 600 back to the wild.	**Open:** daily except Christmas Day, Boxing Day and New Year's Day. **Directions:** north end of Skegness seafront.

FHG GUIDES, ABBEY MILL BUSINESS CENTRE, PAISLEY PA1 1TJ • www.holidayguides.com

FHG READERS' OFFER 2010

THE WORLD OF GLASS
Chalon Way East, St Helens,
Merseyside WA10 1BX
Tel: 01744 22766 • Fax: 01744 616966
e-mail: info@worldofglass.com
www.worldofglass.com

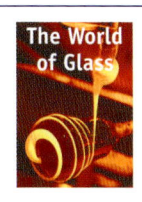

2 for 1 - one FREE with each full paying adult.
Valid until December 2010.

NOT TO BE USED IN CONJUNCTION WITH ANY OTHER OFFER

FHG READERS' OFFER 2010

NEWARK AIR MUSEUM
The Airfield, Winthorpe, Newark,
Nottinghamshire NG24 2NY
Tel: 01636 707170
e-mail: newarkair@onetel.com
www.newarkairmuseum.org

Party rate discount for every voucher (50p per person off normal admission). Valid during 2010.

NOT TO BE USED IN CONJUNCTION WITH ANY OTHER OFFER

FHG READERS' OFFER 2010

FERRY FARM PARK
Ferry Farm, Boat Lane, Hoveringham
Nottinghamshire NG14 7JP
Tel & Fax: 0115 966 4512
e-mail: graham@ferryfarm.fsnet.co.uk
www.ferryfarm.co.uk

20% OFF admission price.
Valid during 2010

NOT TO BE USED IN CONJUNCTION WITH ANY OTHER OFFER

FHG READERS' OFFER 2010

THE HELICOPTER MUSEUM
The Heliport, Locking Moor Road,
Weston-Super-Mare BS24 8PP
Tel: 01934 635227• Fax: 01934 645230
e-mail: helimuseum@btconnect.com
www.helicoptermuseum.co.uk

One child FREE with two full-paying adults
Valid from April to October 2010

NOT TO BE USED IN CONJUNCTION WITH ANY OTHER OFFER

Experience a wonderful day out with a difference at this award-winning visitor attraction, showing how glass has changed our world forever. Live glass-blowing demonstrations, Victorian glass furnace, museum galleries. Artisan shop and Kaleidoscope canalside cafe.	**Open:** 10am-5pm Tues-Sun, plus all Bank Holidays exluding Christmas Day, Boxing Day and New Year's Day. **Directions:** 5 minutes' walk from rail and bus stations in the heart of St Helens. 30 minutes from Manchester and Liverpool - J7 of M62.

FHG GUIDES, ABBEY MILL BUSINESS CENTRE, PAISLEY PA1 1TJ • www.holidayguides.com

A collection of 70 aircraft and cockpit sections from across the history of aviation. Extensive aero engine and artefact displays.	**Open:** daily from 10am (closed Christmas period and New Year's Day). **Directions:** follow brown and white signs from A1, A46, A17 and A1133.

FHG GUIDES, ABBEY MILL BUSINESS CENTRE, PAISLEY PA1 1TJ • www.holidayguides.com

Family-run farm park set in beautiful countryside next to river. 20-acre site with animal handling, pony rides, large indoor soft play area, go-karts, trampolines, pedal tractors, swings, slides, zipline and assault course. Jumicar children's driving activity (small extra charge)	**Open:** daily 10am to 5.30pm. Feb-April and Oct-end Nov: Thurs, Fri, Sat, Sun only. April-Sep: open daily. Please call for December opening times. Closed all January. **Directions:** off A612 Nottingham to Southwell road.

FHG GUIDES, ABBEY MILL BUSINESS CENTRE, PAISLEY PA1 1TJ • www.holidayguides.com

The world's largest helicopter collection - over 70 exhibits, includes two royal helicopters, Russian Gunship and Vietnam veterans plus many award-winning exhibits. Cafe, shop. Flights. **PETS MUST BE KEPT UNDER CONTROL**	**Open:** Wednesday to Sunday 10am to 5.30pm. Daily during school Easter and Summer holidays and Bank Holiday Mondays. November to March: 10am to 4.30pm **Directions:** Junction 21 off M5 then follow the propellor signs.

FHG GUIDES, ABBEY MILL BUSINESS CENTRE, PAISLEY PA1 1TJ • www.holidayguides.com

FHG READERS' OFFER 2010

EXMOOR FALCONRY & ANIMAL FARM
Allerford, Near Porlock, Minehead,
Somerset TA24 8HJ
Tel: 01643 862816
e-mail: exmoor.falcon@virgin.net
www.exmoorfalconry.co.uk

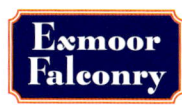

10% off entry to Falconry Centre
Valid during 2010

NOT TO BE USED IN CONJUNCTION WITH ANY OTHER OFFER

FHG READERS' OFFER 2010

THE NATIONAL HORSERACING MUSEUM
99 High Street,
Newmarket,
Suffolk CB8 8JH
Tel: 01638 667333
www.nhrm.co.uk

One FREE adult or concession with on paying full price.
Valid Easter to end October 2010. Museum admission only.

NOT TO BE USED IN CONJUNCTION WITH ANY OTHER OFFER

FHG READERS' OFFER 2010

EASTON FARM PARK
Pound Corner, Easton, Woodbridge,
Suffolk IP13 0EQ
Tel: 01728 746475
e-mail: info@eastonfarmpark.co.uk
www.eastonfarmpark.co.uk

One FREE child entry with a full paying adult
Only one voucher per group. Valid during 2010.

NOT TO BE USED IN CONJUNCTION WITH ANY OTHER OFFER

FHG READERS' OFFER 2010

PARADISE PARK
Avis Road, Newhaven,
East Sussex BN9 0DH
Tel: 01273 512123 • Fax: Fax: 01273 616005
e-mail: enquiries@paradisepark.co.uk
www.paradisepark.co.uk

One child FREE with one full paying adult.
Valid January - end October 2010.

NOT TO BE USED IN CONJUNCTION WITH ANY OTHER OFFER

Falconry centre with animals - flying displays, animal handling, feeding and bottle feeding - in 15th century NT farmyard setting on Exmoor. Also falconry and outdoor activities, hawk walks and riding.	**Open:** 10.30am to 5pm daily **Directions:** A39 west of Minehead, turn right at Allerford, half a mile along lane on left.

FHG GUIDES, ABBEY MILL BUSINESS CENTRE, PAISLEY PA1 1TJ • www.holidayguides.com

Stories of racing, ride the horse simulator, or take a 'behind the scenes' tour of the training grounds and yards.	**Open:** Easter to end October, 7 days a week 11am to 5pm. Last admission 4pm. **Directions:** on the High Street in the centre of Newmarket.

FHG GUIDES, ABBEY MILL BUSINESS CENTRE, PAISLEY PA1 1TJ • www.holidayguides.com

Family day out down on the farm, with activities for children every half hour (included in entry price). Indoor and outdoor play areas. Riverside cafe, gift shop. For more details visit the website.	**Open:** 10.30am-6pm daily March to September. **Directions:** signposted from A12 in the direction of Framlingham.

FHG GUIDES, ABBEY MILL BUSINESS CENTRE, PAISLEY PA1 1TJ • www.holidayguides.com

Discover 'Planet Earth' for an unforgettable experience. A unique Museum of Life, Dinosaur Safari, beautiful Water Gardens with fish and wildfowl, plant houses, themed gardens, Heritage Trail, miniature railway. Playzone includes crazy golf and adventure play areas. Garden Centre and Terrace Cafe.	**Open:** 9am - 6pm daily except Christmas/Boxing Days. **Directions:** signposted from A26 and A259.

FHG GUIDES, ABBEY MILL BUSINESS CENTRE, PAISLEY PA1 1TJ • www.holidayguides.com

227

FHG READERS' OFFER 2010

EARNLEY BUTTERFLIES & GARDENS
133 Almodington Lane, Earnley, Chichester,
West Sussex PO20 7JR
Tel: 01243 512637
e-mail: earnleygardens@msn.com
www.earnleybutterfliesandgardens.co.uk

Earnley Buttterflies & Gardens

£1 per person off normal entry prices.
Valid late March to end October 2010.

NOT TO BE USED IN CONJUNCTION WITH ANY OTHER OFFER

FHG READERS' OFFER 2010

HATTON FARM VILLAGE AT HATTON COUNTRY WORLD
Dark Lane, Hatton, Near Warwick,
Warwickshire CV35 8XA
Tel: 01926 843411
e-mail: hatton@hattonworld.com
www.hattonworld.com

Admit one child FREE with one full-paying adult day ticket. Valid during 2010 except Bank Holidays or for entrance to Santa's Grotto promotion.

NOT TO BE USED IN CONJUNCTION WITH ANY OTHER OFFER

FHG READERS' OFFER 2010

CHOLDERTON CHARLIE'S FARM & YOUTH HOSTEL
Amesbury Road, Cholderton, Salisbury,
Wiltshire SP4 0EW
Tel: 01980 629438 • Fax: 01980 629594
e-mail: choldertonrbf@aol.com
www.choldertoncharliesfarm.com

One child FREE with full paying adult.
Valid September 2009 - end March 2010.

NOT TO BE USED IN CONJUNCTION WITH ANY OTHER OFFER

FHG READERS' OFFER 2010

FALCONRY UK BIRDS OF PREY CENTRE
Sion Hill Hall, Kirby Wiske
Near Thirsk, North Yorkshire YO7 4GU
Tel: 01845 587522
e-mail: mail@falconrycentre.co.uk
www.falconrycentre.co.uk

TWO for ONE on admission to Centre. Cheapest ticket free with voucher. Valid 1st March to 31st October.

NOT TO BE USED IN CONJUNCTION WITH ANY OTHER OFFER

3 attractions in 1. Tropical butterflies, exotic animals of many types in our Noah's Ark Rescue Centre. Theme gardens with a free competition for kids. Rejectamenta - the nostalgia museum.	**Open:** 10am - 6pm daily late March to end October. **Directions:** signposted from A27/A286 junction at Chichester.

Hatton Farm Village offers a wonderful mix of farmyard animals, adventure play, shows, demonstrations, and events, all set in the stunning Warwickshire countryside.	**Open:** daily 10am-5pm (4pm during winter). Closed Christmas Day and Boxing Day. **Directions:** 5 minutes from M40 (J15), A46 towards Coventry, then just off A4177 (follow brown tourist signs).

A farm park that rears and keeps rare breed animals. Animal handling, indoor play equipment etc. Cafe serving delicious home-made food. Plus a newly opened 70-bed youth hostel.	**Open:** April to October 10am-6pm November-March 10am-4pm **Directions:** just off the A303 and the A338 near Stonehenge.

Birds of prey centre with over 60 birds including owls, hawks, falcons, kites, vultures and eagles. 3 flying displays daily. When possible public welcome to handle birds after each display. No dogs allowed.	**Open:** 1st March to 31st October 10.30am to 5pm. Flying displays 11.30am, 1.30pm and 3.30pm daily. **Directions:** on the A167 between Northallerton and the Ripon turn off. Follow brown tourist signs.

FHG READERS' OFFER 2010
K·U·P·E·R·A·R·D

WORLD OF JAMES HERRIOT
23 Kirkgate, Thirsk,
North Yorkshire YO7 1PL
Tel: 01845 524234
Fax: 01845 525333
www.worldofjamesherriot.org

Admit TWO for the price of ONE (one voucher per transaction only). Valid until October 2010

NOT TO BE USED IN CONJUNCTION WITH ANY OTHER OFFER

FHG READERS' OFFER 2010
K·U·P·E·R·A·R·D

MUSEUM OF RAIL TRAVEL
Ingrow Railway Centre, Near Keighley,
West Yorkshire BD21 5AX
Tel: 01535 680425
e-mail: admin@vintagecarriagestrust.org
www.vintagecarriagestrust.org

"ONE for ONE" free admission
Valid during 2010 except during special events (ring to check)

NOT TO BE USED IN CONJUNCTION WITH ANY OTHER OFFER

FHG READERS' OFFER 2010
K·U·P·E·R·A·R·D

EUREKA! THE NATIONAL CHILDREN'S MUSEUM
Discovery Road, Halifax,
West Yorkshire HX1 2NE
Tel: 01422 330069 • Fax: 01422 398490
e-mail: info@eureka.org.uk
www.eureka.org.uk

One FREE child on purchase of full price adult ticket
Valid from 1/10/09 to 31/12/10. Excludes groups. Promo Code 243

NOT TO BE USED IN CONJUNCTION WITH ANY OTHER OFFER

FHG READERS' OFFER 2010
K·U·P·E·R·A·R·D

THE GRASSIC GIBBON CENTRE
Arbuthnott, Laurencekirk,
Aberdeenshire AB30 1PB
Tel: 01561 361668
e-mail: lgginfo@grassicgibbon.com
www.grassicgibbon.com

TWO for the price of ONE entry to exhibition (based on full adult rate only). Valid during 2010 (not groups)

NOT TO BE USED IN CONJUNCTION WITH ANY OTHER OFFER

Visit James Herriot's original house recreated as it was in the 1940s. Television sets used in the series 'All Creatures Great and Small'. There is a children's interactive gallery with life-size model farm animals and three rooms dedicated to the history of veterinary medicine.

Open: daily. Easter-Oct 10am-5pm; Nov-Easter 11am to 4pm

Directions: follow signs off A1 or A19 to Thirsk, then A168, off Thirsk market place

---

A fascinating display of railway carriages and a wide range of railway items telling the story of rail travel over the years.

ALL PETS MUST BE KEPT ON LEADS

Open: daily 11am to 4.30pm

Directions: approximately one mile from Keighley on A629 Halifax road. Follow brown tourist signs

---

As the UK's National Children's Museum, Eureka! is a place where children play to learn and grown-ups learn to play.

Open: daily except 24-26 December, 10am to 5pm

Directions: leave M62 at J24 for Halifax. Take A629 to town centre, following brown tourist signs.

Visitor Centre dedicated to the much-loved Scottish writer Lewis Grassic Gibbon. Exhibition, cafe, gift shop. Outdoor children's play area. Disabled access throughout.

Open: daily March to October 10am to 4.30pm. Groups by appointment including evenings.

Directions: on the B967, accessible and signposted from both A90 and A92.

SCOTTISH MARITIME MUSEUM
Harbourside, Irvine,
Ayrshire KA12 8QE
Tel: 01294 278283
Fax: 01294 313211
www.scottishmaritimemuseum.org

TWO for the price of ONE
Valid from April to October 2010

FHG READERS' OFFER 2010

NOT TO BE USED IN CONJUNCTION WITH ANY OTHER OFFER

GALLOWAY WILDLIFE CONSERVATION PARK
Lochfergus Plantation, Kirkcudbright,
Dumfries & Galloway DG6 4XX
Tel & Fax: 01557 331645
e-mail: info@gallowaywildlife.co.uk
www.gallowaywildlife.co.uk

One FREE child or Senior Citizen with two full paying adults.
Valid Feb - Nov 2010 (not Easter weekend and Bank Holidays)

FHG READERS' OFFER 2010

NOT TO BE USED IN CONJUNCTION WITH ANY OTHER OFFER

BO'NESS & KINNEIL RAILWAY
Bo'ness Station, Union Street,
Bo'ness, West Lothian EH51 9AQ
Tel: 01506 822298
e-mail: enquiries.railway@srps.org.uk
www.srps.org.uk

FREE child train fare with one paying adult/concession. Valid
March-Oct 2010. Not Days Out with Thomas or Santa Steam trains

FHG READERS' OFFER 2010

NOT TO BE USED IN CONJUNCTION WITH ANY OTHER OFFER

MYRETON MOTOR MUSEUM
Aberlady,
East Lothian EH32 0PZ
Tel: 01875 870288
www.myretonmotormuseum.co.uk

One child FREE with each paying adult
Valid during 2010

FHG READERS' OFFER 2010

NOT TO BE USED IN CONJUNCTION WITH ANY OTHER OFFER

| Scotland's seafaring heritage is among the world's richest and you can relive the heyday of Scottish shipping at the Maritime Museum. | **Open:** 1st April to 31st October - 10am-5pm

Directions: situated on Irvine harbourside and only a 10 minute walk from Irvine train station. |

FHG GUIDES, ABBEY MILL BUSINESS CENTRE, PAISLEY PA1 1TJ • www.holidayguides.com

| The wild animal conservation centre of Southern Scotland. A varied collection of over 150 animals from all over the world can be seen within natural woodland settings. Picnic areas, cafe/gift shop, outdoor play area, woodland walks, close animal encounters. | **Open:** 10am to dusk 1st February to 30 November.

Directions: follow brown tourist signs from A75; one mile from Kirkcudbright on the B727. |

FHG GUIDES, ABBEY MILL BUSINESS CENTRE, PAISLEY PA1 1TJ • www.holidayguides.com

| Steam and heritage diesel passenger trains from Bo'ness to Birkhill for guided tours of Birkhill fireclay mines. Explore the history of Scotland's railways in the Scottish Railway Exhibition. Coffee shop and souvenir shop. | **Open:** weekends Easter to October, daily July and August.
See website for dates and timetables.

Directions: in the town of Bo'ness. Leave M9 at Junction 3 or 5, then follow brown tourist signs. |

FHG GUIDES, ABBEY MILL BUSINESS CENTRE, PAISLEY PA1 1TJ • www.holidayguides.com

| On show is a large collection, from 1899, of cars, bicycles, motor cycles and commercials. There is also a large collection of period advertising, posters and enamel signs. | **Open:** March-Oct: open daily 10.30am to 4.30pm.
Nov-Feb: weekends 11am to 3pm or by special appointment.

Directions: off A198 near Aberlady. Two miles from A1. |

FHG GUIDES, ABBEY MILL BUSINESS CENTRE, PAISLEY PA1 1TJ • www.holidayguides.com

FHG
K·U·P·E·R·A·R·D
READERS' OFFER 2010

BRITISH GOLF MUSEUM
Bruce Embankment, St Andrews,
Fife KY16 9AB
Tel: 01334 460046 • Fax: 01334 460064
e-mail: judychance@randa.org
www.britishgolfmuseum.co.uk

*10% off price of admission (one per customer).
Valid during 2010.*

NOT TO BE USED IN CONJUNCTION WITH ANY OTHER OFFER

FHG
K·U·P·E·R·A·R·D
READERS' OFFER 2010

SCOTTISH DEER CENTRE
Cupar,
Fife KY15 4NQ
Tel: 01337 810391
e-mail: info@tsdc.co.uk
www.tsdc.co.uk

One child FREE with one full paying adult on production of voucher. Not valid during December.

NOT TO BE USED IN CONJUNCTION WITH ANY OTHER OFFER

FHG
K·U·P·E·R·A·R·D
READERS' OFFER 2010

LOCH NESS CENTRE & EXHIBITION EXPERIENCE
Drumnadrochit, Loch Ness,
Inverness-shire IV63 6TU
Tel: 01456 450573 • 01456 450770
www.lochness.com

'2 for the price of 1' entry to the world famous Exhibition Centre. Valid during 2010.

NOT TO BE USED IN CONJUNCTION WITH ANY OTHER OFFER

FHG
K·U·P·E·R·A·R·D
READERS' OFFER 2010

NATIONAL CYCLE COLLECTION
Automobile Palace, Temple Street,
Llandrindod Wells, Powys LD1 5DL
Tel: 01597 825531
e-mail: cycle.museum@powys.org.uk
www.cyclemuseum.org.uk

*TWO for the price of ONE
Valid during 2010 except Special Event days*

NOT TO BE USED IN CONJUNCTION WITH ANY OTHER OFFER

The 5-Star British Golf Museum explores 500 years of golfing history using exciting interactives and diverse displays. A visit here makes the perfect break from playing golf.	**Open:** Mon-Sat 9.30am-5pm, Sun 10am-4pm. Closed Christmas and New Year periods. **Directions:** opposite the Old Course in St Andrews.

FHG GUIDES, ABBEY MILL BUSINESS CENTRE, PAISLEY PA1 1TJ • www.holidayguides.com

55-acre park with 10 species of deer from around the world. Guided tours, trailer rides, treetop walkway, children's adventure playground and picnic area. Other animals include wolves, foxes, otters and a bird of prey centre.	**Open:** 10am to 5pm daily except Christmas Day and New Year's Day. **Directions:** A91 south of Cupar. Take J9 M90 from the north, J8 from the south.

FHG GUIDES, ABBEY MILL BUSINESS CENTRE, PAISLEY PA1 1TJ • www.holidayguides.com

VisitScotland 5-Star Visitor Attraction, described by Scottish Natural Heritage as "a portal to the unique natural phenomenon that is Loch Ness". Cafe and restaurant on site with large shopping complex and cruises on Loch Ness.	**Open:** all year except Christmas Day. **Directions:** directly on A82 trunk road, 12 miles south of Inverness.

FHG GUIDES, ABBEY MILL BUSINESS CENTRE, PAISLEY PA1 1TJ • www.holidayguides.com

Journey through the lanes of cycle history and see bicycles from Boneshakers and Penny Farthings up to modern Raleigh cycles. Over 250 machines on display **PETS MUST BE KEPT ON LEADS**	**Open:** 1st March to 1st November daily 10am onwards. **Directions:** brown signs to car park. Town centre attraction.

FHG GUIDES, ABBEY MILL BUSINESS CENTRE, PAISLEY PA1 1TJ • www.holidayguides.com

Index of Towns and Counties

Abergele, North Wales	WALES	Bude, Cornwall	SOUTH WEST
Abington, Lanarkshire	SCOTLAND	Bungay, Suffolk	EAST
Alford, Lincolnshire	MIDLANDS	Buxton, Derbyshire	MIDLANDS
Alton, Staffordshire	MIDLANDS	Caernarfon, Anglesey & Gwynedd	WALES
Ambleside, Cumbria	NORTH WEST	Caister-on-Sea, Norfolk	EAST
Anglesey, Anglesey & Gwynedd	WALES	Chichester, West Sussex	SOUTH EAST
Antrim, Co. Antrim	NORTHERN IRELAND	Chudleigh, Devon	SOUTH WEST
Arisaig, Highlands	SCOTLAND	Combe Martin, Devon	SOUTH WEST
Aviemore, Highlands	SCOTLAND	Coniston, Cumbria	NORTH WEST
Ayr, Ayrshire & Arran	SCOTLAND	Cotswolds, Gloucestershire	SOUTH WEST
Bala, Anglesey & Gwynedd	WALES	Coverack, Cornwall	SOUTH WEST
Bamburgh, Northumberland	NORTH EAST	Crackington Haven, Cornwall	SOUTH WEST
Barmouth, Anglesey & Gwynedd	WALES	Craven Arms, Shropshire	MIDLANDS
Barnstaple, Devon	SOUTH WEST	Crieff, Perth & Kinross	SCOTLAND
Battle, East Sussex	SOUTH EAST	Cullompton, Devon	SOUTH WEST
Beaconsfield, Buckinghamshire	SOUTH EAST	Dalbeattie, Dumfries & Galloway	SCOTLAND
Beauly, Highlands	SCOTLAND	Dartmouth, Devon	SOUTH WEST
Benllech, Anglesey & Gwynedd	WALES	Dawlish, Devon	SOUTH WEST
Biddenden, Kent	SOUTH EAST	Devizes, Wiltshire	SOUTH WEST
Birchington, Kent	SOUTH EAST	Dial Post, West Sussex	SOUTH EAST
Bishop Auckland, Durham	NORTH EAST	Diss, Norfolk	EAST
Blackpool, Lancashire	NORTH WEST	Dolgellau, Anglesey & Gwynedd	WALES
Blairgowrie, Perth & Kinross	SCOTLAND	Dollar, Stirling & The Trossachs	SCOTLAND
Blandford, Dorset	SOUTH WEST	Dorchester, Dorset	SOUTH WEST
Bodiam, East Sussex	SOUTH EAST	Dornoch, Highlands	SCOTLAND
Bodmin, Cornwall	SOUTH WEST	Dumfries, Dumfries & Galloway	SCOTLAND
Boston, Lincolnshire	MIDLANDS	East Calder, Edinburgh & Lothians	SCOTLAND
Botallack, Cornwall	SOUTH WEST	Eastbourne, East Sussex	SOUTH EAST
Branscombe, Devon	SOUTH WEST	Elgin, Aberdeen, Banff & Moray	SCOTLAND
Brechin, Angus & Dundee	SCOTLAND	Exmouth, Devon	SOUTH WEST
Bridgwater, Somerset	SOUTH WEST	Filey, North Yorkshire	YORKSHIRE

INDEX OF TOWNS AND COUNTIES

Flamborough, East Yorkshire	YORKSHIRE	Lauragh, Co Kerry	IRELAND
Fort William, Highlands	SCOTLAND	Laurencekirk, Aberdeen, Banff & Moray	
Glaisdale, North Yorkshire	YORKSHIRE		SCOTLAND
Glencoe, Highlands	SCOTLAND	Leominster, Herefordshire	MIDLANDS
Grange-over-Sands, Cumbria	NORTH WEST	Little Asby, Cumbria	NORTH WEST
Grantham, Lincolnshire	MIDLANDS	Llandysul, Ceredigion	WALES
Great Yarmouth, Norfolk	EAST	Loch Rannoch, Perth & Kinross	SCOTLAND
Greenlaw, Borders	SCOTLAND	Lochinver, Highlands	SCOTLAND
Harrogate, North Yorkshire	YORKSHIRE	London (Central & Greater)	LONDON
Hastings, East Sussex	SOUTH EAST	Looe, Cornwall	SOUTH WEST
Haverfordwest, Pembrokeshire	WALES	Lower Wick, Gloucestershire	SOUTH WEST
Hawes, North Yorkshire	YORKSHIRE	Lowestoft, Suffolk	EAST
Hayle, Cornwall	SOUTH WEST	Lune Valley, Lancashire	NORTH WEST
Hayling Island, Hampshire	SOUTH EAST	Lyng, Norfolk	EAST
Helensburgh, Argyll & Bute	SCOTLAND	Maidenhead, Berkshire	SOUTH EAST
Helmsley, North Yorkshire	YORKSHIRE	Marston, West Midlands	MIDLANDS
Helston, Cornwall	SOUTH WEST	Mawgan Porth, Cornwall	SOUTH WEST
Hexham, Northumberland	NORTH EAST	Merthyr Tydfil, South Wales	WALES
Hunstanton, Norfolk	EAST	Milford-on-Sea, Hampshire	SOUTH EAST
Huntly, Aberdeen, Banff & Moray	SCOTLAND	Minehead, Somerset	SOUTH WEST
Ilfracombe, Devon	SOUTH WEST	Mundesley, Norfolk	EAST
Inverness, Highlands	SCOTLAND	Newby Bridge, Cumbria	NORTH WEST
John O'Groats, Highlands	SCOTLAND	Newcastle-upon-Tyne, Tyne & Wear	NORTH EAST
Kendal, Cumbria	NORTH WEST	Newquay, Cornwall	SOUTH WEST
Keswick, Cumbria	NORTH WEST	Newton Abbot, Devon	SOUTH WEST
Killorglin, Co Kerry	IRELAND	Newton Stewart, Dumfries & Galloway	
Kingsbridge, Devon	SOUTH WEST		SCOTLAND
Kinlochleven, Argyll & Bute	SCOTLAND	Northallerton, North Yorkshire	YORKSHIRE
Kirkbymoorside, North Yorkshire	YORKSHIRE	Oban, Argyll & Bute	SCOTLAND
Kirkwall, Orkney	SCOTLAND	Otterburn, Northumberland	NORTH EAST
Knutsford, Cheshire	NORTH WEST	Padstow, Cornwall	SOUTH WEST
Laide, Highlands	SCOTLAND	Paignton, Devon	SOUTH WEST
Lairg, Highlands	SCOTLAND	Penrith, Cumbria	NORTH WEST
Launceston, Cornwall	SOUTH WEST	Penzance, Cornwall	SOUTH WEST

INDEX OF TOWNS AND COUNTIES

Pickering, North Yorkshire	YORKSHIRE	Stratford-upon-Avon, Warwickshire	MIDLANDS
Pidsley, Cambridgeshire	EAST	Strathnaver, Highlands	SCOTLAND
Pitlochry, Perth & Kinross	SCOTLAND	Swansea, South Wales	WALES
Polzeath, Cornwall	SOUTH WEST	Tal-y-Llyn, Anglesey & Gwynedd	WALES
Poole, Dorset	SOUTH WEST	Tarbert, Argyll & Bute	SCOTLAND
Porlock, Somerset	SOUTH WEST	Taunton, Somerset	SOUTH WEST
Redruth, Cornwall	SOUTH WEST	Tavistock, Devon	SOUTH WEST
Rhayader, Powys	WALES	Thornbury, Devon	SOUTH WEST
Ringwood, Hampshire	SOUTH EAST	Totnes, Devon	SOUTH WEST
Ripley, Derbyshire	MIDLANDS	Trearddur Bay, Anglesey & Gwynedd	WALES
Riseley, Berkshire	SOUTH EAST	Truro, Cornwall	SOUTH WEST
Romsey, Hampshire	SOUTH EAST	Tuxford, Nottinghamshire	MIDLANDS
St Agnes, Cornwall	SOUTH WEST	Tyndrum, Perth & Kinross	SCOTLAND
St Austell, Cornwall	SOUTH WEST	Ullswater, Cumbria	NORTH WEST
St Ives, Cornwall	SOUTH WEST	Wadebridge, Cornwall	SOUTH WEST
Salcombe, Devon	SOUTH WEST	Wareham, Dorset	SOUTH WEST
Saltash, Cornwall	SOUTH WEST	West Bexington	SOUTH WEST
Scarborough, North Yorkshire	YORKSHIRE	Westray, Orkney	SCOTLAND
Scourie, Highlands	SCOTLAND	Wetherby, North Yorkshire	YORKSHIRE
Sea Palling, Norfolk	EAST	Weymouth, Dorset	SOUTH WEST
Seaton, Devon	SOUTH WEST	Whicham Valley, Cumbria	NORTH WEST
Selkirk, Borders	SCOTLAND	Whitby, North Yorkshire	YORKSHIRE
Shielbridge, Highlands	SCOTLAND	Wimborne, Dorset	SOUTH WEST
Silloth-on-Solway, Cumbria	NORTH WEST	Wokingham, Berkshire	SOUTH EAST
Slimbridge, Gloucestershire	SOUTH WEST	Wolvey, Leicestershire	MIDLANDS
Snowdonia, Anglesey & Gwynedd	WALES	Wool, Dorset	SOUTH WEST
South Molton, Devon	SOUTH WEST	Woolacombe, Devon	SOUTH WEST
Stranraer, Dumfries & Galloway	SCOTLAND	York, North Yorkshire	YORKSHIRE

www.holidayguides.com

Looking for Holiday Accommodation?

for details of hundreds of properties throughout the UK, visit our website

www.holidayguides.com

Other FHG titles for 2010

239

FHG Guides Ltd have a large range of attractive holiday accommodation guides for all kinds of holiday opportunities throughout Britain. They also make useful gifts at any time of year.

Our guides are available in most bookshops and larger newsagents but we will be happy to post you a copy direct if you have any difficulty. POST FREE for addresses in the UK. We will also post abroad but have to charge separately for post or freight.

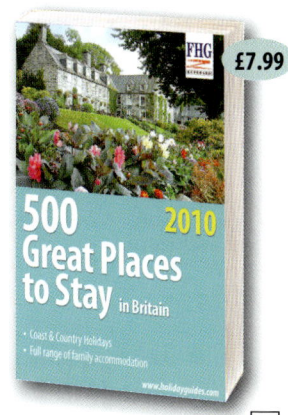

FHG KUPERARD

£7.99

500 Great Places to Stay in Britain
- Coast & Country Holidays
- Full range of family accommodation

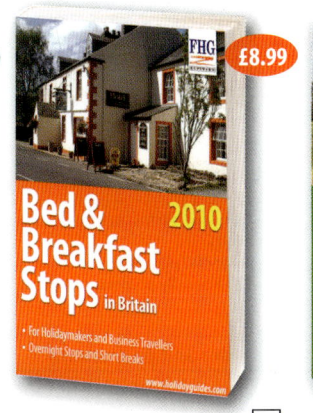

£8.99

Bed & Breakfast Stops in Britain
- For holidaymakers and business travellers
- Overnight stops and Short Breaks

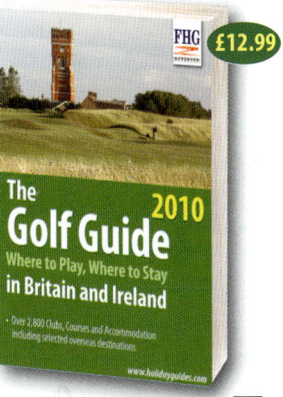

£12.99

The Golf Guide
Where to play, Where to stay.
- Over 2800 golf courses in Britain with convenient accommodation.
- Holiday Golf in France, Portugal, Spain, USA and Thailand.

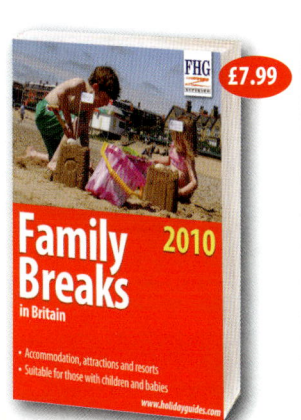

£7.99

Family Breaks in Britain
- Accommodation, attractions and resorts
- Suitable for those with children and babies

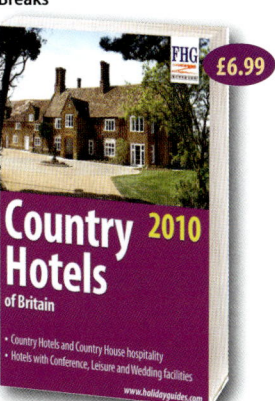

£6.99

Country Hotels of Britain
- Hotels with Conference, Leisure and Wedding Facilities

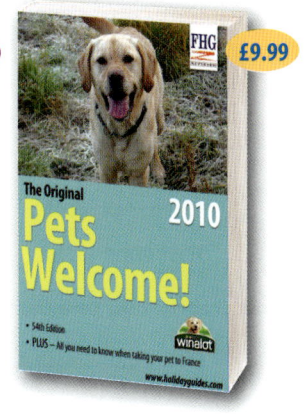

£9.99

The Original Pets Welcome!
- The bestselling guide to holidays for pets and their owners

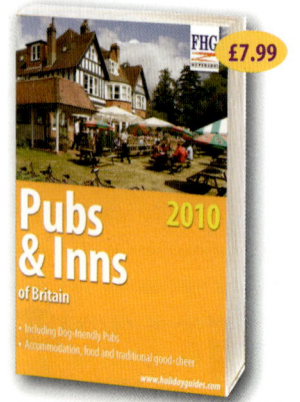

Pubs & Inns £7.99
of Britain
• Including Dog-friendly Pubs
• Accommodation, food and traditional good cheer

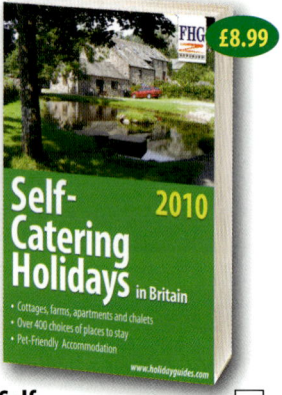

Self-Catering Holidays £8.99
in Britain
• Cottages, farms, apartments and chalets
• Over 400 places to stay
• Pet-Friendly accommodation

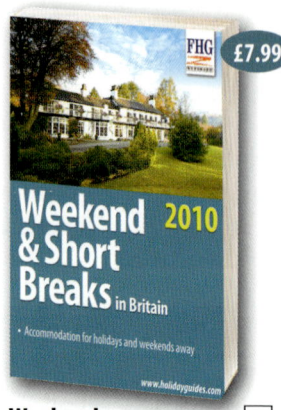

Weekend & Short Breaks £7.99
in Britain
• Accommodation for holidays and weekends away

Tick your choice above and send your order and payment to

**FHG Guides Ltd. Abbey Mill Business Centre
Seedhill, Paisley, Scotland PA1 1TJ
TEL: 0141- 887 0428 • FAX: 0141- 889 7204
e-mail: admin@fhguides.co.uk**

Deduct 10% for 2/3 titles or copies; 20% for 4 or more.

Send to: NAME ....

ADDRESS ....

....

....

POST CODE ....

I enclose Cheque/Postal Order for £ ....

SIGNATURE ....DATE ....

Please complete the following to help us improve the service we provide.
How did you find out about our guides?:

☐ Press   ☐ Magazines   ☐ TV/Radio   ☐ Family/Friend   ☐ Other